"In *Developing Competencies for Recovery: Mastering Addiction, Living Well, and Doing Good*, Dr. Rasmussen, a thoughtful scholar and practitioner, has created a masterplan for recovery based on the principle that, 'recovery is an idea whose time has come'. To affirm and advance recovery, her book weaves theory, practice, learning and serves as a guide for individuals, group residential settings, outpatient programs, and correction facilities. Developing Competencies for Recovery complements medication-assisted treatment and will be especially appropriate for Recovery-Oriented Systems of Care.

Dr. Rasmussen recognizes that recovery requires commitment, courage, and work. Her book's 12 chapters begin with real stories about real people and their recovery process, followed by a detailed framework for the recovery process."

Elizabeth M. George, *Chief Executive Officer of the North American Training Institute, and the American Academy of Health Care Providers in the Addictive Disorders*

"Faculty and students in addiction studies, counselors, and therapists can and will benefit from this book. I state this because recovery is a dynamic process that is dependent on developing a holistic and dynamic approach, which is rooted in possessing skills and competencies. As depicted in Dr. Rasmussen's book, recovery cannot occur without knowledge and guidance of strategic ways to encourage the acknowledgment of use and desire to change. What I find most appealing about this book is that it provides a no-nonsense approach to addiction management by clearly depicting core competencies in a manner that will allow the clinician, instructor, and subsequently the client the ability to clearly understand and develop a pathway and/or direction on how to manage recovery successfully."

Dr. Samantha Leigh Fields-Salain, *Behavioral Counselor II, State of Georgia Department of Community Supervision*

"Born from lifetimes of experience, practice, and theory, Rasmussen's *Developing Competencies for Recovery: Mastering Addiction, Living Well, and Doing Good* provides an exceptional template for those working or planning to work in a field that has frequent contact with people struggling with addiction. Rasmussen has managed to create a fine-tuned resource that is both comprehensive and formulaic, yet still flexible and harmonious with the individualistic nature of addiction. Behavioral health professionals and peer workers: clear a spot by your *DSM-5*, you're going to be using this one just as much."

Bob Cabaniss, Founder of Williamsville Wellness & Summit Hill Wellness

"As our world struggles to redefine itself, the changes to the cycles of addiction and recovery are formidable. Addiction built upon the devastation of trauma can be reassessed and a life recreated through *Developing Competencies for Recovery:*

Mastering Addiction, Living Well, and Doing Good. This book lights brave new paths towards recovery in our changing times. One's ability to grasp the eclectic competencies of addiction, its models, treatment, and application lead to mastering addiction which will reinforce recovery leading to a full life of goodness. *Developing Competencies for Recovery: Mastering Addiction, Living Well, and Doing Good* highlights this path."

Alessandre Singher, *PhD, LPC, LCADC, CAACD, CCJP.*
Professor, Addiction Curriculum Developer, and Therapist

"In *Developing Competencies for Addiction*, Dr. Sandra Rasmussen provides a cutting-edge guide to competencies for addiction treatment and recovery management. Often addiction treatment is focused on the drug or problematic behavior. These competencies effectively examine the broader context of the recovery process. This journey begins with freedom from the problem substance or behavior, but is about the recovery of our self-respect, relationships, meaning, motivation, and hope. This guide effectively integrates the whole person as they return to living well!"

Kenneth Martz, *PsyD, author of* Manage My Emotions *and* Manage My Addiction

"*Developing Competencies for Recovery: Mastering Addiction, Living Well, and Doing Good* provides a sound and timely theoretical and competency-based framework for persons in recovery and for practitioners in the recovery field. It is a must-read for recovering addicts, practitioners, and public health professionals."

Damon Grew Peter Syphers, *PhD, Lewiston, ME*

Developing Competencies for Recovery

Developing Competencies for Recovery aims to help people struggling with addiction realize recovery by developing core competencies that will equip, enable, and empower them to master addiction, live well, and do good.

Competencies are clusters of related knowledge, skills, and attitudes (KSAs) that prepare a person to act effectively and reflect cognitive, affective, and psychomotor domains of learning. This book provides a cutting-edge guide to recovery by depicting these core competencies in a manner that will prepare the reader with the ability to understand and develop a course of action on how to manage recovery successfully. The first section of each chapter presents facts, concepts, principles, and theories about a particular competency, and it shares real stories about real people and their own recovery journeys. The following section suggests applications of the competency with questions, worksheets, exercises, and projects. In the final section, readers can evaluate their recovery work and competency development. Resources for recovery and references can be found at the end of the book.

Behavioral health practitioners and instructors and students of addiction studies will find this book a best-practice template for recovery work.

Sandra Rasmussen, PhD, RN, LMHC, CAS-F is a registered nurse, a licensed mental health counselor, and a certified addiction specialist with many years of academic, professional, and personal experience with addiction, relapse, and recovery.

Developing Competencies for Recovery

Mastering Addiction, Living Well, and Doing Good

Sandra Rasmussen

R Routledge
Taylor & Francis Group

NEW YORK AND LONDON

Cover image: Getty Image

First published 2023
by Routledge
605 Third Avenue, New York, NY 10158

and by Routledge
4 Park Square, Milton Park, Abingdon, Oxon OX14 4RN

Routledge is an imprint of the Taylor & Francis Group, an informa business

© 2023 Sandra Rasmussen

Library of Congress Cataloging-in-Publication Data
Names: Rasmussen, Sandra, author.
Title: Developing competencies for recovery : mastering addiction, living
well, and doing good / by Sandra Rasmussen.
Description: New York, NY : Routledge, 2023. | Includes bibliographical
references and index. |
Identifiers: LCCN 2022015286 (print) | LCCN 2022015287 (ebook) |
Subjects: LCSH: Addicts--Rehabilitation. | Recovering addicts.
Classification: LCC HV4998 .R373 2023 (print) | LCC HV4998 (ebook) |
DDC 362.29--dc23/eng/20220805
LC record available at https://lccn.loc.gov/2022015286
LC ebook record available at https://lccn.loc.gov/2022015287

ISBN: 978-1-032-27465-2 (hbk)
ISBN: 978-1-032-27464-5 (pbk)
ISBN: 978-1-003-29294-4 (ebk)

DOI: 10.4324/9781003292944

Typeset in Baskerville
by Taylor & Francis Books

Matt and Michele H. are Mastering Addiction, Living Well, and Doing Good

Contents

Figures

Tables

Boxes

Preface

Addiction jeopardizes the health and well-being of individuals, families, communities, even society itself. Yet, prevention, treatment, and recovery services mitigate disability, devastation, and death from addiction. *Developing Competencies for Recovery: Mastering Addiction, Living Well, and Doing Good* describes core competencies people with addiction can develop to realize recovery. *Recovery* is the ability to master addiction, live well, and do good, as evidenced by abstinence or harm reduction and relapse prevention; health, wellness, and well-being; together with helping, service, and altruism.

Competencies are clusters of related knowledge, skills, and attitudes (KSAs) that prepare a person to act effectively. Competencies reflect cognitive, affective, and psychomotor domains of learning. Tertiary prevention provides the conceptual framework for the book. *Competencies for Recovery* has one chapter for each competency. Chapters open with a short story from a recovering person followed by a stated **purpose**, a list of **objectives,** and a topical **outline**. Each chapter has three sections. Section I presents facts, concepts, principles, and theories about the competency. Section II suggests applications of the competency with questions, worksheets, exercises, and projects. In Section III, readers evaluate recovery work and competency development. Chapters end with a comprehensive paragraph summary. Resources for recovery, references, and an index complete the book.

This book affirms and advances recovery, an idea whose time has come. Behavioral health practitioners and instructors and students of addiction studies will find this book a best-practice template for recovery work. Use the book to help people with addiction acquire, apply, and appreciate the knowledge, skills, and attitudes they need for recovery. *Competencies for Recovery* equips, enables, and empowers people to master addiction, live well, and do good. This is recovery!

Acknowledgments

Recovery has been the focus of my professional, academic, and personal life for the past 20 years when I lived in Virginia.

Thank you for the opportunity to work with caring, competent behavioral health practitioners who provided best-practice addiction and mental health services for men, women, children, and families at:

- **The Farley Center** for evaluation, detox, partial hospitalization, and IOP addiction treatment for adults and families, particularly its professionals' program.
- **Eastern State Hospital**, the first public facility in the U.S. dedicated to the care and treatment of the mentally ill, providing safety and care for people admitted for acute treatment.
- **Cumberland Hospital for Children and Adolescents** for residential treatment and hospital services for youths with brain injury, chronic illness, and neurobehavioral issues.
- **Williamsville Wellness**, offering many types of therapy in a historic residential center and online, with an emphasis on individual sessions for adults and families with alcohol, other drugs, and gambling problems.
- **The Master Center for Addiction Medicine**, an accessible physician-led practice that utilizes Peer Recovery Coaches as personal patient helpers, guides, teachers, and care navigators; its state-of-the-art Medication-Assisted Treatment (MAT) program combines FDA-approved medications with behavioral therapies.
- **The American Academic of Health Care Providers in the Addictive Disorders**, an international credentialing body devoted to establishing and upholding the highest standards for the treatment of alcohol, drugs, gambling, eating disorders, and sexual addiction.
- **The Virginia Health Practitioners' Monitoring Program** (VA HPMP), an alternative to disciplinary action for qualified healthcare practitioners with substance use, mental health, or physical diagnoses, which may alter their ability to practice their profession safely.

- **SpiritWorks Foundation**, a Recovery Community Organization (RCO) of peer-to-peer programs and services for children, youth, and adults living in recovery from the disease of addiction.

Thank you for the privilege of supervising hundreds of doctoral students in psychology at Walden University. Your research contributed to positive social change. As scholar-practitioners, you created and applied ideas, strategies, and actions to promote the worth, dignity, and development of individuals, communities, and society itself.

Thank you for the call to service as a Stephen Minister at King of Glory Lutheran Church and as a health advocate at the WindsorMeade Continuing Care Retirement Community.

And most of all, a humble thank you to the many people with addiction who shared their experience, strength, and hope with me. You showed me that recovery works!

About the Author

Sandra Rasmussen holds a PhD in Clinical Psychology and Public Practice from Harvard University, an MA in Child Welfare and Development from the University of Minnesota, an MS in Nursing Management from Anna Maria College, and a BS in Nursing from the University of Minnesota. She is an RN (registered nurse), an LMHC (licensed mental health counselor), and a CAS-F (certified addiction specialist in alcohol, other drugs, and gambling).

Dr. Rasmussen is recognized for her:

- Practice *expertise* in addiction/mental health with adults, children, and families; with health practitioners and inmates. She is a Fellow in the American Academy of Health Care Providers in the Addictive Disorders.
- Management *competence* in the public, private, and for-profit sectors.
- Teaching *excellence* in graduate, undergraduate, and vocational programs. In 2015, she received the Walden University Presidential Faculty Excellence Award and the Walden University College of Social & Behavioral Sciences Faculty Excellence Award.
- Research *production* in addiction, mental health, psychology, and nursing.
- Scholarship *evidence* with many journal and book publications including *Ready, Set, Go! Addiction Management for People in Recovery* (2015) and *Addiction Treatment: Theory and Practice* (2000): AJN Book of the Year Award.
- Service *commitments* including **a.** Virginia Public Health Association Recognition Award 2004 for "outstanding leadership, commitment, and support to the public health of Virginia," **b.** University of Minnesota School of Nursing *100 Distinguished Alumni* (1909–2009) for addiction work, **c.** local and state committees for healthy aging, and **d.** Stephen Minister for King of Glory Lutheran Church.

With many years of personal, professional, and academic experience with addiction, relapse, and recovery, Sandra writes as a recovering peer, nurse/counselor, and teacher.

1   Begin Recovery Work

Bill C. Begins Recovery Work

I began my recovery five years ago when I saw the light. It was a flashing blue light that followed me as I swerved home about 3 am on Route 2. I missed a turn and rolled the car. Fortunately, only bruises and minor cuts when the EMTs brought me to Riverside Hospital ER. Riverside has a behavioral health unit where I was admitted for detox; they call it withdrawal management. Filled with shame and remorse, and certain I was the only High School teacher in the country that ever experienced such "indignities," I reluctantly agreed to treatment in an Intensive Outpatient Program (IOP). Fortunately, it was summer, and I had time to "get my act and story together" before school began. However, the teacher learned! I learned about addiction, relapse prevention, and the promises of recovery: if I worked for them. And I did. My name is Bill C. I am a proud social studies teacher at Franklin County Regional High School. Last year I helped launch a Recovery Home Room. I have a quality-of-life second to none I choose to call recovery.

Purpose: This chapter introduces 12 core competencies people with addiction can develop to realize recovery.

Objectives

- Recognize addiction as a social problem and an individual challenge.
- Embrace recovery as an idea whose time has come.
- Herald the establishment of the federal Office of Recovery.
- Define recovery.
- Recognize recovery as work.
- Understand the dimensions and dynamics of competencies.
- Use developmental-learning theory.
- Employ principles from Competency-Based Education (CBE).
- Build upon competencies developed by the Substance Abuse Mental Health Services Administration (SAMHSA) for behavioral health professionals and peer workers.
- Grasp the concept of core competencies from the business world.
- Consider 12 core competencies as a template for recovery work.

DOI: 10.4324/9781003292944-1

Outline

People with Addiction

A Social Problem
An Individual Challenge

Recovery

An Idea Whose Time has Come
Definition of Recovery
The Office of Recovery
Recovery is Work

Developing Competencies for Recovery

Dimensions and Dynamics of Competencies
Developmental Learning
Competency-Based Education (CBE)
SAMHSA Competencies
Core Competencies from the Business World
12 Core Competencies

I

Section I presents facts, concepts, principles, and theories about people with addiction, recovery, and developing competencies for recovery.

People with Addiction

Addiction jeopardizes the health and well-being of individuals, families, communities, even society itself. Addiction is a major social problem and a life-threatening individual challenge.

A Social Problem

Addiction is a major public health problem, causing disability and death for populations across the lifespan and around the world. Excessive alcohol use causes over 90,000 deaths in the United States each year. Worldwide, 3 million deaths every year result from harmful use of alcohol, this represents 5.3% of all deaths. Drug overdose is the leading cause of accidental death in the U. S., with over 107,000 overdose deaths reported in 2021, a 15% increase over the previous year, setting a staggering record, attributed in part to Fentanyl use and the COVID pandemic. The 2020 National Survey on Drug Use and Health (NSDUH) documents the adverse impact of the COVID-19 pandemic on mental health, including the exacerbating use of alcohol and other drugs with an increase in overdose deaths. Abuse of tobacco, alcohol, and illicit drugs costs the U.S. more than $800 billion annually from crime, lost work productivity, and health.

A troubling report in the January 13, 2022, Thursday Styles section of the *New York Times* titled "The Clouds of Smoke Return," reported that cigarettes, once shunned, have made a comeback among young people. Contributing factors include the stress of the pandemic, a rejection of e-cigarettes, with many online posts of smoking as a social activity. Although many young adults acknowledge the harmful effects of smoking cigarettes and abhor the cost, "it looks and feels cool."

Behaviors like gambling, binge eating, exercise, work, love, sex, shopping, the Internet, gaming, mobile phone use, and other reward experiences may become addictive. According to the National Council on Problem Gambling (NCPG), 15% of Americans gamble at least once per week. NCPG notes the annual cost associated with gambling (crime, addiction, and bankruptcy) is $17 billion. Illegal wagers on professional and amateur sports in America total an estimated $150 billion every year. In May 2018, the U.S. Supreme Court allowed sports betting by States. TV ads for sports betting abound! Recently, the World Health Organization reported massive, unprecedented growth in commercial gambling in recent decades, with expectations for this trend to continue, expanding to new, high-risk populations and driven by ready online access.

Access to addiction treatment is complicated and cost-prohibitive for many people. Even with the passage of the Mental Health Parity and Addiction Equity Act of 2008 and the Affordable Care Act in 2010, 90% of individuals with substance use disorders (SUD) receive no treatment. Rarely, do we see a continuum of addiction service including pre-screening, referral, treatment, continuing care, and recovery support services.

Treatment for problem gambling is scarce. Insurance often requires a primary diagnosis of depression or substance use and considers problem gambling secondary. According to the WHO,

> There is an urgent need to place gambling on national and international public health agendas and strengthen evidence-based policy and prevention strategies, as well as greatly extend early intervention and treatment provision. These measures are critical to reducing current and future harm and social costs associated with commercial gambling.
>
> (WHO 2017, p. 1)

Addiction treatment has become a growth industry. Unfortunately, profit incentives contribute to clinical and financial abuse of clients by unscrupulous providers: a major concern of the National Association of Addiction Treatment Providers (NAATP).

An Individual Challenge

Addiction is a complex brain-based disorder, a compulsive, harmful, lethal habit that defies knowledge and resists change. It is a treatable, chronic medical disease involving complex interactions among brain circuits, genetics, the environment, and an individual's life experiences. *Facing Addiction in America* (The Surgeon General's Report on Alcohol, Drugs, and Health 2016), explains how repeated use of alcohol, other drugs, or addicting behaviors "hijacks" the brain changing the normal functions of the brain circuits that are involved in pleasure (the reward systems), learning, stress, decision making, and self-control.

Alcohol, other drugs, and addictive behaviors increase the severity of mental disorders. Excessive alcohol use is associated with suicides, interpersonal violence, traffic injuries, liver cirrhosis, hypertensive heart disease, tuberculosis, pancreatitis, as well as cancer of the mouth, breast, and colorectal area.

Why is it so difficult for an individual to interrupt the addictive process, let alone realize recovery? *The Diagnostic and Statistical Manual of Mental Disorders* (5th ed.) criteria for substance-related and addictive disorders describe recurrent, persistent, compulsive, and continued substance use despite harmful and hazardous consequences. This lethal habit becomes an addictive lifestyle that evades reason and eludes recovery. Individuals develop tolerance and experience withdrawal. Meanwhile, craving calls out for "more, more."

Many addiction professionals consider addiction a progressive disease. According to the Surgeon General's Report on Alcohol, Drug, and Health *Facing Addiction in America*:

> As individuals continue to misuse alcohol or other substances, progressive changes, called *neuroadaptations*, occur in the structure and function of the brain. These neuroadaptations compromise brain function and also drive the transition from controlled, occasional substance use to chronic misuse, which can be difficult to control. Moreover, these brain changes endure long after an individual stops using substances. They may produce continued, periodic craving for the substance that can lead to relapse: More than 60 percent of people treated for a substance use disorder experience relapse within the first year after they are discharged from treatment, and a person can remain at increased risk of relapse for many years.
>
> (2016, p. 2–2)

(Chapter 2 "Face Addiction" examines addiction, profiles faces of addiction, reviews addictive disorders and treatment, and comments on addiction treatment and monitoring of impaired professionals.)

Recovery

An Idea Whose Time has Come

As stated, addiction jeopardizes the health and well-being of individuals, families, communities, even society itself. Yet, prevention, treatment, and recovery services mitigate disability, devastation, and death from addiction.

Even though addiction is a major social problem and a life-threatening individual challenge, people recover. Today, increasing numbers of addiction/

recovery practitioners, together with thousands of recovering men and women, affirm and advance recovery as an idea whose time has come.

Definition of Recovery

This book defines *recovery as the ability to master addiction, live well, and do good as evidenced by abstinence or harm reduction and relapse prevention; health, wellness, and well-being; together with helping, service, and altruism.*

(Chapter 3 "Affirm Recovery" chronicles the evolution of the concept recovery.)

The Office of Recovery

On September 30, 2021, SAMHSA launched the Office of Recovery to advance the agency's commitment to, and support of, recovery for all Americans. September marks National Recovery Month, and in establishing this new office, SAMHSA now has a dedicated team with a deep understanding of recovery to promote policies, programs, and services to those in or seeking recovery. (See Chapter 3 Affirm Recovery for more information about the new Office of Recovery.)

Recovery is Work

Recovery is work. So, say faculty and students learning about recovery, recovery providers, and especially recovering people. Chapter 5 of *Alcoholic Anonymous* is titled "How it Works," beginning with the sentence "Rarely have we seen a person fail who has thoroughly followed our path." The chapter then describes 12 steps, which are suggested as a program of recovery. Chapter 6 is called "Into Action." The AA Promises conclude by affirming "Are these extravagant promises? We think not. They are being fulfilled among us - sometimes quickly, sometimes slowly. They will always materialize if we work for them."

Most addiction treatment includes psychoeducation, counseling, as well as exercises and assignments for individuals, groups, and families. Addiction treatment/recovery workbooks abound. Consider *The Staying Sober Workbook* by Terence T. Gorski, *Addiction Recovery Skills Workbook* by Suzette Glasner-Edwards, and *The Relapse Prevention Workbook* by Judy Lohr, to name a few. The SMART Recovery Toolbox provides a variety of methods, worksheets, and exercises.

Developing Competencies for Recovery is work! Tertiary prevention provides the conceptual framework for recovery work, supported by developmental-learning theory, Competency-Based Education (CBE), and the lived experiences of thousands of recovering men and women. Three assumptions—actually, three strong beliefs—ground and guide recovery work. We believe:

1 People can develop competencies to master addiction, live well, and do good.
2 Developing competencies for recovery requires commitment, courage, and change over time.
3 Recovery is work.

Developing Competencies for Recovery

Dimensions and Dynamics Competencies

THE DIMENSIONS: KNOWLEDGE, SKILLS, AND ATTITUDES (KSA)

Competencies are clusters of related knowledge, skills, and attitudes (KSAs) that equip, enable, and empower a person to act effectively, usually with proficiency. Diana Vinke, an education policy leader at the Eindhoven University of Technology, defines competency as the ability of an individual to select and use the knowledge, skills, and attitudes that are necessary for effective behavior in a specific professional, social, or learning situation. Competencies reflect cognitive, affective, and psychomotor domains of learning.

In the 1950s and continuing into the 1970s, Dr. Benjamin Bloom and colleagues identified three domains of learning: *cognitive, affective,* and *psychomotor.* The cognitive (mental) domain involves knowledge including the recall or recognition of specific facts, procedural patterns, and concepts that serve in the development of intellectual abilities. The affective (attitude) domain reflects emotional phenomena, especially values and feelings such as appreciation, enthusiasm, and motivation. The psychomotor (skill) domain includes physical movement, coordination, and use of the motor-skill areas. Each domain has a taxonomy of processes ranging from simple to complex. Widely recognized and referred to as KSA (knowledge, skills, and attitudes), these three learning domains constitute the dimensions of competency.

Yet, competencies are more than KSA dimensions. Empowerment is the central dynamic of competency. As such, empowerment drives and directs actions toward the experience and expression of excellence.

THE DYNAMICS: EMPOWERMENT

Empowerment is personal or social agency that enables an individual or group to act in a responsible, determined way. Empowerment theory drives and directs the development of competencies for recovery, specifically the knowledge, skills, and attitudes necessary to master addiction, live well, and do good. Empowerment for recovery has historical origins and current support in social movements, mental health reforms, Alcoholics Anonymous, and recovery initiatives.

Empowerment is rooted in individual actions and social supports. Personal empowerment develops when individuals seek to acquire capabilities to overcome their psychological and intellectual obstacles and attain self-determination, self-sufficiency, and decision-making abilities. Personal empowerment requires a strong, authentic, positive sense of self as experienced and expressed by self-worth, self-regulation, self-efficacy, self-in-relation, and self-care.

Social or collective empowerment occurs when people join forces to overcome barriers or obstacles to social change. People experience a sense of collective belonging through social empowerment. With social empowerment, an individual moves beyond self to family and friends; into the community, even society and culture. Mutual support groups like Alcoholic Anonymous (AA), as well as Recovery-Oriented Systems of Care (ROSC), exemplify social empowerment for recovery.

Step One of Narcotics Anonymous (NA) reads "We admitted we were powerless over our addiction, that our lives had become unmanageable." Recovery practitioners help people with addiction overcome their sense of powerlessness and develop empowerment for recovery.

Developmental Learning

Developmental learning is a sound way to develop competencies for recovery. Learning is concerned with the acquisition of knowledge, skills, and attitudes. Development is the broadening and deepening of this learning over a lifetime. Developmental-learning theory integrates learning theory and developmental psychology.

The goal of developmental learning is to enhance, expand, extend the thoughts, feelings, and actions of individuals or groups. It helps people perform well and reach their full potential for success. Developmental learning can help people with addiction develop competencies to master addition, live well, and do good.

Competency-Based Education (CBE)

Developing Competencies for Recovery builds upon the principles and practice of Competency-Based Education (CBE). Competency-based learning is a system of education where individuals demonstrate mastery of content or performance proficiency. Competency-Based Education (CBE) is different from traditional learning which is governed by time: e.g., the time required to complete a class, receive a diploma, or earn a degree. Sometimes competencies are part of traditional educational programs.

Home-schooling and online teaching often employ a competency-learning model. An increasing number of K-12 school systems and higher education institutions are developing Competency-Based Education (CBE). CBE programs provide greater flexibility for adult learners, reduce costs for institutions, and provide students with validated skills that are highly valued by employers. More health practitioners are completing Competency-Based Education programs. Increasingly, continuing education (CEUs) for licensed practitioners is competency-based.

In the 1980s, insurance companies and addiction treatment providers began to replace a "one size fits all" philosophy of treatment with the idea of "different strokes for different folks." While time and tradition still prevail, addiction treatment today reflects the ASAM placement criteria and levels of care, medication-assisted treatment (MAT), a shift to ambulatory settings for services, and an increasing emphasis on recovery.

SAMHSA Competencies

Two publications from the Substance Abuse Mental Health Services Association (SAMHSA) ground and guide the development of competencies for recovery:

- *Addiction Counseling Competencies: Knowledge, Skills, and Attitudes of Professional Practice.*
- *Core Competencies for Peer Workers in the Behavioral Health Services.*

In 1998, the Substance Abuse and Mental Health Services Administration (SAMHSA) and the Center for Substance Abuse Treatment (CSAT) published Addiction Counseling Competencies: The Knowledge, Skills, and Attitudes of Professional Practice (The Competencies) as Technical Assistance Publication (TAP) 21. The guide identified four generic KSAs, eight professional practice needs or dimensions, and 123 specific competencies. TAP 21 was last updated in 2017. Note: *Competencies for Supervision in Substance use Disorder Treatment: An Overview* (TAP 21-A may be of special interest to addiction/recovery faculty and supervisors).

More recently, the Substance Abuse Mental Health Services Administration identified the critical knowledge, skills, and abilities needed by individuals who provide peer support services to people with or in recovery from a mental health or substance use condition: *Core Competencies for Peer Workers in Behavioral Health Services*. SAMHSA suggested 12 Competency Categories with specific behaviors for each category. Additional competencies may be required to provide peer support services in settings such as clinical, school, or correctional settings or to groups such as families, veterans, people in medication-assisted recovery from a SUD, senior citizens, or members of specific ethnic, racial, or gender-orientation groups.

If competencies ground and guide treatment and recovery work by behavioral health professionals and peer workers, why not extend this model of learning and practice to people with addiction?

Core Competencies from the Business World

In the business world, core competencies foster performance that is efficient, effective, excellent, and competitive by a company, team, and individual. Most effective business organizations employ core competencies: a corporate competency framework, team core competencies, and personal core competencies.

A competency framework reflects the values, vision, mission, and goals of an organization. This competency framework drives the organization toward excellence and gives it a competitive advantage in industry and market. These core competencies are expected of all employees. Team core competencies reflect the behavioral, technical, and leadership expectations within a division and relate to its abilities, products, and services that equip it to perform in an efficient, effective way. Specialty competencies are expected of team members. Personal core competencies include honesty, leadership, accountability, intelligence, and skill set specific to the job. Competency-based job descriptions are used for hire and performance review. Core competencies at all levels include knowledge, skills, and abilities.

12 Core Competencies

The dimensions and dynamics of competencies, developmental learning, and the many concepts from Competency-Based Education (CBE), the SAMHSA competencies, and the idea of core competencies from the business world collectively support the idea of core competencies for recovery. As stated, competencies are clusters of related knowledge, skills, and attitudes (KSAs) that equip, enable, and empower a person to act effectively, usually with proficiency.

Developing Competencies for Recovery: Mastering Addiction, Living Well, and Doing Good describes 12 core competencies people with addiction can develop to realize recovery. Consider the core competencies:

1 Begin recovery work
2 Face addiction
3 Affirm recovery
4 Develop a strategic recovery plan
5 Set recovery goals
6 Determine motivation for recovery
7 Inventory resources and risks for recovery
8 Draft recovery objectives
9 Act for recovery
10 Evaluate recovery work and competency development
11 Record recovery work and competency development
12 Construct a recovery lifestyle

But how do people with addiction develop the competencies? Often addiction treatment practitioners initiate recovery work. Yet, we know that some 90% of people with substance-use disorders (SUDs) and other addictive disorders never receive treatment. Access to treatment in the U.S. is challenging.

Ideally, people with addiction work with a treatment/recovery professional, peer-support worker, or volunteer to develop competencies for recovery. The book has 12 chapters, one for each competency, and there is a reasonable order for the sequence of the chapters, much like the steps in a recipe. Yet, practitioners and people with addiction can vary the order in which they develop competencies for recovery, especially when it comes to competencies 5, 6, 7, and 8:

1 Develop a Strategic Recovery Plan
2 Set recovery goals
3 Determine motivation for recovery
4 Inventory resources and risks for recovery

There may be situations where goals come first. Motivation may drive and direct recovery. Obtaining resources for recovery may pre-empt setting goals or developing strategic plans.

- Ralph G. is two years clean and sober from alcohol, pot, and cocaine. He tells an addiction counselor, "I want to be in solid recovery when I walk my daughter down the aisle in May." Ralph and the counselor develop a recovery plan and agree to work together to reach this goal.
- "I will do anything, so my wife lets me attend our son's bar mitzvah," Josh W. tells an admissions nurse as he checks into a residential rehabilitation program for health practitioners. Staff acknowledge his motivation and work with Josh to develop a goal-oriented treatment/recovery plan.
- Sue Ellen T. knows she needs recovery housing to continue recovery. "What about childcare? How much will the Oxford house cost?"

Her Parish Nurse reassures Sue Ellen they can meet these needs together.

Directions to a good multiple-choice test often read "Choose the one BEST answer." We urge recovery practitioners and people with addiction to choose the best approach for them to develop competencies for recovery.

Section I presented facts, concepts, principles, and theories about people with addiction, recovery, and developing competencies for recovery. Continue recovery work in Section II with applications for this competency.

II

Section II suggests applications about people with addiction, recovery, and developing competencies for recovery.

People with Addiction

1   You are presenting a program on addiction as a social problem to a middle-school civics class. Outline your presentation.
2   You are receiving a three-year medallion and cake at your NA home-group. Describe your challenge with addiction.

Recovery

3   Recovery is an idea whose time has come. What does this mean for you?
4   What are your expectations from the new federal Office of Recovery?
5   This book defines *recovery as the ability to master addiction, live well, and do good as evidenced by abstinence or harm reduction and relapse prevention; health, wellness, and well-being; together with helping, service, and altruism.* What does each indicator of recovery mean for you?

- Abstinence
- Harm reduction
- Relapse prevention
- Health
- Wellness
- Well-being
- Helping
- Service
- Altruism

6   Why is recovery work?

Developing Core Competencies for Recovery

7   Think of something you do especially well such as a competency for cooking, coaching, biking, or singing. What knowledge, skills, and attitudes ground and guide this competency?

Competency: _____

- Knowledge
- Skills
- Attitude

8 How does developmental learning help people with addiction develop competencies to master addition, live well, and do good?
9 What ideas from Competency-Based Education (CBE) are especially useful in developing competencies for recovery?
10 Why is it so useful to build on competencies for behavioral health professionals and peer workers developed by the Substance Abuse Mental Health Services Administration (SAMHSA)?
11 What is your experience with core competencies or shared common expectations?
12 How can you use the 12 core competencies for recovery work?

Section II suggested applications about people with addiction, recovery, and developing competencies for recovery. Complete Chapter 1 with evaluations of recovery work and competency development.

III

Evaluate recovery work and competency development.

1 Evaluate recovery work with a short True/False Quiz and a review of the outcome, effort, process, and decisions of work.

a Quiz: Based on your learning from Chapter 1 "Begin Recovery," indicate whether each of the following statements is True (T) or False (F).

1 T or F Addiction is a major public health problem.
2 T or F It is easy for an individual to interrupt the addictive process.
3 T or F Prevention, treatment, and recovery services can mitigate disability, devastation, and death from addiction.
4 T or F Many addiction professionals consider addiction a progressive disease.
5 T or F "I'll Quit Tomorrow" is a sound plan for people to manage their addiction.
6 T or F The U.S. Office of Recovery has supported recovery work for many years.
7 T or F Recovery is work.
8 T or F According to *The Promises* from Alcoholics Anonymous (AA), recovery is a gift.
9 T or F Competency-based learning is time-based.
10 T or F Competencies from the Substance Abuse Mental Health Services Association (SAMHSA) ground and guide this book.

(True: 1, 3, 4, 7, 10. False: 2, 5, 6, 8, 9)

b   Outcome, Effort, Process, and Decisions

Examine the outcome, effort, process, and decision-making of your recovery work in Chapter 1.

Outcome

Did you meet **objectives** for Chapter 1? Use Table 1.1 to review objectives and rank as:

Strongly disagree = 1
Disagree = 2
Undecided = 3
Agree = 4
Strongly agree = 5

Effort

Effort evaluation reviews the input or energy you invested in recovery work. Ask and answer the following questions.

- How hard did you work on Chapter 1?
- How much time did you dedicate to Chapter 1?
- What resources did you employ for Chapter 1 work?

Table 1.1 Objectives

Objectives	Rank
I recognize addiction as a social problem and an individual challenge.	1, 2, 3, 4, 5
I embrace recovery as an idea whose time has come.	1, 2, 3, 4, 5
I herald the coming of the federal Office of Recovery.	1, 2, 3, 4, 5
I define recovery.	1, 2, 3, 4, 5
I recognize recovery as work.	1, 2, 3, 4, 5
I understand the characteristics of competencies.	1, 2, 3, 4, 5
I use developmental-learning theory.	1, 2, 3, 4, 5
I employ principles from Competency-Based Education (CBE).	1, 2, 3, 4, 5
I build upon competencies developed by the Substance Abuse Mental Health Services Administration (SAMHSA) for behavioral health professionals and peer workers.	1, 2, 3, 4, 5
I grasp the concept of core competencies from the business world.	1, 2, 3, 4, 5
I consider 12 core competencies as a template for recovery work.	1, 2, 3, 4, 5

Table 1.2 Process

Process	Yes or No	Comment
I read the narrative. (Section I)		
I completed the applications. (Section II)		
I evaluated recovery work and competency development. (Section III)		

Process

Process evaluation is especially valuable when you want to improve outcome and increase the efficiency of your recovery work. Use Table 1.2 to evaluate process.

Decisions

Based on evaluation of your recovery work from Chapter 1, decide to celebrate, continue, correct, or change your approach to recovery work. Reward yourself with a positive thought, feeling, or action. Keep doing what you are doing if "it works." Modify or adjust anything that is not working well. Plan and welcome change that supports your recovery work as you move on to Chapter 2. Ask and answer the following questions.

- Did you **celebrate** your recovery work from Chapter 1 "Begin Recovery?"
- Will you **continue** to approach recovery work in Chapter 2 in the same way?
- Do you plan to **correct** your recovery work to learning in Chapter 2?
- Do you plan to **change** your approach to recovery work in Chapter 2?

2   Evaluate competency development using a KSA/Topic Matrix and a Rubric Review

    a   What knowledge, skills, and attitudes are you using to develop Competency 1 Begin Recovery Work? Document KSA examples in Table 1.3 KSA/Topic Matrix.

    b   Evaluate development of Competency 1 Begin Recovery Work with a Rubric Review. The chapter outline provides the criteria to evaluate competency development. Rank competency development on Table 1.4 as:

- **Exceeds expectations**. Understands, applies, and evaluates competency criteria > 90% of the time.
- **Meets expectations**: Understands, applies, and evaluates competency criteria 75% to 90% of the time.
- **Needs improvement**: Understands, applies, and evaluates competency criteria < 75% of the time.

Table 1.3 KSA/Topic Matrix

Topics	Knowledge	Skills	Attitudes
People with Addiction A Social Problem An Individual Challenge			
Recovery An Idea Whose Time has Come The Office of Recovery Definition of Recovery Recovery is Work			
Developing Competencies for Recovery Dimensions and Dynamics of Competencies Developmental Learning Competency-Based Education (CBE) SAMHSA Competencies Core Competencies from the Business World 12 Core Competencies			

Table 1.4 Competency 1 Begin Recovery Work

Criteria	Exceeds Expectations 3	Meets Expectations 2	Needs Improvement 1
People with Addiction A Social Problem An Individual Challenge	. .		
Recovery An Idea Whose Time has Come The Office of Recovery Definition of Recovery Recovery is Work			
Developing Competencies for Recovery Dimensions and Dynamics of Competencies Developmental Learning Competency-Based Education (CBE) SAMHSA Competencies Core Competencies from the Business World 12 Core Competencies			

Summary

This chapter introduced 12 core competencies people with addiction can develop to realize recovery. Topics that provided the organizing framework for the chapter included People with Addiction, Recovery, and Developing Competencies for Recovery. The chapter described addiction as a social problem and an individual challenge. It suggested recovery is an idea whose time has come and heralded the establishment of the federal Office of Recovery. We defined recovery as the ability to master addiction, live well, and do good. Recovery is work. The chapter explained the dimensions and dynamics of competencies: specifically, knowledge, skills, and attitudes, plus empowerment. It used developmental-learning theory, principles from Competency-Based Education, the competencies for behavioral health professionals and peer workers developed by the Substance Abuse Mental Health Services Administration, and the concept of core competencies from the business world to formulate 12 core competencies people with addiction can develop to realize recovery. The chapter suggested applications—questions, worksheets, exercises, and projects—for the competency. Chapter 1 concluded with evaluations of recovery work and competency development.

2 Face Addiction

Clay W. Refuses to Face Addiction

Face addiction? No way! Yes, I am angry, bored, and perhaps a little depressed, but no addiction. Because of COVID, my basketball scholarship went up in smoke when Tech went online. No sports; no college. Of course, I drink. Weed is legal in our state, and I am mellow most of the time. I covet a little Special K, Crystal, or anything I can get cheap. I have become a 24/7 gamer. I believe I am increasing my executive functioning skills. I prefer creative challenges rather than "shoot-em-up" games. My name is Clay W. I am 20 years old. I live with my mother while I wait for the world to change.

Purpose: This chapter examines addiction: the faces of addiction, addictive disorders, addiction treatment, and monitoring of impaired professionals.

Objectives

- Examine theories, models, and definitions of addiction.
- Profile the many faces of addiction.
- Identify addictive disorders.
- Review and dimensions and dynamics of addiction treatment.
- Acknowledge the monitoring needs of impaired professionals.

Outline

Addiction

Theories and Models of Addiction
The Neurobiology of Addiction
American Society of Addiction Medicine (ASAM)

Faces of Addiction

Addiction Across the Lifespan
Gender Differences in Addiction

DOI: 10.4324/9781003292944-2

Addiction and the Family
LGBTQ Individuals with Addiction
Diversity, Disparities, and Addiction

Addictive Disorders

Substance Use Disorders (SUDs)
Other Addictive Disorders
Co-Occurring Mental Illness and Substance Use Disorders

Addiction Treatment

Assessment and Diagnosis
Treatment Goals
Treatment Settings
Treatment Approaches
Treatment Duration

Monitoring for Impaired Professionals

I

Face addiction. Section I presents facts, concepts, principles, and theories about addiction, the many faces of addiction, addictive disorders, addiction treatment, and monitoring for impaired professionals.

Addiction

Theories of addiction are legion: a moral model, a legal model, the disease concept or medical model, a pharmacological model, a public health agent-host-environment model, and other biopsychosocial models of addiction to name a few. We review the neurobiological model of addiction from the Surgeon General's Report *Facing Addiction in America* and include the 2019 definition of addiction from the American Society of Addiction Medicine (ASAM).

Theories and Models of Addiction

A MORAL MODEL

The use of alcohol and other intoxicating substances is well-documented throughout world history. However, overindulgence was scorned and usually punished. Many cultures have a specific place for use of alcohol and other drugs in their religious rites. Yet, according to the *Quran*, the use of alcohol and other intoxicants is a bad habit that drives people away from the remembrance of God. Islamic dietary law bans alcohol.

Gambling is an ancient human activity found in most cultures and parts of the world, although acceptance of gambling varies with the zeitgeist. Currently, gambling occurs in most countries openly and extensively. The video gaming industry is huge and shows no signs of slowing down. While there were almost two billion video gamers across the world in 2015, this figure is expected to rise to over three billion gamers by 2023. Gaming, especially by youth, is epidemic in China.

Today, certain individuals, groups, religions, and cultures still consider the use of intoxicants or other addictive behaviors as immoral, even a sin. Addicts are considered depraved, dissolute degenerates who should be scorned, punished, banished, not treated.

THE LEGAL MODEL

As knowledge about the actual or potential harm from addiction increased, so too did laws to prohibit, control, regulate, even punish possession, use, or sale of substances and addictive behaviors. Beginning mid-20th century, addiction treatment and later prevention legislation was passed. Note the following U.S. federal laws and trends.

The **Harrison Narcotic Act of 1914**, the first such act passed by any nation, established the word *narcotic* as a legal term. The law regulated the importation, manufacture, sale, and use of opium and cocaine, and their compounds and by-products, as well as other synthetic compounds capable of producing physical or psychological dependence. In 1919, Congress ratified the **18th Amendment**, which prohibited the manufacture, sale, or transportation of intoxicating liquors within the United States; this amendment was repealed in 1933.

Significant drug legislation passed in the latter half of the 20th century was the **Comprehensive Drug Abuse Prevention and Control Act** of 1970, also known as the **Controlled Substances Act**. This law provided for increased research into drug abuse prevention and treatment for drug dependency; it strengthened existing law enforcement and established drug schedules. The pharmacological model of addiction that follows has more information about this law.

Recent legislation addresses treatment and prevention, including:

- **Sober Truth on Preventing (STOP) Underage Drinking Act of 2006.** The STOP Act provides additional funds to current or former grantees under the Drug-Free Communities Act of 1997 to prevent and reduce alcohol use among youth ages 12–20.
- **Americans with Disabilities Act (ADA) of 1990/2008.** The Americans with Disabilities Act (ADA) establishes requirements for equal opportunities in employment, state and local government services, public accommodations, commercial facilities, transportation, and telecommunications for citizens with disabilities—including people with mental illnesses and addictions.

- **Mental Health Parity and Addiction Equity Act of 2008.** The Mental Health Parity and Addiction Equity Act requires insurance groups offering coverage for mental health or substance use disorders to make these benefits comparable to general medical coverage. Deductibles, copays, out-of-pocket maximums, and treatment limitations, for mental health or substance use disorders, must be no more restrictive than the same requirements or benefits offered for other medical care.
- **Tribal Law and Order Act (TLOA) of 2010.** The purpose of TLOA is to institutionalize reforms within the federal government so that justice, safety, education for youth, and alcohol and substance abuse prevention and treatment issues relevant to the Indian country remain the subject of consistent focus, not only in the current administration but also in future administrations.
- **Affordable Care Act (ACA) of 2010.** The Affordable Care Act makes health insurance more affordable for individuals, families, and small business owners. People living with mental health challenges or substance use disorders often have problems getting private health insurance.
- **Comprehensive Addiction and Recovery Act (CARA) of 2016.** The Comprehensive Addiction and Recovery Act (CARA) of 2016 authorizes over $181 million each year (must be appropriated each year) to respond to the epidemic of opioid abuse and is intended to greatly increase both prevention programs and the availability of treatment programs.
- **21st Century Cures Act of 2016.** The Cures Act addresses many critical issues including leadership and accountability for behavioral health disorders at the federal level, the importance of evidence-based programs and prevention of mental and substance use disorders, and the imperative to coordinate efforts across government.
- **SUPPORT Act of 2018.** The Substance Use-Disorder Prevention that Promotes Opioid Recovery and Treatment (SUPPORT) for Patients and Communities Act of 2018 was made law to address the nation's opioid overdose epidemic.

THE DISEASE CONCEPT OR MEDICAL MODEL

The idea that drunkenness is a disease was common among doctors in the 18th century. In 1790, Dr. Benjamin Rush described a disease syndrome caused by alcohol and characterized by individual moral and physical decay. According to Rush, the diseased condition of dependence could be cured by total abstinence from hard liquor. The American Association for the Study and Cure of Inebriates, organized in 1870, confirmed a commitment to the disease model and campaigned for institutional care based on the following beliefs:

- Inebriety is a disease.
- It is curable as other diseases are.
- The constitutional tendency to this disease may be either inherited or acquired.

- The disease is often induced by the habitual use of alcohol or other narcotic substances.
- Hence, the establishing of hospitals for the special treatment of inebriety, in which such conditions are recognized, becomes a positive need of the age.

The British Society for the Study and Cure of Inebriety, founded in 1884, recognized inebriety as a true disease.

- Inebriety is a disease caused by an abnormality in brain function and characterized by craving.
- The causes of this disease are multiple: genetic predisposition, adverse life events or fatigues, and drinking long continued.
- Total abstinence is the treatment goal.
- Inebriety must be studied with the same scientific method as other forms of disease to acquire a more exact acquaintance with the phenomena, causation, and condition of inebriety.

Unfortunately, the disease concept gained little ground in late 19th and early 20th century America because of the influence of the temperance movement and Prohibition. Stringent licensing controls in Britain brought alcohol consumption to an all-time low and support for the disease concept waned. In the 1940s, especially after World War II, the disease concept of alcoholism reemerged as a dominant explanation of etiology and guide for treatment.

The disease concept was championed by Alcoholic Anonymous, the Yale Center on Alcohol Studies, the National Council on Alcoholism, and E. M. Jellinek's prestigious 1960 publication *The Disease Concept of Alcoholism*. Subsequently, the American Medical Association, American Psychiatric Association, American Public Health Association, World Health Association, National Institute on Alcohol Abuse and Alcoholism, and National Institute on Drug Abuse recognized alcoholism and other drug addictions as diseases. Reimbursement by insurers for addiction treatment exists in large part today because substance-related and other addictive disorders meet medical criteria to be considered diseases.

Yet, Carl Erik Fisher, professor of clinical psychiatry at Columbia, believes that the emphasis on addiction of a disease ignores its many socio-cultural influences. Fisher advocates for language that minimizes social stigma and personal shame when talking about addiction. See his compelling personal and professional story of addiction, treatment, and recovery in the 2022 book *The Urge: Our History of Addiction*.

THE PHARMACOLOGICAL MODEL

By the 1800s, Americans believed alcohol to be a serious threat to the social order, a menace as great as the gin epidemic in London between 1720 and

1750. In addition to the widespread use of alcohol, increasing numbers of people were using and becoming addicted to drugs. Doctors universally prescribed opium to relieve pain; it was cheap and easily available. Laudanum (tincture of opium) was the faithful companion of many women. Patent medicines were fortified with alcohol, opium, or cocaine. Morphine addiction surfaced in the United States following the Civil War (1861–1865). Concerns about the ravages of distilled spirits and drugs culminated with the passage of the 18th Amendment which prohibited the manufacture, sale, and transportation of intoxicating liquors within the United States.

Many laws have been passed to regulate licit and illicit drugs. Of special note is the **Controlled Substances Act (CSA)**. Drugs and other substances that are considered controlled substances are divided into five schedules. An updated and complete list of the schedules is published annually. Substances are placed in their respective schedules based on whether they have a currently accepted medical use in treatment within the United States, their relative abuse potential, and the likelihood of causing dependence when abused. Warnings for potential abuse appear on bottles or package inserts. The pharmacological model of addiction is current and contributes to our overall understanding of addiction.

PUBLIC HEALTH AGENT-HOST-ENVIRONMENT MODEL

The public health model of disease and disorders, including addiction, emphasizes a dynamic agent-host-environment interaction. The *agent* is any internal or external factor that by its presence or absence can lead to a disease or disorder. Alcohol, some other drug, or a behavior such as gambling, pornography, or shopping must be present for an addiction to develop. Yet, the presence of the substance or behavior alone does not cause addiction.

The *host* is the individual who may be susceptible or resilient to addiction. Host factors such as a family history of addiction, co-occurring mental illness, trauma, chronic pain, and acute stress increase susceptibility to addiction. Protective factors including genetics, a functional family, personal competence, and healthy coping mechanisms increase resilience and resistance to misuse and addiction.

The *environment* is all physical and social conditions external to the host: including where people were born, live, learn, work, play, worship, and age. Adverse conditions like poverty, homelessness, unemployment, systemic racism, war, natural disasters, and pandemics increase the risk for addiction. A stable family, satisfying work, access to health care, and community services mitigate against addiction.

The public health agent-host-environment model of addiction is congruent with the ASAM definition of addiction and *DSM-5* diagnostic criteria.

OTHER THEORIES AND MODELS OF ADDICTION

Genetic theory emphasizes the role of heredity in the etiology of addictive disorders. Genograms often reveal a history of addiction in families. Individuals with a family history of addiction are at 40–60% greater risk to develop an addiction. However, genetic predisposition and vulnerability alone do not account for the development of addiction.

Many psychological theories extend our understanding of addiction. Classical conditioning theory helps explain craving, tolerance, and withdrawal. Operant conditioning underscores the significant role reinforcement plays in the development and maintenance of an addiction. Psychodynamic theory gives us the concepts id, ego, and super-ego, and the ego mechanisms of defense. Trait theory suggests that certain personality traits predispose individuals to addiction such as thrill-seeking and low harm avoidance. Cognitive-behavioral factors such as self-awareness, expectancy, and attribution help clinicians and clients manage addiction. Stress-management theory recognizes the need for people to reduce tension and anxiety. Unfortunately, many people use alcohol and other drugs (especially prescription medications) to manage stress.

Sociocultural theories, especially family theory and systems theory, consider the role of the family, environment, culture, and other socioeconomic factors in the development and expression of addiction. Addiction is a synthesis of biological, psychological, sociocultural, and ecological variables. Many addiction professionals employ the biopsychosocial model of illness developed by George Engel and Uri Bronfenbrenner's ecological systems theory of development to understand people with addiction.

Consider transcendental/spiritual theories of addiction too. In his book *Addiction and Grace* (2008), psychiatrist Gerald May says all human beings long for wholeness, completion, and fulfillment. We hunger to love, to be loved, and to move closer to the source of love, God. This longing gives meaning to life. Yet, "life happens," and modern experience often creates a sense of aloneness, alienation, and pain. Addiction offers temporary relief. Psychiatrists Carl Jung and more recently Stanislav Grof describe craving as the equivalent of the spiritual thirst for wholeness. People also crave release from pain, a desire for joy, a "rush," a "high." Spirituality is an important component of 12-step recovery programs.

The Neurobiology of Addiction

The 2016 Surgeon General's report on alcohol, drugs, and health, *Facing Addiction in America*, highlights the key issues and important research findings of addiction in America. The section, The Neurobiology of Substance Use, Misuse, and Addiction reviews brain research on the neurobiological processes that turn casual substance use into a compulsive disorder.

According to the report, repeated use of alcohol, other drugs, or addicting behaviors "hijacks" the brain, changing the normal functions of brain circuits involved in pleasure (the reward systems), learning, stress, decision making, and self-control. Three main circuits in the brain are involved in addiction: the basal ganglia, extended amygdala, and prefrontal cortex. Use (intoxication) produces a surge of the neurotransmitter dopamine in the region of the brain called the basal ganglia and people feel pleasure. With repeated use, the brain associates the rewarding high with cues in the individual's life: persons, places, and things. The extended amygdala controls our stress response. Withdrawal is the distress people experience when they are not using. Use is the only way "to spell relief." The pre-frontal cortex governs decision-making, judgment, and impulse control. However, the prefrontal cortex is disrupted in individuals with addiction. Craving is the preoccupation with anticipation of reward from drinking, using, gambling, or other addictive behavior. Self-control is compromised; cues dominate, and people return to active addiction. This is relapse. The intensity of symptoms and progression vary; a person may go through the cycle over months, weeks, or several times a day. As the cycle continues, addiction severity increases with greater physical and psychological harm. See Figure 2.1 areas of the human brain that are especially important in addiction from *Facing Addiction in America*, pp. 2–5.

American Society of Addiction Medicine (ASAM) Definition of Addiction

The Board of Directors of the American Society of Addiction Medicine (ASAM) adopted the following definition of addiction on September 15, 2019.

> Addiction is a treatable, chronic medical disease involving complex interactions among brain circuits, genetics, the environment, and an individual's life experiences. People with addiction use substances or engage in behaviors that become compulsive and often continue despite harmful consequences.

Prevention efforts and treatment approaches for addiction are generally as successful as those for other chronic diseases.

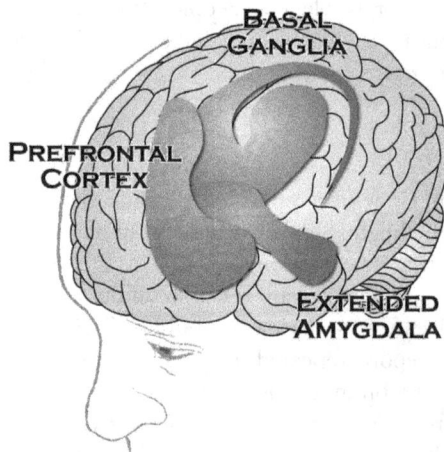

Figure 2.1 Areas of the Human Brain that are Important in Addiction, from *Facing Addiction in America*, p. 2–5

Faces of Addiction

One in seven people develops a substance use disorder some time in life. An increasing number of people gamble, game, and engage in other addictive behaviors. Faces of addiction profiles addiction across the lifespan; gender differences and addiction; addiction and the family; LGBTQ individuals with addiction; as well as ethnic/ racial/cultural diversity and disparities.

Addiction Across the Lifespan

Addiction across the lifespan wears many faces.

- An infant born six weeks premature to a mother who drank, smoked, and used cocaine during her pregnancy.
- Two little girls playing dress-up and using lipstick to draw red lines up their arms to look like mom: an IV drug user.
- A 16-year-old girl, "dumped" by her 25-year-old boyfriend, admitted to a hospital psychiatric unit after ingesting a quart of vodka and 50 Tylenol.
- "What do you have: gold or green OCs?" asks a teen to a street drug dealer.
- Four high-school seniors "high" on Adderall before taking their Scholastic Aptitude Tests (SATs).
- A young adult dead from cardiac arrest after a 40-hour marathon session of Diablo 3, an action role-playing game.
- An evening TV news anchor and sports gambler praying for a long commercial so he can check scores on his cell phone.
- A homeless soldier with four deployments to Iraq and Afghanistan admitted to a Veterans Administration (VA) Hospital, with delirium tremens (DTs).
- A board-certified oncologist dismissed from his position at a prestigious University Hospital facing loss of license and incarceration for selling pain prescriptions to finance his gambling.
- A hospice nurse, employee of the year, who has been suspended from work because she diverted narcotics to self-medicate her back pain.
- An executive vice-president of a major insurance company admitted to a locked psychiatric ward for self-inflicted gunshot wounds, a botched suicide attempt, related to embezzlement to pay gambling debts.
- A retired electric utility worker who drinks himself into a stupor every evening to cope with his depression after the recent death of his wife.
- A 78-year-old woman visiting her daughter and family who gets up during the night, falls, and breaks a hip. Her daughter discovers prescribed medications for Percocet, Xanax, and Ambien in her mother's purse.

Addiction has adverse biopsychosocial consequences across the lifespan. Alcohol and other drug use by pregnant women can affect the developing fetus and newborn adversely, often with lifelong deleterious effects. Children cared for by people with addictions are at greater risk for neglect and abuse. This stress, plus genetic predispositions, increases the probability these children may develop an addiction.

Adolescents risk and experiment with life, often through drinking, using, and other dangerous behaviors. Heavy substance use can affect teen brain development and contribute to the likelihood of addiction. Most people who meet the criteria for a substance use disorder started using substances during adolescence and met diagnostic criteria by age 20–25. Many young adult lifestyles include substance use and other addictive behaviors.

Addiction can exact a heavy toll on middle-aged adults who may be wrestling with job and career loss, financial and legal problems, divorce, alienation from children, and the onset of health problems. Life expectancy in the U.S. has fallen for several years because of opioid deaths, especially among adults. Biopsychosocial vulnerabilities increase the risk of substance misuse and other addictive behaviors by older adults, especially baby boomers. Note: There is strong interest in intergenerational studies of trauma, racism, and addiction.

Gender Differences and Addiction

Addiction is an equal opportunity disorder, yet there are some differences between men and women with addiction. Men tend to drink and use more substances than women; however, progression is greater in women. In the U.S., drinking, using, and gambling have been associated with men and an alpha-male lifestyle. Historically, addiction treatment often reflected male needs. Addiction has been less visible and less acceptable for women: especially pregnant women and mothers. Perception of addiction differs for men and women. Men tend to focus on behavior: "I did bad things when I was high." Women personalize addiction: "I was a bad person when I used." Unemployment, criminal behavior, and homelessness are more common in men with addiction. We see more depression, abuse, eating disorders, and social media dependencies in women. Co-occurring medical conditions challenge both men and women with addiction. Pain, physical disabilities, and HIV/AIDs increase addiction severity irrespective of gender.

Addiction and the Family

A family is a social unit of two or more persons related by blood, marriage, or choice living together. Traditional families include parents and children, yet today we see many single-parent families, grandparents raising children, or blended families. Friends living together constitute a family. Even people who live alone are still part of a family. Pets are important parts of many families. Children are socialized within a family. A healthy family promotes the growth and development of all its members.

Addiction affects families in two ways. First, addicts come from families, and families of origin often contribute to the development of addiction through genetics and family dysfunction. Second, addicted individuals adversely affect their immediate families in many ways. Addiction in the family damages trust, respect, and relationships; children experience neglect and abuse. Life often revolves around the addicted person. Rules become rigid, unrealistic, and difficult to keep. When children live in homes with active addiction, they often adapt to family dysfunction by playing certain roles: hero, scapegoat, lost child, or mascot. Role reversal among spouses is stressful. Intimate partner violence (IPV) is frequent. Underemployment and unemployment happen; financial losses are great. Reputations suffer as addiction becomes public. See the moving book by Beverly Conyers titled *Addict in the Family: Stories of Loss, Hope, and Recovery*.

Enabling and codependency characterize many families with addiction. Enabling includes all actions by family or friends that prevent people who drink, use, or gamble from experiencing the full impact of the negative consequences of their addiction. Enablers protect the addict: e.g., a wife calls in sick for her husband when he is hungover. Although the intention is care, concern, and protection, enabling allows the person to continue in addiction. Codependency describes a pattern of unhealthy behavior family and friends may develop to survive the stress caused by a loved one's drinking, using, or other addictive behavior. Symptoms of codependency include control, distrust, perfectionism, avoidance of feelings, problems with intimacy, excessive caretaking, hyper-vigilance, physical illness, and even clinical depression. Check out books by Melody Beattie such as *Codependent No More*.

Several self-help support groups attest to the relationship between addiction and the family. Adult Children of Alcoholics (ACOA) is an organization that provides a forum for individuals who desire to recover from the effects of growing up in an alcoholic or otherwise dysfunctional family. Al-Anon, Nar-Anon, and Gam-Anon are self-help groups for family and friends of individuals with drinking, using, or gambling problems.

LGBTQ Individuals with Addiction

Addiction prevalence is higher among LGBTQ individuals, especially youth, than in the general population, addiction severity is higher when LGBTQ individuals enter treatment. Understanding the developmental and social experiences of LGBTQ individuals is critical for addiction providers and practitioners. Treatment that offers specialized groups for LGBTQ people is most effective. Co-occurring problems that complicate treatment and recovery for LGBTQ individuals include family issues and social isolation; abuse, battering, even violence, co-occurring psychiatric problems, and positive HIV status.

Diversity and Disparities and Addiction

Research found brain differences in smoking rates between African Americans and Whites. Some East Asians have a gene that alters the metabolism of alcohol. Gambling and gaming are almost endemic among Asian populations.

Alcohol prevalence is high, and the current opioid epidemic is rampant among Native Americans. Ethnicity, race, and culture influence personal health beliefs and practices about addiction. Some label the opioid epidemic in the U.S. a white person's disease, because white people were prescribed opioids in greater amounts than black/brown populations.

Disparities in addiction service are great and most minority populations with addiction are underserved. Discrimination, acculturation, ethnic pride, shame, and cultural mistrust prevent many "minority" groups from seeking addiction services. See Resources for Recovery at the back of the book, especially the annual National *Drug Use Survey and Health* (NDUSH) for current substance use and mental illness among different ethnic/racial populations.

Best-practice treatment reflects the cultural beliefs and practices of the population being served. Recovery support, like AA groups and literature, exists for African Americans, Latinos, Asians, and Native Americans.

Addictive Disorders

Addictive disorders include substance use disorders (SUDs), other addictive disorders such as gambling, and co-occurring substance use and mental disorders.

Substance Use Disorders (SUDs)

According to the *Diagnostic and Statistical Manual of Mental Disorders* (5th ed.), substance-related disorders encompass ten separate classes of drugs including alcohol; caffeine; cannabis; hallucinogens; inhalants; opioids; sedatives, hypnotics, and anxiolytics; stimulants; tobacco; and other or unknown substances. The *DSM-5* includes diagnostic criteria and codes for substance use, intoxication, and withdrawal for each of these classes of drugs. Note: the *DSM-5-TR* was published in March 2022. There are no major changes from *DSM-5* in the diagnostic criteria. The DSM-5-TR uses ICD-10-CM codes, with anticipation of ICD 11. ICD-10-CM stands for the International Classification of Diseases, 10th Edition, Clinical Modification. There is more attention to culture, racism, and discrimination in the *DSM-5-TR*.

Substance use is the use of any of these substances—even one time. *Substance misuse* is the use of any substance in a manner, situation, amount, or frequency that can cause harm to users or those around them: e.g., a fight, a motor vehicle crash, an overdose, or a job loss. Severe substance use disorders that meet diagnostic criteria for significant clinical impairment and distress are called *addictions*. Drug overdose is the leading cause of accidental death in the United States. According to the Centers for Disease Control and Prevention, over 96,000 people in the U.S. died as the result of accidental drug overdoses in 2020, an increase of 30% from the previous year, attributed in part to the COVID pandemic. Fentanyl is one driving force behind this spike in deaths.

Other Addictive Disorders

Behaviors like gambling, binge eating, exercise; work, love, sex, shopping; Internet use, gaming, mobile phone use, and other reward experiences may become addictive. Research by Dr. Kenneth Blum and others on reward deficiency syndrome (RDS) suggests a genetic basis for a broad array of addictive disorders. Many of these "behaviors" are treated as addictions. The *DSM-5* considers gambling an addictive disorder. In 2018, the World Health Organization (WHO) listed gaming addiction as a mental health condition.

Co-occurring Mental Illness and Substance Use Disorders

Substance use and mental disorders are closely linked. Mental illness is a risk factor for substance use and other addictive behaviors. Individuals with mental illness often "self-medicate" with alcohol, other drugs, and addictive behaviors. In 2020, stress from COVID-19 was associated with a surge in substance use, online gambling, pornography, and suicidality, intimate partner violence (IPV), and child abuse.

Co-occurring substance use and mental disorders are common in teens, adults, and older adults, especially depression, anxiety, and post-traumatic stress disorder (PTSD). Any mental illness (AMI), let alone serious mental illness (SMI), worsens with substance use or other addictive behaviors. Severity and impairment increase while daily functioning and quality of life decrease markedly. Suicide thoughts, plans, and attempts are higher among individuals with addiction. Treatment is limited and, when available, often addresses only one problem. See especially the most recent *National Surveys on Drug Use and Health.*

Addiction Treatment

As mentioned in Chapter 1, people with addiction need treatment. Even with the passage of the Mental Health Parity and Addiction Equity Act of 2008 and the Affordable Care Act in 2010, 90% of individuals with substance use disorders receive no treatment. The National Council on Problem Gambling refers gamblers to treatment, yet insurance often requires a primary diagnosis of depression or substance use and considers problem gambling secondary. Why this gap between need and treatment? The reasons are legion. Public stigma and personal shame about addiction prevail. Addiction education for health professionals is limited. Access to addiction treatment is complicated and cost-prohibitive for many. Rarely do we see a continuum of addiction service including pre-screening, referral, treatment, continuing care, and recovery support services? And perhaps more important, there is no consensus within the addiction community about what constitutes best treatment.

Best-practice addiction treatment begins with a comprehensive holistic, biopsychosocial assessment followed by a *DSM-5* diagnosis. Treatment goals reflect addiction stage and severity. Treatment settings suggest a range of providers with multiple levels of care. Because "one size does not fit all," addiction practitioners employ many approaches to addiction treatment. Relapse happens. Recovery is often a distant goal.

See also the World Health Organization publication 2020 *International Standards for the Treatment of Drug Use Disorders* (2020). Download a free copy and note especially:

- Key principles and standards for the treatment of drug use disorders
- Treatment systems for drug use disorders
- Treatment settings, modalities, and intervention
- Populations with special treatment and care needs

According to the World Health Organization (WHO) and its Office of Drugs and Crime (UNODC), treatment aims to improve the health and quality of life of people with drug use disorders. Specific treatment goals are to:

- stop or reduce drug use
- improve health, well-being, and social functioning of the affected individual
- prevent future harms by decreasing the risk of complications and relapse.

Assessment and Diagnosis

ASSESSMENT

The ASAM Criteria: Treatment Criteria for Addictive Substance-Related and Co-Occurring Conditions suggests six dimensions for a holistic, biopsychosocial assessment of individuals with addiction:

1 Acute Intoxication and/or Withdrawal Potential
2 Biomedical Conditions and Complications
3 Emotional, Behavior, or Cognitive Conditions, and Complications
4 Readiness to Change
5 Relapse, Continued Use, of Continued Problem Potentials
6 Recovery/Living Environment

Biopsychosocial assessment elements include a history of the present episode; family history, developmental history; alcohol, tobacco other drug use, addictive behavior history; personal/social history; legal history; psychiatric history; medical history; spiritual history; review of systems, mental status examination, physical examination; formulation and diagnosis; survey of assets, vulnerabilities, and supports; culmination in treatment recommendations. See Table 2.1 for an example of ASAM Dimensions and a Holistic, Biopsychosocial Assessment.

Table 2.1 ASAM Dimensions and Holistic, Biopsychosocial Assessment

ASAM Dimension	Holistic, Biopsychosocial Assessment
1. Acute Intoxication and/or Withdrawal Potential	Exploring an individual's past and current experiences of substance use and withdrawal.
2. Biomedical Conditions and Complications	Exploring an individual's health history and current physical condition
3. Emotional, Behavioral or Cognitive Conditions and Complications	Exploring an individual's thoughts, emotions, and mental health issues.
4. Readiness to Change	Exploring an individual's readiness and interest in change.
5. Relapse/Continued Use, Continued Problem Potential	Exploring an individual's unique relationship with relapse or continued use or problems.
6. Recovery/Living Environment	Exploring an individual's recovery or living situation and the surrounding people, places, and things.

DIAGNOSIS

As stated in the *DSM-5*, substance-related disorders encompass ten separate classes of drugs including alcohol; caffeine; cannabis; hallucinogens; inhalants; opioids; sedatives, hypnotics, and anxiolytics; stimulants; tobacco; and other or unknown substances. Substance use is the use of any of these substances—even one time. Substance misuse is the use of any substance in a manner, situation, amount, or frequency that can cause harm to users or those around them: e.g., a fight, a motor vehicle crash, an overdose, or a job loss. Severe substance use disorders that meet diagnostic criteria for significant clinical impairment and distress are called addictions.

Treatment Goals

Treatment goals follow assessment and diagnosis. Goals for substance use disorders address intoxication, withdrawal, and the severity of the SUD itself. Goals begin with intoxication management and withdrawal management followed by interventions to promote abstinence or harm reduction and relapse prevention. Goals for other addictive behaviors are similar, except for chemical detoxification.

Ideally, recovery begins in early treatment. Abstinence or harm reduction and relapse prevention are early, continuing recovery goals. Health, wellness, and well-being are personal growth goals that build on early recovery. Helping, service, and altruism are recovery goals that transcend the self.

Treatment Settings

According to 2019 The National Survey of Drug Use and Health, 19.3 million Americans received treatment for substance use disorders. Mutual groups and outpatient settings provided most SUD treatment, yet it behooves us to examine recognized addiction providers, levels of care, and addiction practitioners.

Increasingly, health care providers employ core competencies as an organizing framework, for team collaboration, and practitioner expectations. The book *Health Professional Education: A Bridge to Quality*, edited by Ann C. Greiner and Elisa Knebel (2003) identified simple, core competencies for all providers and practitioners:

- Provide patient-centered care
- Work in interdisciplinary teams
- Employ evidence-based practice
- Apply quality improvement
- Utilize informatics.

ADDICTION PROVIDERS

Service for people with addiction is often a "stand-alone" specialty provided by public, private, and for-profit organizations and facilities. Settings for addiction service include the community, professional offices, treatment centers, clinics, hospitals, as well as prisons, churches, and schools. With the advent of the concept of behavioral health, more providers began to offer both substance abuse and mental health services. The 2016 U.S. Surgeon's Report *Facing Addiction in America* recommends full integration of the continuum of service for substance use disorders with the rest of health care as the most promising way to address access to improve access and quality of treatment: an idea whose time has yet to come. Addiction treatment has become a growth industry and profit incentives bring clinical and financial abuse of clients by unscrupulous providers: a major concern of the National Association of Addiction Treatment Providers (NAATP).

LEVELS OF CARE

According to the Substance Abuse Mental Health Services Administration (SAMHSA), the treatment system for substance use disorders is comprised of multiple service components and levels of care including the following:

- Individual and group counseling
- Inpatient and residential treatment
- Intensive outpatient treatment
- Partial hospital programs
- Case or care management
- Medication
- Recovery support services
- 12-step fellowship

The American Society of Addiction Medicine identifies levels of care for withdrawal and/or intoxication management and for addiction treatment: from ambulatory/outpatient care to clinically managed intensive inpatient services. *ASAM-3* provides exact matrices for matching severity with treatment intensity. Insurance providers and addiction professionals employ these tools for effective, efficient addiction treatment. Usually, level of care placement is the lowest treatment level possible to achieve a favorable outcome. Irrespective of private or public insurance, we need to remember these guidelines when we are helping someone access treatment. The 2016 U.S. Surgeon's Report *Facing Addiction in America* recommends full integration of the continuum of service for substance use disorders with the rest of health care as the most promising way to address access to improve access and quality of treatment.

ADDICTION PRACTITIONERS

Addiction professionals, paraprofessionals, peer supports, and volunteers provide service for people with addiction: physicians, psychologists, counselors, nurses, social workers, clergy, recovery coaches, sponsors, and a host of recovery supports. Practitioners are licensed and/or certified by states or their respective professional associations. Competencies and codes of ethics guide practice. Addiction professionals also direct prevention services, manage programs, teach practitioners, and conduct research. Increasingly, health practitioners in general practice offer screening and early intervention services to people with addiction. Recovering men and women, support individuals with addiction through mutual self-help groups like AA, NA, GA, and SMART Recovery.

Treatment Approaches

"One size does not fit all." Today, we have many approaches to addiction treatment. The vision and mission of treatment providers often reflect one dominant philosophy. Practitioners usually embrace and use a treatment approach commensurate with their training and experience. Providers and practitioners may modify, blend, or integrate different therapeutic approaches to facilitate individual goal achievement. For example, Hazelden/Betty Ford launched COR-12: Comprehensive Opioid Response with the Twelve Steps. Caron integrated COVID-19 stress management into its family programs. Recognized treatment approaches for individuals with addiction include:

- **Twelve-step-oriented treatment** helps clients achieve abstinence and prevent relapse through understanding the principles of Alcoholics Anonymous and other 12-step groups, group counseling, psychoeducation, and homework assignments. The 12-step approach emphasizes cognitive, behavioral, spiritual, and health aspects of recovery. It is effective with diverse populations.

- **Cognitive-behavioral therapy** focuses on teaching people with addiction skills that can help them understand addiction, maintain abstinence and/or harm reduction, and reduce risks for relapse. CBT is effective when people are motivated; practitioners must be CBT-trained specifically for therapy to succeed.

- **Motivational approaches**, such as motivational interviewing and motivational enhancement therapy, rely on extensive practitioner training and high levels of client self-awareness. Through empathic listening, practitioners explore individual attitudes toward addiction and treatment, support past successes, and encourage problem-solving strategies. Motivational approaches are person-centered, goal-driven, and encourage individual self-sufficiency.

- **The Matrix model** integrates several treatment approaches, including mutual-help, cognitive-behavioral, and motivational interviewing. A strong therapeutic relationship between client and practitioner is the centerpiece of the Matrix approach. Other features include learning about withdrawal and cravings, practicing relapse prevention and coping techniques, and submitting to drug screens.

- **Medication-Assisted Treatment (MAT)** is an evidence-based treatment that includes FDA-approved medication combined with counseling and psychosocial support. Acamprosate, disulfiram, and naltrexone are the most common medications used to treat alcohol use disorder. Medications approved to treat opioid use disorder (OUD) include methadone, buprenorphine, and naltrexone. These medications decrease cravings associated with addiction. Buprenorphine and methadone also help to relieve withdrawal symptoms.

- **SMART Recovery (Self-Management and Recovery Training)** builds on Rational Emotive Behavior Therapy (REBT) developed by the psychologist Albert Ellis. SMART Recovery emphasizes the power of choice through a 4-Point Program. 1. Building and Maintaining Motivation, 2. Coping with Urges, 3. Managing Thoughts, Feelings and Behaviors, and 4. Living a Balanced Life. SMART Recovery may be used by providers, practitioners, and people with substance and behavior addictions, especially individuals who opt out of a 12-step approach. SMART Recovery sponsors face-to-face meetings around the world and daily online meetings. Their online message board and 24/7 chat rooms are excellent forums to learn about SMART Recovery and obtain addiction recovery support.

The National Institute on Drug Abuse (NIDA) *Principles of Drug Addiction Treatment: A Research-Base Guide* can help addiction treatment providers and practitioners select a best-practice treatment approach.

- Addiction is a complex but treatable disease that affects brain function and behavior.
- No single treatment is appropriate for everyone.

- Treatment needs to be readily available.
- Effective treatment attends to multiple needs of the individual, not just his or her drug abuse.
- Remaining in treatment for an adequate period of time is critical.
- Behavioral therapies—including individual, family, or group counseling—are the most commonly used forms of drug abuse treatment.
- Medications are an important element of treatment for many patients, especially when combined with counseling and other behavioral therapies.
- An individual's treatment and service plan must be assessed continually and modified as necessary to ensure that it meets his or her changing needs.
- Many drug-addicted individuals also have other mental disorders.
- Medically assisted detoxification is only the first stage of addiction treatment and by itself does little to change long-term drug abuse.
- Treatment does not need to be voluntary to be effective.
- Drug use during treatment must be monitored continuously, as lapses during treatment do occur.
- Treatment programs should test patients for the presence of HIV/AIDS, hepatitis B and C, tuberculosis, and other infectious diseases as well as provide targeted risk-reduction counseling, linking patients to treatment if necessary.

(https://www.drugabuse.gov/publications/principles)

Treatment Duration

Addiction is a chronic condition that requires management and monitoring over time. Treatment helps. The 90-day rehabilitation program is considered a gold standard for addiction treatment. However, practical considerations such as cost, work, school, family, and dropout limit participation. A "one size fits all philosophy" characterized addiction treatment in the 1970s with a flourish of 28-day residential programs. Today, level of care criteria match addiction severity with treatment intensity. Level of care placement is the lowest treatment level possible to achieve a favorable outcome.

Granted, hospital-based and residential programs have many benefits. Alcohol detoxification may require medical treatment in the case of delirium tremens, a life-threatening alcohol withdrawal syndrome that occurs with heavy or long-term drinking. Some drugs, such as benzodiazepines, must be tapered slowly. Longer treatment programs provide patients with extended time to address factors that contributed to addiction. Relapse prevention is a major goal of longer treatment.

Increasingly, treatment goals can be met in ambulatory settings, especially with the aid of medications to manage safe withdrawal and address craving. Recovery coaches support treatment. Participating in a mutual support group reinforces and extends the benefits of professional treatment and provides much-needed support for long-term recovery.

Monitoring for Impaired Professionals

Licensed health care professionals, lawyers, pilots, and other professionals may struggle with substance use disorders, other addictive disorders, and mental health problems. These professionals often are "HFAs," that is, high functioning alcoholics/addicts. Addiction severity is high when HFAs begin treatment; "intellectualizing" works against them. Appropriate treatment and monitoring are necessary for public safety and the health and well-being of the professionals.

Most states have five-year monitoring programs for health practitioners. For example, the Virginia Health Practitioners' Monitoring Program (VA HPMP) is an alternative to disciplinary action for qualified healthcare practitioners with a substance use diagnosis, mental health or physical diagnoses, that may alter their ability to practice their profession safely.

In New York State, with almost 100 licensed professionals, the Professional Assistance Program (PAP) assists professionals who have substance abuse problems, but who have not harmed patients or clients. Such professionals may voluntarily surrender their licenses while receiving treatment rather than face charges of professional misconduct. All applications to the program are confidential. The criteria for admission to the PAP include:

- total abstinence from all mood-altering substances including alcohol
- temporary, voluntary surrender of the professional license
- participation in treatment at an agency approved by the PAP
- an agreement to be monitored by the PAP for at least two years after reinstatement of the license.

Lawyers Helping Lawyers exists to help attorneys reduce the pain and loss that result from the misuse of alcohol, other drugs, and mental and emotional disorders. In the 2016 study conducted by the ABA Commission on Lawyer Assistance Programs and the Hazelden Betty Ford Foundation, more than 20% of lawyers and judges reported problematic alcohol use.

The Federal Aviation Association (FAA) has a drug and alcohol monitoring program for pilots. Any commercial airline pilot who tests positive for alcohol or who has a diagnosis of a substance use disorder (SUD) is required to be monitored and evaluated through the Human Intervention Motivation program.

See Resources for Recovery at the end of the book for descriptions of mutual self-help groups for health professionals, lawyers, and pilots:

- Caduceus Group for Health Professionals
- American Bar Association (ABA) Lawyer Assistance Program (LAP)
- Human Intervention Motivation for Pilots (HIMS)

Section I presented facts, concepts, principles, and theories about addiction, the many faces of addiction, addictive disorders, addiction management, and addiction treatment and monitoring for impaired professionals. Continue recovery work in Section II with applications to the competency.

II

Section II suggests applications about addiction, the many faces of addiction, addictive disorders, addiction treatment, and addiction treatment and monitoring for impaired professionals.

Addiction

1   What theory or model best explains addiction for you? Why?
2   Comment on the ASAM definition of addiction that follows.

Addiction is a treatable, chronic medical disease involving complex interactions among brain circuits, genetics, the environment, and an individual's life experiences. People with addiction use substances or engage in behaviors that become compulsive and often continue despite harmful consequences. Prevention efforts and treatment approaches for addiction are generally as successful as those for other chronic diseases.

3   Write your definition of addiction.

Faces of Addiction

4   Profile a person with an addiction.
5   Add your profile to the faces of addiction.

Addictive Disorders

6   Describer your experience with substance use disorders.

- use
- misuse
- addiction

7   Describe your experience with "other addictions" such as:

- gambling
- gaming
- pornography
- binge eating
- exercise
- other

8   Discuss the challenges of having co-occurring substance use and mental disorder diagnoses.

- impairment
- treatment
- recovery

Addiction Treatment

9   What is your experience with an assessment and diagnosis of addiction?
10 What is your experience with addiction treatment providers?
11 How have addiction practitioners helped or hindered your recovery?
12 What is your experience with different addiction treatment approaches?

Monitoring for Impaired Professionals

13 What is the responsibility of licensed professionals with addiction to the people they serve?
14 What is your experience with high functioning alcoholics/addicts (HFAs)?
15 If you are a licensed professional, please think about your experience with addiction, treatment, monitoring, and recovery.

Section II suggested applications about addiction, the many faces of addiction, addictive disorders, addiction treatment, and addiction treatment and monitoring for impaired professionals. Complete Chapter 2 with evaluations of recovery work and competency development in Section III.

III

Evaluate recovery work and competency development.

1   Evaluate recovery work with a short True/False Quiz and a review of the outcome, effort, process, and decisions of work.

   a   Quiz: Based on your learning from Chapter 2 Face Addiction, indicate whether each of the following statements is True (T) or False (F).

      1   T or F   Some individuals, groups, religions, and cultures believe the use of intoxicants or other addictive behavior is immoral, even a sin.
      2   T or F   The disease concept of addiction was widely accepted in the early 1900s in the United States.
      3   T or F   The Controlled Substances Act (CSA) prohibited the manufacture, sale, or transportation of intoxicating liquors within the United States.
      4   T or F   The Surgeon General's Report *Facing Addiction in America* describes the neurobiology of substance use, misuse, and addiction.
      5   T or F   According to the American Society of Addiction Medicine (ASAM), it is more difficult to treat addiction than chronic diseases like diabetes, arthritis, or congestive heart failure.

6   T or F   Addiction has adverse biopsychosocial consequences across the lifespan.

7   T or F   Addiction and recovery are similar for men and women.

8   T or F   A co-occurring mental disorder increases the severity of a substance use disorder.

9   T or F   There are many effective treatment approaches for people with addiction.

10   T or F   Professionals who are high functioning alcoholics/addicts (HFAs) require little if any monitoring.

(True: 1, 4, 6, 8, 9. False: 2, 3, 5, 7,10)

b   Outcome, Effort, Process, and Decisions

Examine the outcome, effort, process, and decisions of your recovery work in Chapter 2.

Outcome

Did you meet **objectives** for Chapter 2? Use Table 2.2 to review objectives and rank as:

Strongly disagree = 1
Disagree = 2
Undecided = 3
Agree = 4
Strongly agree = 5

Effort

Effort evaluation reviews the input or energy you invested in recovery work. Ask and answer the following questions.

- How hard did you work on Chapter 2?
- How much time did you dedicate to Chapter 2?
- What resources did you employ for Chapter 2 work?

Table 2.2 Objectives

Objectives	Rank
I consider theories, models, and definitions of addiction.	1, 2, 3, 4, 5
I profile the many faces of addiction.	1, 2, 3, 4, 5
I identify addictive disorders.	1, 2, 3, 4, 5
I review the dimensions and dynamics of addiction treatment.	1, 2, 3, 4, 5
I recognize monitoring for impaired professionals.	1, 2, 3, 4, 5

Table 2.3 Process

Process	Yes or No	Comment
I read the narrative (Section I).		
I completed the applications (Section II).		
I evaluated recovery work and competency development (Section III).		

Process

Process evaluation is especially valuable when you want to improve outcome and increase the efficiency of your recovery work. Use Table 2.3 to evaluate process.

Decisions

Based on the evaluation of your recovery work from Chapter 2, decide to celebrate, continue, correct, or change your approach to recovery work. Reward yourself with a positive thought, feeling, or action. Keep doing what you are doing if "it works." Modify or adjust anything that is not working well. Plan and welcome change that supports your recovery work as you move on to Chapter 3. Ask and answer the following questions.

- Did you **celebrate** your recovery work from Chapter 2 "Face Addiction"?
- Will you **continue** to approach recovery work in Chapter 3 in the same way?
- Do you plan to **correct** your approach to recovery work in Chapter 3?
- Do you plan to **change** your approach to recovery work in Chapter 3?

2   Evaluate competency development using a KSA/Topic Matrix and a Rubric Review.

    a   What knowledge, skills, and attitudes are you using to develop Competency 2 Face Addiction. Document KSA examples in Table 2.4 KSA/Topic Matrix.

    b   Evaluate the development of Competency 1 Begin Recovery Work with a Rubric Review. The chapter outline provides the criteria to evaluate competency development. Rank competency development on Table 2.5 as:

- **Exceeds expectations**: Understands, applies, and evaluates competency criteria > 90% of the time.
- **Meets expectations**: Understands, applies, and evaluates competency criteria 75% to 90% of the time.
- **Needs improvement**: Understands, applies, and evaluates competency criteria < 75% of the time.

Table 2.4 KSA/Topic Matrix

Topics	Knowledge	Skills	Attitudes
Addiction			
Theories and Models of Addiction			
The Neurobiology of Addiction			
American Society of Addiction Medicine (ASAM)			
Faces of Addiction			
Addiction Across the Lifespan			
Gender Differences and Addiction			
Addiction and the Family			
LGBTQ Individuals with Addiction			
Diversity, Disparities, and Addiction			
Addictive Disorders			
Substance Use Disorders (SUDs)			
Other Addictive Disorders			
Co-Occurring Mental Illness (MI) and SUDs			
Addiction Treatment			
Assessment and Diagnosis			
Treatment Goals			
Treatment Settings			
Treatment Approaches			
Treatment Duration			
Monitoring for Impaired Professionals			

Table 2.5 Competency 2 Face Addiction

Criteria	Exceeds Expectations 3	Meets Expectations 2	Needs Improvement 1
Addiction Theories and Models of Addiction The Neurobiology of Addiction American Society of Addiction Medicine (ASAM)			
Faces of Addiction Addiction Across the Lifespan Gender Differences and Addiction Addiction and the Family LGBTQ Individuals with Addiction Diversity, Disparities, and Addiction			
Addictive Disorders Substance Use Disorders (SUDs) Other Addictive Disorders Co-Occurring Mental Illness (MI) and SUDs			
Addiction Treatment Assessment and Diagnosis Treatment Goals Treatment Settings Treatment Approaches Treatment Duration			
Monitoring for Impaired Professionals			

Summary

This chapter examined addiction: the faces of addiction, addictive disorders, addiction treatment, and monitoring of impaired professionals. Topics that provided the organizing framework for the chapter included Addiction, Faces of Addiction, Addictive Disorders, Addiction Treatment, and Monitoring for Impaired Professionals. The chapter examined theories, models, and definitions of addiction. It profiled the many faces of addiction. The chapter reviewed addictive disorders and current approaches to addiction treatment. It acknowledged the monitoring needs of impaired professionals. The chapter suggested applications—questions, worksheets, exercises, and projects—for the competency. Chapter 2 concluded with evaluations of recovery work and competency development.

3 Affirm Recovery

April G. Sees What Recovery Looks Like

I am attending a DUI first offender class. The Driver Alcohol Education program consists of 16 weekly sessions and at least two mandatory AA meetings. Tonight, I am attending the Thursday night Some of Us Are Sicker Than Others speaker meeting. After listening to three speakers tell their stories, the Chair begins the chip ceremony. "Anyone with one day of sobriety? Several people file up to the podium and receive a white chip. The Chair smiles and shakes their hands and continues asking "30 days? 60 days? 90 days?" The Chair hands out different colored chips for various lengths of sobriety. Then, "Bill, come and get your one-year medallion." Bill blows out one candle on a cake. We all clap. "Brenda, come on up and celebrate your 5-year anniversary." Brenda received a 5-year medallion blows out five candles. We clap. Then the Chair asks for a show of hands of men and women with more than five years recovery. To my surprise, many hands of healthy, happy-looking people go up. I wonder why these people still attend meetings. We close the meeting linking hands and proclaiming together "Keep coming back. It works if you work it." My name is April G. and I guess this is what recovery looks like.

Objectives

- Understand the public health classification of disease as proposed by the Commission on Chronic Illness, especially tertiary prevention.
- Applaud the New Freedom Commission on Mental Health for advancing the concept *recovery*.
- Use the many recovery resources available from the Substance Abuse and Mental Health Services Administration (SAMHSA), especially the new Office of Recovery.
- Join the Faces and Voices of Recovery to promote the right to recovery through advocacy, education. and the power of long-term recovery.
- Recognize emerging recovery research, theories, and practice.
- Embrace recovery as the ability to master addiction, live well, and do good.

Purpose: This chapter chronicles the evolution of recovery as an idea whose time has come.

DOI: 10.4324/9781003292944-3

Outline

The Idea

Commission on Chronic Illness
Tertiary Prevention
New Freedom Commission on Mental Health

Substance Abuse Mental Health Services Administration (SAMHSA)

Definition
Dimensions
Principles
Strategic Plan
2020 National Survey on Drug Use and Health
Office of Recovery

A Movement

Faces and Voices of Recovery
Recovery Initiatives

Recovery Defined

I

Affirm recovery. Section I presents facts, concepts, principles, and theories about the idea of recovery, the Substance Abuse Mental Health Services Administration (SAMHSA), the recovery movement, and a working definition of recovery.

The Idea

The Commission on Chronic Illness

In 1957, the Commission on Chronic Illness proposed a public health classification of disease prevention as primary, secondary, and tertiary prevention. We describe primary and secondary prevention briefly. Tertiary prevention provides the theoretical framework for this book. General examples and specific applications to substance use and other addictive disorders follow.

PRIMARY PREVENTION

Primary prevention includes those preventive measures that come before the onset of illness or injury and before the disease process begins. Examples include childhood immunizations and COVID vaccinations. Healthy choices about nutrition, exercise, sleep, weight, smoking, drinking, sex, and stress reduction can promote health, reduce risks, and prevent disease. Primary prevention practices are especially important for populations at risk. For example, family history is a major *risk factor* for coronary artery disease.

Children of alcoholics have a high risk of developing a *drinking* problem. Social determinants of disease such as poverty, unequal access to health care, health literacy, stigma, and racism increase risks for many diseases and disorders, including addiction. Most K-12 school health curricula include mental health and substance use. See also the resources Center for Substance Abuse Prevention (CSAP) within the Substance Abuse Mental Health Services Administration (SAMHSA), especially its model Substance Abuse Prevention Programs.

SECONDARY PREVENTION

Secondary prevention includes those preventive measures that lead to early diagnosis and prompt treatment of a disease, illness, or injury. These measures aim to limit disability, impairment, or dependency and prevent more severe health problems from developing in the future. Testing for COVID-19 is secondary prevention.

Secondary prevention includes screening, case finding, early intervention, and prompt treatment for a substance use or other addictive disorder. The Affordable Care Act (ACA) launched SBIRT. Screening, Brief Intervention, and Referral to Treatment is a comprehensive, integrated, public health approach for early identification and intervention with patients whose patterns of alcohol and/or drug use put their health at risk. Even with the passage of the Mental Health Parity and Addiction Equity Act of 2008 and the Affordable Care Act in 2010, 90% of individuals with substance use disorders receive no treatment.

Tertiary Prevention

Tertiary prevention includes those preventive measures aimed at rehabilitation following a significant illness. At this level, health practitioners work to retrain, re-educate, and rehabilitate the individual who has already had an impairment or disability.

Tertiary prevention emphasizes relapse prevention and chronic disease management for people with addiction. As discussed in Chapter 2, addiction is a treatable, chronic medical disease. Treatment approaches for addiction are generally as successful as those for other chronic diseases.

RELAPSE PREVENTION

According to G. Alan Marlatt and Katie Witkiewitz (2007), the major goal of relapse prevention (RP) is to address the problem of relapse and to generate techniques for preventing or managing its occurrence. Based on a cognitive-behavioral framework, RP seeks to identify high-risk situations in which an individual is vulnerable to relapse and to use both cognitive and behavioral coping strategies to prevent future relapses in similar situations. RP can be described as a tertiary prevention strategy with two specific aims: (1) preventing an initial lapse and maintaining abstinence or harm reduction treatment goals, and (2) providing lapse management if a lapse occurs, to prevent further relapse. The goal is to provide the skills to prevent a complete relapse, regardless of the situation or impending risk factors.

CHRONIC DISEASE MANAGEMENT

An effective chronic disease management program is a pro-active, population-based approach that addresses chronic diseases early in the disease cycle to prevent disease progression and reduce potential health complications. Successful chronic disease management programs share the following characteristics. They:

• are evidenced-based
• use multiple strategies and interventions
• are patient-centered
• empower individuals to increase control over and improve their health
• promote collaboration among providers, organizations, individuals, families, and community groups
• include an evaluation component to ensure that programs are achieving their objectives.

Today we have sound guidelines for chronic disease management, primarily for physical conditions such as diabetes, heart disease, stroke, cancer, osteoporosis, asthma, arthritis, Alzheimer's dementia, and increasingly for mental health disorders. Probably the best known and most highly regarded self-management program for people with chronic conditions is the Stanford Chronic Disease Self-Management Program (CDSMP). Stanford granted the National Council on Aging (NCOA) an exclusive U.S. license to distribute the online version of the CDSMP program, called Better Choices, Better Health®. Self-efficacy is a key component of the Stanford Program and BCBH.

Addiction practitioners are familiar with the useful publications from the Substance Abuse and Mental Health Services Association (SAMHSA) that support treatment and recovery. See especially Treatment Improvement Protocols (TIPs) and Evidence-based Practices (EBPs).

The New Freedom Commission on Mental Health

Deinstitutionalization from mental hospitals, a national movement beginning in the mid-1960s, resulted in more individuals living in the community. Simultaneously, a recovery approach gained impetus as a social movement due in large part to a perceived failure of traditional mental health/addiction services. Moreover, the realization that people recover surfaced. Influenced in part by the philosophy of Alcoholics Anonymous and social movements of the 60s and 70s, the New Freedom Commission on Mental Health established by President George W. Bush proposed a shift from the traditional medical psychiatric model of care toward the concept of recovery. The report, *Achieving the Promise: Transforming Mental Health Care in America*, boldly recommended recovery from mental illness as the expected goal of this transformed system of care.

> *Recovery* refers to the process in which people are able to live, work, learn and participate fully in their communities. For some individuals, recovery is the ability to live a fulfilling and productive life despite a disability. For others, recovery implies the reduction or complete remission of symptoms. Science has shown that having hope plays an integral role in an individual's recovery.
> (The President's New Freedom Commission in Mental Health 2003, p. 7)

A recovery approach to mental disorder or substance dependence emphasizes and supports a person's potential for recovery. Recovery is generally seen as a personal journey rather than a destination. Recovery involves hope, basic security, and empowerment as evidenced by a durable sense of self, self-determination, self-management, self-help, and self-care.

SAMHSA Recovery Definition, Dimensions, Principles, Initiatives, and the Office of Recovery

The Substance Abuse Mental Health Services Administration (SAMHSA) is the agency within the U.S. Department of Health and Human Services (HHS) that leads public health efforts to advance the behavioral health of the nation. SAMHSA's mission is to reduce the impact of substance misuse and mental illness on America's communities.

Definition of Recovery

In December 2011, SAMHSA defined recovery from mental disorders and substance use disorders *as a process of change through which individuals improve their health and wellness, live a self-directed life, and strive to reach their full potential.*

Four Recovery Dimensions

SAMHSA identified four recovery dimensions: 1. *Health*: overcoming or managing one's disease(s) as well as living in a physically and emotionally healthy way; 2. *Home*: a stable and safe place to live; 3. *Purpose*: meaningful daily activities, such as a job, school, volunteerism, family caretaking, or creative endeavors, and the independence, income, and resources to participate in society; and 4. *Community*: relationships and social networks that provide support, friendship, love, and hope.

Principles for Recovery

SAMHSA advanced ten guiding principles for recovery.

- Recovery emerges from hope.
- Recovery is person-driven.
- Recovery occurs via many pathways.
- Recovery is holistic.
- Recovery is supported by peers and allies.
- Recovery is supported through relationships and social networks.
- Recovery is culturally based and influenced.
- Recovery is supported by addressing trauma.
- Recovery involves individual, family, and community strengths and responsibilities.
- Recovery is based on respect.

2020 National Survey on Drug Use and Health (NSDUH)

Although the findings from the 2020 National Survey on Drug Use and Health document the negative impact of the COVID-19 pandemic on mental health, including the exacerbating use of alcohol or other drugs and increase in overdose deaths, it is interesting to note that recovery is now part of the "big three:" prevention, treatment, and recovery. According to Regina LaBelle, Acting Director of National Drug Control Policy, the federal government is taking steps to quickly reduce barriers to evidence-based prevention, harm reduction, treatment, and recovery services.

Strategic Plan 2019–2023

In its Strategic Plan for 2019–2023, SAMHSA identified five priority areas to better meet the behavioral health care needs of individuals, communities, and service providers. Two of the five priorities include Recovery Support Services.

Office of Recovery

The U.S. strategy to address addiction has four priorities: primary prevention, harm reduction, evidence-based treatment, and recovery support. On September 30, 2021, SAMHSA launched the Office of Recovery to advance the agency's commitment to, and support of, recovery for all Americans. September marks National Recovery Month, and in organizing this new office, SAMHSA now has a dedicated team with a deep understanding of recovery to promote policies, programs, and services to those in or seeking recovery. SAMHSA believes

> Recovery is enhanced by peer-delivered services. These peer support services have proven to be effective as the support, outreach, and

engagement with new networks help sustain recovery over the long term. Peer services are critical, given the significant workforce shortages in behavioral health. SAMHSA's new Office of Recovery will promote the involvement of people with lived experience throughout agency and stakeholder activities, foster relationships with internal and external organizations in the mental health and addiction recovery fields and identify health disparities in high-risk and vulnerable populations to ensure equity for support services across the Nation.

(SAMHSA 2021a)

A Movement

Faces and Voices of Recovery

Beginning in the early 90s, recovering men and women, their families and friends, mental health and addiction professions, together with concerned communities began organizing recovery initiatives. We may remember the work of Senator Harold Hughes and the Society of Americans for Recovery (SOAR). Faces and Voices of Recovery incorporated in 2004, is dedicated to organizing and mobilizing millions of Americans in recovery from addiction to alcohol and other drugs, their families, friends and allies, into recovery organizations and networks. Faces and Voices of Recovery promotes the right and resources for recovery through advocacy, education, and demonstrating the power and proof of long-term recovery. See especially its *Recovery Bill of Rights*. Note: The *Recovery Bill of Rights* is ten years old and presently under revision. Watch for the update on the Faces and Voices of Recovery website https://facesandvoicesofrecovery.org.

In December 2012, Faces and Voices of Recovery conducted the first nationwide survey of persons in recovery from drug and alcohol problems about their experiences in active addiction and recovery. Some 9000 people who met medical criteria for severe substance disorder described recovery as *abstinence, personal growth,* and *service* to others. Findings documented the many costs of active addiction to individuals and society in terms of health, finances, work, family life, and criminal justice involvement. However, the survey also found that people in recovery are employed, pay bills and taxes, vote, volunteer in their communities, and take care of their health and their families. Today, millions of recovery men and women affirm and advance recovery in personal, public, and political ways.

In 2017, Faces and Voices of Recovery, in collaboration with addiction/recovery research colleagues in the United Kingdom, amended the Life in Recovery survey to document the lives of Families Living with Addiction and Recovery. While much is known about the many costs of addiction and problematic drug use, we know less about what happens to family members of those using or in recovery.

Recovery Initiatives

Although there is a shared understanding of addiction by professionals and the public, recovery has many meanings. Is recovery a process or an outcome, a journey, or a destination? What is the difference between remission and recovery, between sobriety and recovery? Is recovery a concept, a theory, or perhaps a science? Today, scholar-practitioners conduct recovery research, develop recovery theories, and practice in recovery-oriented systems of care (ROSC). Several examples demonstrate these recovery initiatives.

THE RECOVERY RESEARCH INSTITUTE

The Recovery Research Institute of Massachusetts General Hospital and Harvard of Harvard Medical School, founded in 2012, is a nonprofit research institute dedicated to the advancement of addiction treatment and recovery. Its vision to mission statement reads:

> To enhance the public health impact of addiction recovery science through the summary, synthesis, and dissemination of scientific findings and the conduct of novel research.
>
> (https://www.recoveryanswers.org)

The Institute believes that addiction is one of the greatest public health crises of our time, with staggeringly high rates of mortality, disease, and disability. The Institute defines recovery from a substance use disorder as a process of improved physical, psychological, and social well-being and health after having suffered from a substance-related condition. It believes that stable and long-term recovery from alcohol and other drug use disorders is possible and that rates of recovery can continue to be improved through focused scientific investigation and a commitment to public education.

The Institute conducts research to improve the effectiveness of addiction treatment and recovery efforts, to find out what is and what is not working, and why certain pathways to recovery work for some individuals and not others. It offers a course *Recovery 101* that includes Fast Facts, Pathways to Recovery, The Brain, and Recovery, with Special Topics and Resources.

Check out The ADDICTIONary with its scientific definitions of addictive disorders and stigma alerts to words like "alcoholic." See also several landmark recovery studies. The 2017 National Recovery Study found that people recover from addiction. Around 75% of people seeking recovery from a substance use problem reach their goal, though it may take them some time to achieve full remission. They also go on to do good things. With time in recovery psychological distress decreases and quality of life improves.

A 2021 study by David Eddie and colleagues at the Institute titled "Reasons to be Cheerful: Personal, Civic, and Economic Achievements After Resolving an Alcohol or Drug Problem in the United States Population" found that the majority of Americans who resolved an alcohol or other drug problem reported achievements in 1. self-improvement (e.g., changes in educational and employment circumstances), 2. family engagement (e.g., family reunification, financial support of family), 3. civic participation (e.g., volunteering, voting, helping others), and 4. economic participation (e.g., purchasing a car or home).

THE *JOURNAL OF RECOVERY SCIENCE (JORS)*

The *Journal of Recovery Science (JORS)* was established in 2018, with the specific aim to create a recovery-centric academic journal that has minimal barriers to knowledge dissemination and transfer. The areas of focus for the journal— recovery support services, recovery support institutions, recovery outcomes, recovery policy, and recovery in special populations—were selected so that both established and early career/student researchers could find a suitable platform for high-quality contributions in the behavioral health recovery field. The JORS is an open-access, peer-reviewed, international journal devoted to publishing original research in behavioral health recovery. Accepted articles are published on a rolling basis with numbered issues released twice per year.

RECOVERY THEORY

Published in January 2019, Austin M. Brown and Robert D. Ashford describe "Recovery-Informed Theory: Situating the Subjective in the Science of Substance Use Disorder Recovery." The authors propose a grand theory of recovery science, built upon the seminal theories of recovery capital, recovery-oriented systems of care, and socioecological theory. This grand theory, called recovery-informed theory (RIT), states that successful long-term recovery is self-evident and is a fundamentally emancipatory set of processes. The essentials of recovery include hope and flourishing, identity, authenticity, and agency. A recovery-informed approach takes the aggregate knowledge of those in recovery, translates it into science, and further translates knowledge into practice, education, prevention, and treatment.

Recovery Defined

Building on Federal initiatives and resources, listening to the voices of thousands of recovering men and women, and recognizing current recovery research, theories, and practice, we define recovery as *the ability to master addiction, live well, and do good* as evidenced by:

- abstinence or harm reduction and relapse prevention
- health, wellness, and well-being
- helping, service, and altruism

What does recovery look like? People in recovery:

- maintain abstinence or
- continue harm reduction.
- prevent relapse.
- promote health.
- achieve wellness.
- experience well-being.
- help others.
- serve society.
- do the right thing.

Although often used interchangeably, recovery is different from sobriety. Sobriety means no drinking, using, gambling, or engaging in other addictive behaviors: what we call abstinence. Recovery includes sobriety plus health, wellness, well-being, and often service to others.

People with addiction learn how to master addiction. Treatment programs and relapse prevention plans emphasize abstinence or harm reduction, health, and beginning recovery. Individuals in early recovery learn how to live well. Personal work and recovery support promote wellness and well-being. With continuing recovery, people with addiction "do good" through helping, service, and altruism. Recovery is for good!

Section I presented facts, concepts, principles, and theories about the idea of recovery, the SAMHSA, the recovery movement, and a working definition of recovery. Continue recovery work in Section II with applications about the competency.

II

Section II suggests applications about the idea of recovery, the SAMHSA, the recovery movement, and definitions of recovery.

The Idea

1 Explain and give examples of primary, secondary, and tertiary prevention of substance use or other addictive disorders. Use Table 3.1.

Table 3.1 Primary, Secondary, and Tertiary Prevention

Explanation	Example
Primary prevention:	
Secondary prevention:	
Tertiary prevention:	

2   The New Freedom Commission on Mental Health advanced the concept recovery. Imagine recovery as a freedom coin with freedom from addiction on one side and freedom for life on the other.

   a   Describe your emancipation from addiction.

   b   Describe your empowerment for recovery.

SAMHSA

3   The Substance Abuse Mental Health Services Administration (SAMHSA) identified four recovery dimensions. What does each dimension mean for you?

- *Health*:
- *Home:*
- *Purpose:*
- *Community:*

4   Check out the SAMHSA website for information about the Office of Recovery, launched on September 30, 2021: https://www.samhsa.gov.

A Movement

5   In a survey study, some 9000 people who met medical criteria for severe substance disorder described recovery as:

- *abstinence,*
- *personal growth*, and
- *service to others.*

If you were part of this survey, how would you describe recovery?

Recovery Defined

6   SAMHSA defines recovery from mental disorders and substance use disorders:

as a process of change through which individuals improve their health and wellness, live a self-directed life, and strive to reach their full potential.

Comment on this definition.

7   This book defines recovery as the ability to master addiction, live well, and do good as evidenced by abstinence of harm reduction and relapse prevention; health, wellness, and well-being; and helping, service, and altruism.

Comment on this definition.

8 Write your definition of recovery.

Section II suggested applications about the idea of recovery, the SAMHSA, the recovery movement, and definitions of recovery. Complete Chapter 3 with evaluations of recovery work and competency development.

III

Evaluate recovery work and competency development.

1 Evaluate recovery work with a short True/False Quiz and a review of the outcome, effort, process, and decisions of recovery work.

   a Quiz: Based on your learning from Chapter 3 Affirm Recovery, indicate whether each of the following statements is True (T) or False (F).

   1 T or F   Relapse prevention and chronic disease management are examples of tertiary prevention.

   2 T or F   The Substance Abuse Mental Health Services Administration (SAMHSA) is the federal agency that leads public health efforts to advance the behavioral health of the nation.

   3 T or F   SAMHSA's mission is to reduce the incidence and prevalence of substance misuse and mental illness in America's communities.

   4 T or F   According to SAMHSA, four dimensions of recovery include self, family, community, and society.

   5 T or F   The U.S. Office of Recovery believes recovery is enhanced by professional-delivered services.

   6 T or F   Faces and Voices of Recovery is a federal agency that promotes the right to recovery through advocacy, education. and the power of long-term recovery.

   7 T or F   The Life in Recovery Survey describes recovery as *abstinence, personal growth,* and *service to others.*

   8 T or F   Recovery initiatives advance theory, research, practice, and education about recovery.

   9 T or F   Recovery and sobriety are the same.

   10 T or F   Developing Competencies for Recovery defines recovery as the ability to master addiction, live well, and do good.

   (True: 1, 2, 7, 8, 10. False: 3, 4, 5, 6, 9)

   b Outcome, Effort, Process, and Decisions

Examine the outcome, effort, process and decision-making of your recovery work in Chapter 3.

Outcome

Did you meet objectives for Chapter 3? Use Table 3.2 to review objectives and rank as:

Strongly disagree = 1
Disagree = 2
Undecided = 3
Agree = 4
Strongly agree = 5

Effort

Effort evaluation reviews the input or energy you invested in recovery work. Ask and answer the following questions.

- How hard did you work on Chapter 3?
- How much time did you dedicate to Chapter 3?
- What resources did you employ for Chapter 3 work?

Process

Process evaluation is especially valuable when you want to improve outcome and increase the efficiency of your recovery work. Use Table 3.3 to evaluate process.

Table 3.2 Objectives

Objectives	Rank
I understand the public health classification of disease as proposed by the Commission on Chronic Illness, especially tertiary prevention.	1, 2, 3, 4, 5
I applaud the New Freedom Commission on Mental Health for advancing the concept *recovery*.	1, 2, 3, 4, 5
I use the many recovery resources available from the Substance Abuse and Mental Health Services Administration (SAMHSA), especially the new Office of Recovery.	1, 2, 3, 4, 5
I join the Faces and Voices of Recovery to promote the right to recovery through advocacy, education and the power of long-term recovery.	1, 2, 3, 4, 5
I recognize emerging recovery research, theories, and practice.	1, 2, 3, 4, 5
I embrace recovery as the ability to master addiction, live well, and do good.	1, 2, 3, 4, 5

Table 3.3 Process

Process	Yes or No	Comment
I read the narrative (Section I).		
I completed the applications (Section II).		
I evaluated recovery work and competency development (Section III).		

Decisions

Based on the evaluation of your recovery work from Chapter 3, decide to celebrate, continue, correct, or change your approach to recovery work. Reward yourself with a positive thought, feeling, or action. Keep doing what you are doing if "it works." Modify or adjust anything that is not working well. Plan and welcome change that supports your recovery work as you move on to Chapter 4. Ask and answer the following questions.

- Did you **celebrate** your recovery work from Chapter 3 "Affirm Recovery"?
- Will you **continue** to approach recovery work in Chapter 4 in the same way?
- Do you plan to **correct** your recovery work in Chapter 4?
- Do you plan to **change** your approach to recovery work in Chapter 4?

2   Evaluate competency development using a KSA/Topic Matrix and a Rubric Review.

    a   What knowledge, skills, and attitudes are you using to develop Competency 3 Affirm Recovery? Document KSA examples in Table 3.4 KSA/Topic Matrix.

    b   Evaluate the development of Competency 3 Affirm Recovery with a Rubric Review. The chapter outline provides the criteria to evaluate competency development. Rank competency development on Table 3.5 as:

- **Exceeds expectations**. Understands, applies, and evaluates competency criteria > 90% of the time.
- **Meets expectations**: Understands, applies, and evaluates competency criteria 75% to 90% of the time.
- **Needs improvement**: Understands, applies, and evaluates competency criteria < 75% of the time.

Table 3.4 KSA/Topic Matrix

Topics	Knowledge	Skills	Attitudes
The Idea			
Commission on Chronic Illness			
Tertiary Prevention			
New Freedom Commission on Mental Health			
SAMHSA			
Definition			
Dimensions			
Principles			
Strategic Plan			
National Survey on Drug Use and Health			
Office of Recovery			
A Movement			
Faces and Voices of Recovery			
Recovery Initiatives			
Recovery Defined			

Table 3.5 Competency 3 Affirm Recovery

Criteria	Exceeds Expectations 3	Meets Expectations 2	Needs Improvement 1
The Idea Commission on Chronic Illness Tertiary Prevention New Freedom Commission on Mental Health			
SAMHSA Definition Dimensions Principles Strategic Plan National Survey on Drug Use and Health Office of Recovery			
A Movement Faces and Voices of Recovery Recovery Initiatives			
Recovery Defined			

Summary

This chapter chronicled the evolution of recovery as an idea whose time has come. Topics that provided the organizing framework for the chapter included The Idea, Substance Abuse Mental Health Services Administration, A Movement, and Recovery Defined. The chapter explained the public health classification of disease as proposed by the Commission on Chronic Illness, specifically tertiary prevention. It applauded the New Freedom Commission on Mental Health for advancing the concept *recovery*. The chapter highlighted the many resources available from the Substance Abuse and Mental Health Services Administration, especially the new Office of Recovery. It described the vision and mission of Faces and Voices of Recovery. It recognized emerging recovery research, theory, and practice. Recovery is the ability to master addiction, live well, and do good. The chapter suggested applications—questions, worksheets, exercises, and projects—for the competency. Chapter 3 concluded with evaluations of recovery work and competency development.

4 Develop a Strategic Recovery Plan

Josh N. Develops a Strategic Recovery Plan

My name is Josh N. I had some tough years with sports betting during my college and young adult years. Residential treatment for my gambling disorder helped. I attend GA once or twice a month, "just to keep my memory green." Thank goodness my gambling days were before legal online sports betting. The growth and acceptance of gambling today, plus the easy access to online phone betting are scary. My life is good. I am married; we have two children, and I am beginning my third year as a District Sales Manager for a major appliance company. Recently, I was part of a leadership team that completed a 5-year Strategic Business Plan for the company. Why can't I use the same strategic planning process to develop a Strategic Recovery Plan? One of my close co-workers has solid recovery from a drug problem. Perhaps we can support each other with parallel recovery plans, goals, and achievements.

Purpose: This chapter proposes a strategic plan to guide recovery work.

Objectives

- Review the principles and practice of strategic management.
- Consider several chronic disease management programs.
- Examine the origins and characteristics of strategic planning, including the SWOT analysis.
- Develop a Strategic Recovery Plan.

Outline

Strategic Management

Chronic Disease Management

Chronic Disease
Chronic Care Model (CCM)
Chronic Disease Self-Management Program (CDSMP)

DOI: 10.4324/9781003292944-4

Strategic Planning

Plans
Strategic Planning
SWOT

A Strategic Recovery Plan

I

Develop a strategic recovery plan. Section I presents facts, concepts, principles, and theories about strategic management, chronic disease management, strategic planning, and a Strategic Recovery Plan.

Strategic Management

Strategic management is the planned use of an organization's resources to meet specific objectives and reach major goals. This book builds on strategic management tenets. Strategic management involves formulating goals and initiatives that reflect the mission and purpose of an organization and its stakeholders.

Strategic management considers the resources available for goal achievement. It includes an assessment of internal and external environments in which the organization operates. Strategic management provides an overall direction for goal achievement by specifying objectives, allocating resources, managing risks, and implementing action plans with strategies and tactics to meet objectives and reach goals.

Strategic management is dynamic in nature. There is a feedback loop to monitor and evaluate the execution of the plan and inform the next round of work. Strategic managers in business, education, and health organizations developed and use models and frameworks to assist in strategic planning and decision-making.

Chronic Disease Management

Addiction is a chronic disease. Several chronic disease management models and programs support the mission of this book: *Developing Competencies for Recovery: Mastering Addiction, Living Well, and Doing Good.*

Chronic Disease

Chronic disease is defined by the World Health Organization (WHO) as being of long duration, generally slow in progression. The term chronic is often applied when the course of a disease lasts for more than three months. Common chronic diseases include arthritis, asthma, cancer, chronic obstructive pulmonary disease, diabetes, and some viral diseases such as hepatitis C and acquired immunodeficiency syndrome. Mental illness and addiction are rarely included in lists of chronic diseases.

Yet, as indicated in Chapter 2, the American Society of Addiction Medicine (ASAM) defines addiction as a treatable, chronic medical disease involving complex interactions among brain circuits, genetics, the environment, and an individual's life experiences. People with addiction use substances or engage in behaviors that become compulsive and often continue despite harmful consequences. Prevention efforts and treatment approaches for addiction are generally as successful as those for other chronic diseases (ASAM, 2019).

Addressing chronic disease is a major challenge for healthcare systems around the world, which have largely developed to deal with acute episodic care, rather than to provide organized care for people with long-term conditions. This is most certainly true for addiction where health care systems have focused on treatment, to a lesser extent on prevention, and only recently on recovery.

Chronic Care Model (CCM)

In the 1990s, Edward H. Wagner, MD, MPH, and colleagues at the MacColl Institute for Healthcare Innovation, Group Health Cooperative of Puget Sound, developed and disseminated the CCM, which is an evidence-based framework for health care that has guided a shift in focus of health care systems from acute to chronic disease management and proactive care. It is an organizational approach to caring for people with chronic disease that is particularly applicable in the primary care setting The CCM operates within the context of the individual, community, provider organization, and the health care system. Recovery-Oriented Systems of Care (ROSC) are compatible with the Chronic Care Model (CCM).

Chronic Disease Self-Management Program (CDSMP)

The Stanford Chronic Disease Self-Management Program (CDSMP) is a more personal empowerment model. CDSMP was developed by a team of researchers at Stanford University. Individuals with chronic conditions attend self-management education workshops. Participants learn about self-efficacy and how to build confidence in managing their health, keep active, and engage in life. The Center for Disease Control and Prevention embraced the idea of self-management for chronic disease and promulgates The Chronic Disease Self-Management Program (CDSMP) for adults with at least one chronic health condition, which may include arthritis. The program focuses on disease management skills including decision making, problem-solving, and action planning. The interactive program aims to increase confidence; physical and psychological well-being; knowledge of ways to manage chronic conditions, and motivation to manage challenges associated with chronic disease. Workshop leaders can either be two peer health leaders or one health professional and one peer leader. At least one of the leaders should have a chronic condition.

The Stanford Chronic Disease Self-Management Program validates the tenets of this book, that people with addiction can develop competencies for recovery.

Strategic Planning

Plans

Plans are part of our individual, family, social, and global lives. A plan may be a detailed proposal for doing or achieving something "big" like a United Nations' Peace Plan. A plan may be an individual intention or decision about what one is going to do: "I plan to retire at the end of June this year." Familiar examples of plans include:

- a postpartum exercise plan for mind and body
- a family plan to visit Grandma Caroline on Sunday
- an aftercare plan to attend 90 AA meetings in 90 days
- a food plan for three vegetarian dinners each week
- a backpacking plan to hike the Appalachian Trail with friends
- a financial plan for college
- a work plan for the auto mechanic
- a lesson plan for fun with fractions for first-grade children
- a treatment plan for diabetic foot care for adults.

Strategic Planning

Business corporations, educational institutions, health care companies, professional associations, community organizations, religious bodies, and sports teams develop strategic plans to reach their goals: launch a new product, increase student retention, expand membership, renovate the community center, build a new church, or strengthen the offensive line. Purpose and direction characterize strategic planning. Strategies are a big part of negotiation and mediation between parties and even countries. Game theory employs strategies. A strategic plan is an effective, efficient way for individuals with addiction can realize recovery.

Strategic planning emerged in the 1950s and 1960s, although the idea dates back thousands of years, especially to military strategy and tactics. *The Art of War*, an ancient Chinese military treatise dating from the 5th century BC attributed to the ancient Chinese military strategist Sun Tzu. The book has 13 chapters, each one devoted to an aspect of warfare and how it applies to military strategy and tactics. A strategy is an *approach* taken to reach a goal, while *tactics* describe the specific actions taken to achieve the goal.

In 1911, Frederick W. Taylor published *The Principles of Scientific Management*, taking the scientific aspect of strategic planning into the 20th century. Management by Objectives (MBO), a concept so widely used for planning today in business, education, and health care, was first coined by Peter F. Drucker in his 1954 book *The Practice of Management*. The November 1981 issue of *Management Review* contained a paper by George T. Doran called "There's a S.M.A.R.T. way to write management's goals and objectives." In general, the letters mean:

S = specific
M = measurable
A = attainable
R = relevant
T = timely

See especially Chapter 8 "Draft Recovery Objectives."

Strategic planning entails three ongoing processes: analysis, decision, and actions. More specifically, strategic planning involves specifying the organization's vision, mission, goals, and objectives; developing policies and plans, which are designed to meet objectives and reach goals; and then allocating resources to implement the policies and plans through action.

SWOT

A SWOT analysis is often part of strategic planning. The origin of the SWOT analysis technique is credited to Albert Humphrey, who led a research project at Stanford University in the 1960s and 1970s using data from many top companies. The goal was to identify why corporations failed. SWOT is an acronym for Strengths, Weaknesses, Opportunities, and Threats. These four factors make up the SWOT Matrix. See Figure 4.1.

Organizations and individuals conduct a SWOT Analysis to identify factors that guide goal achievement. Internal features are scrutinized by looking at the strengths and weaknesses of the organization or individual. Opportunities and threats are examined to reveal external factors facing the organization or individual. Strengths and opportunities help goal achievement. Weaknesses and threats harm goal achievement.

Chapter 7 "Inventory Resources and Risks for Recovery" provides categories of factors to consider in performing a SWOT analysis. Internal strengths and weaknesses include personal assets and liabilities such as age, sex and gender, race and ethnicity, and self. External opportunities and threats are a. social capital and deficits including family and friends, the community, society itself, and culture; b. professional services and limitations including providers and practitioners and recovery-oriented systems of care (ROSC); and c. support services and scarcities such as mutual self-help groups, peer-based support, the Office of Recovery, and recovery residencies. See also Section II of this chapter for assignments in completing a SWOT analysis.

A Strategic Recovery Plan

Individuals with addiction need a strategic recovery plan. What is a strategic recovery plan? A strategic recovery plan is a guide for recovery work. The plan describes what the person intends to do to meet recovery objectives and reach recovery goals. A strategic recovery plan is an effective, efficient way for people to realize recovery. Men and women who begin recovery work can develop a recovery plan by themselves or with the help of addiction/recovery professionals and peers.

SWOT Matrix

Strengths	Weaknesses
Opportunities	Threats

Figure 4.1 SWOT Matrix

The principles and practice of strategic management guide developing competencies for recovering, specifically, the Strategic Recovery Plan. The Plan is a template people can use to set recovery goals, determine motivation for recovery, inventory resources and risks to recovery, draft objectives, act to meet objectives and reach goals, evaluate the recovery work, and then decide "what's next."

Consider using the Strategic Recovery Plan. Print copies of the Plan or create a digital file The plan reflects the signature features of strategic plans. The plan also incorporates knowledge, skills, and attitudes from the competencies for recovery. Study the Strategic Recovery Plan especially the sections for recovery *goals, motivation* for recovery, inventory *resources* and *risks* for recovery, recovery *objectives, action* to meet recovery objectives, and *evaluation* of recovery work. See Table 4.1 Strategic Recovery Plan.

Section I presented facts, concepts, principles, and theories about strategic management, chronic disease management, strategic planning, and a Strategic Recovery Plan. Continue recovery work in Section II with applications about the competency.

II

Section II suggests applications about strategic management, chronic disease management, strategic planning, and a Strategic Recovery Plan.

Strategic Management

1   What is your experience, if any, with strategic management?

Chronic Disease Management

2   What is your personal experience (self, family, friend, or work) with a chronic disease or condition?
3   Think about and comment on the chronic nature of addiction.

Strategic Planning

4   Strategic planning emerged in the 1950s and 1960s, although the idea dates back thousands of years. Remember and describe briefly some notable historic strategic plans.
5   Management by Objectives (MBO) is part of most strategic plans. What is your familiarity with SMART objectives?
6   What is a SWOT Matrix?
7   Think of a recovery goal. Use Table 4.2 to complete a SWOT Matrix Worksheet. Note what helps or hinders recovery goal achievement.

A Strategic Recovery Plan

A strategic plan is an effective, efficient way for individuals with addiction can realize recovery.

Table 4.1 Strategic Recovery Plan

Strategic Recovery Plan
Name: Date:
Goal:

Motivation	Resources	Risks
Importance: 1–10 = **Confidence:** 1–10 = **Readiness:** 1–10 =		
Objectives	**Action**	**Evaluation**
1 ·	1	**Outcome** Did you meet each objective? Yes, or No Did you reach the goal? Yes, or No
2	2	**Effort** How hard did you work to meet objectives and reach the goal? Consider time and resources.
3	3	**Process** How useful was the Strategic Recovery Plan?
4	4	**Decisions** Celebrate: Continue: Correct: Change:

Table 4.2 SWOT Matrix Worksheet

Internal Strengths	Internal Weaknesses
External Opportunities	**External Threats**

8   Study the Strategic Recovery Plan. What is the purpose of each major section of the Plan?

- Goal:
- Motivation:
- Resources:
- Risks:
- Objectives:
- Action:
- Evaluation:

  - Outcome:
  - Effort:
  - Process:
  - Decisions:

Section II suggested applications about strategic management, chronic disease management, strategic planning, and a Strategic Recovery Plan. Complete Chapter 4 with evaluations of recovery work and competency development in Section III.

III

Evaluate recovery work and competency development.

1   Evaluate recovery work with a short True/False Quiz and a review of the outcome, effort, process, and decisions of recovery work.

  a   Quiz: Based on your learning from Chapter 4 "Develop a Strategic Recovery Plan", indicate whether each of the following statements is True (T) or False (F).

  1   T or F   According to ASAM, addiction is an acute disease.
  2   T or F   Management by objectives (MBO) is primarily a business strategy.
  3   T or F   SMART objectives are part of a sound Strategic Plan.
  4   T or F   SWOT is an acronym for Strengths, Weaknesses, Opportunities, and Threats.

5 T or F According to the SWOT matrix, strengths and weaknesses are external factors that influence goal achievement.

6 T or F According to the SWOT matrix, opportunities and threats are internal factors that influence goal achievement.

7 T or F A strategic recovery plan is a guide for recovery work.

8 T or F Professionals develop strategic recovery plans for people with addiction.

9 T or F This book suggests a Strategic Recovery Plan that builds on the principles and practice of strategic management.

10 T or F A Strategic Recovery Plan is an effective, efficient way individuals with addiction can realize recovery.

(True: 3, 4, 7, 9, 10. False: 1, 2, 5, 6, 8)

b Outcome, Effort, Process, and Decisions

Examine the outcome, effort, process, and decisions of your recovery work in Chapter 4.

Outcome

Did you meet **objectives** for Chapter 4? Use Table 4.3 to review objectives and rank as:

Strongly disagree = 1
Disagree = 2
Undecided = 3
Agree = 4
Strongly agree = 5

Effort

Effort evaluation reviews the input or energy you invested in recovery work. Ask and answer the following questions.

- How hard did you work on Chapter 4?
- How much time did you dedicate to Chapter 4?
- What resources did you employ for Chapter 4 work?

Table 4.3 Objectives

Objectives	Rank
I review the principles and practice of strategic management.	1, 2, 3, 4, 5
I consider several chronic disease management programs.	1, 2, 3, 4, 5
I examine the origins and characteristics of strategic planning, including the SWOT analysis.	1, 2, 3, 4, 5
I develop a develop a Strategic Recovery Plan.	1, 2, 3, 4, 5

Table 4.4 Process

Process	Yes or No	Comment
I read the narrative (Section I).		
I completed the applications (Section II).		
I evaluated recovery work and competency development (Section III).		

Process

Process evaluation is especially valuable when you want to improve outcome and increase the efficiency of your recovery work. Use Table 4.4 to evaluate process.

Decisions

Based on the evaluation of your recovery work from Chapter 4, decide to celebrate, continue, correct, or change your approach to recovery work. Reward yourself with a positive thought, feeling, or action. Keep doing what you are doing if "it works." Modify or adjust anything that is not working well. Plan and welcome change that supports your recovery work as you move on to Chapter 5. Ask and answer the following questions.

- Did you **celebrate** your recovery work from Chapter 4 "Develop a Strategic Recovery Plan?"
- Will you **continue** to approach recovery work in the same way in Chapter 5?
- Do you plan to **correct** your approach to recovery work in Chapter 5?
- Do you plan to **change** your approach to recovery work in Chapter 5?

2   Evaluate competency development using a KSA/Topic Matrix and a Rubric Review.

    a   What knowledge, skills, and attitudes are you using to develop Competency 4 Develop a Strategic Recovery Plan? Document KSA examples in Table 4.5 KSA/Topic Matrix.

    b   Evaluate the development of Competency 4 Develop a Strategic Recovery Plan with a Rubric Review. The chapter outline provides the criteria to evaluate competency development. Rank competency development on Table 4.6 as:

- **Exceeds expectations**. Understands, applies, and evaluates competency criteria > 90% of the time.
- **Meets expectations**: Understands, applies, and evaluates competency criteria 75% to 90% of the time.
- **Needs improvement**: Understands, applies, and evaluates competency criteria < 75% of the time.

Table 4.5 KSA/Topic Matrix

Topics	Knowledge	Skills	Attitudes
Strategic Management			
Chronic Disease Management Chronic Disease Chronic Care Model Chronic Disease Self-Management Program			
Strategic Planning Plans Strategic Planning SWOT			
A Strategic Recovery Plan			

Table 4.6 Competency 4 Develop a Strategic Recovery Plan

Criteria	Exceeds Expectations 3	Meets Expectations 2	Needs Improvement 1
Strategic Management			
Chronic Disease Management			
Chronic Disease			
Chronic Care Model			
Chronic Disease Self-Management Program			
Strategic Planning			
Plans			
Strategic Planning			
SWOT			
A Strategic Recovery Plan			

Summary

Develop a strategic recovery plan in Chapter 4. This chapter proposed a strategic plan to guide recovery work. Topics that provided the organizing framework for the chapter included Strategic Management, Chronic Disease Management, Strategic Planning, and A Strategic Recovery Plan. The chapter reviewed the principles and practice of strategic management. It considered several chronic disease management models and programs. It examined the origins and characteristics of strategic planning, including SMART objectives and a SWOT analysis. It introduced A Strategic Recovery Plan for recovery work. The chapter suggested applications—questions, worksheets, exercises, and projects—for the competency. Chapter 4 concluded with evaluations of recovery work and competency development.

5   Set Recovery Goals

Phil and Brian Set Recovery Goals

Phil and Brian met four years ago at a Narcotics Anonymous (NA) LGBTQ meeting in Southern California. Both men are in sustained recovery. Each man has an undergraduate college degree. Phil and Brian decided to live together and eventually married. They have "reasonable" understanding and acceptance by their families. Their relationship strengthened and developed during the COVID pandemic when they worked remotely from their apartment with limited outside social engagements. In 2020, they developed long-term goals for their personal lives and collected life: 1. pursue and complete graduate work; 2. advance careers with balance. 3. focus on family, possibly adopting a child; and 4. commit to a community through civic involvement. "Wait a minute?" questioned Phil. "What if you or I relapsed? Are we taking our recovery for granted? Because of our recovery, we can set these life goals." Brian agrees. "I think we need to develop some long-term recovery goals as a foundation for our life goals." "Yeah," agrees Phil. "Kind of like the rhythm section of a jazz ensemble, the piano, bass, and drums support the brass, reeds, and strings."

Purpose: This chapter identifies essential recovery goals.

Objectives

- Define goals, objectives, and outcomes.
- Acknowledge the contributions from existential self-states, Maslow's Hierarchy of Needs, and the Life in Recovery Survey to the development of recovery goals.
- Embrace recovery as *the ability to master addiction, live well, and do good.*
- Recognize abstinence or harm reduction and relapse prevention as early, continuing recovery goals.
- Welcome health, wellness, and well-being as personal growth goals that build on early recovery.
- Affirm helping, service, and altruism are recovery goals that transcend self.
- Explain initial, early, sustained, and stable recovery.

DOI: 10.4324/9781003292944-5

Outline

Recovery Goals

Goals, Objectives, and Outcome
Being, Becoming, and Beyond
Maslow's Hierarchy of Needs
Life in Recovery Survey
Recovery Defined

Mastering Addiction

Abstinence
Harm Reduction
Relapse Prevention

Living Well

Health
Wellness
Well-being

Doing Good

Helping
Service
Altruism

Remission and Recovery

Remission
Initial Recovery
Early Recovery
Sustained Recovery
Stable Recovery

I

Set recovery goals. Section I presents facts, concepts, principles, and theories about recovery goals, mastering addiction, living well, doing good, and remission and recovery.

Recovery Goals

Goals, Objectives, Outcome

Goals are an essential part of strategic plans. Goals are broad declarations of future aspirations. Corporations, groups, and individuals work for months, often years, to reach goals. Objectives are specific action plans, measurable steps with time-bound schedules, that people draft to reach goals. Outcomes are the final results of meeting objectives and reaching goals.

Being, Becoming, and Beyond

Existentialism captures well the angst of active addiction: its dread and despair, its alienation and isolation, together with overwhelming feelings of impending doom and possible death. Yet, existential philosophy, existential psychology, and existential therapy support practitioners and people with addiction on their recovery journey.

Being, becoming, and *beyond* are three existential self-states that structure recovery goals.

Being means existence: the individual in the world and at one with the world. Because existence is never static, a person is always *becoming* something new. Becoming implies direction and development. The goal is to become a complete human being. Yet, individuals long to go *beyond*: to transcend the world, to experience and express human possibility and potential. Through such self-actualization, individuals live authentic lives. Beyond also signifies the belief that "we are social" and as such responsible for others.

Existentialism grounds our understanding of these three constructs. The proposed recovery goals reflect the essence, experience, and expression of being, becoming, and beyond.

Note: existential therapy is adaptable and often used with other approaches to addiction treatment and recovery work. While existential therapy addresses broad goals like purpose and meaning for life, cognitive-behavioral therapy (CBT) can focus on immediate craving for a fix. Combining approaches can help maximize the effectiveness of treatment and promote greater recovery.

Maslow's Hierarchy of Needs

Needs are conditions and situations people satisfy for a good life. Most people are familiar with Maslow's theory of motivation and his hierarchy of needs, usually depicted as a triangle. Usually, people meet needs at a lower level and then move on and up the hierarchy. Increasingly, people recognize overlap among the needs. Later in his life, Maslow added a need beyond self-actualization he called transcendence. This six-level hierarchy of needs is widely accepted today. After his death, Maslow scholars added two additional needs: cognitive needs and aesthetic needs located between esteem and self-actualization.

A brief description with examples of Maslow's original needs, the two "new" needs, and his sixth need for self-transcendence follows together with an eight-level triangle.

Physiological needs for air, water, food, sleep, shelter, warmth, and sexual reproduction.

Safety needs for protection from elements, financial security, law and order, freedom from fear, safety against accidents and injury, health, and wellness.

Love and belongingness needs for friendship, intimacy, trust, and acceptance, receiving and giving affection and love, being part of a group such as family, friends, work, or church.

Esteem needs for oneself (dignity, achievement, mastery, independence) and the need to be accepted and valued by others (status, prestige).

Cognitive needs for knowledge and understanding, curiosity, exploration, need for meaning and predictability.

Aesthetic needs for appreciation and search for beauty, balance, and form.

Self-actualization needs to realize personal potential, self-fulfillment, seeking personal growth and peak experiences; to become everything one can become by seeking personal growth and through peak experiences.

Self-transcendence needs wherein person is motivated by values that transcend beyond the personal self. "Be all that you can be" through the full experience and expression of talents, capabilities, and potentialities. See Figure 5.1.

Life in Recovery Survey

Faces & Voices of Recovery conducted the first nationwide survey of persons in recovery from alcohol and other drug problems. The survey was developed, conducted, and analyzed in collaboration with Alexandre Laudet, Ph.D., Director of the Center for the Study of Addictions and Recovery at the National Development and Research Institutes, Inc. The study recruited over

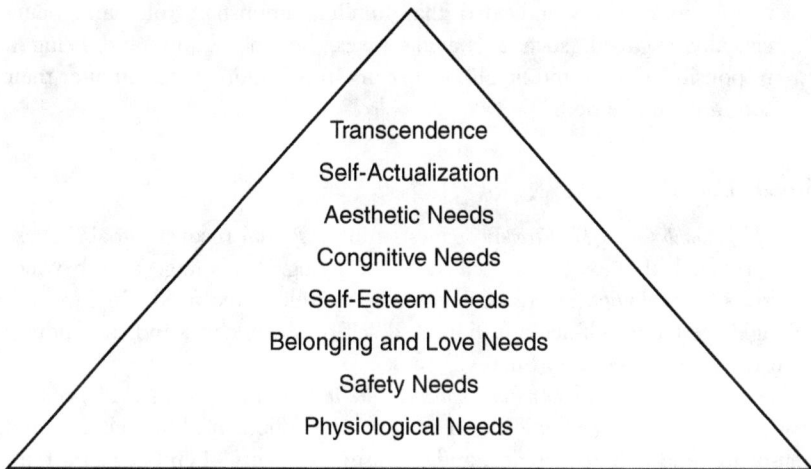

Transcendence
Self-Actualization
Aesthetic Needs
Congnitive Needs
Self-Esteem Needs
Belonging and Love Needs
Safety Needs
Physiological Needs

Figure 5.1 Maslow's Hierarchy of Needs

9,000 individuals with previous substance use disorders. Almost all (98%) reported characteristics that met formal medical criteria for a severe substance use disorder; three-quarters of the participants considered themselves "in recovery." Three dominant recovery themes emerged from the Life in Recovery Survey: **abstinence, personal growth,** and **service to others.**

The Surgeon General's Report on Alcohol, Drugs, and Health, *Facing Addiction in America* (2016), reported study findings in Chapter 5. Recovery: The Many Paths to Wellness.

- **Abstinence:** 86.0% saw abstinence as part of their recovery. The remainder either did not think abstinence was part of recovery in general or felt it was not important for their recovery. Endorsement of abstinence as "essential" was most common among those who were affiliated with 12-step mutual aid groups. This finding was consistent with previous research showing that the great majority of people (about 6 in 7) who have experienced serious substance use disorders consider abstinence essential for recovery.
- **Personal growth:** "Being honest with myself" was endorsed as part of recovery by 98.6% of participants. Others almost universally endorsed elements including "handling negative feelings without using alcohol or drugs" and "being able to enjoy life without alcohol or drugs." Almost all study participants viewed their recovery as a process of growth and development, and about two-thirds saw it as having a spiritual dimension.
- **Service to others:** Engaging in service to others was another prominent component of how study participants defined recovery, perhaps because, during periods of heavy substance use, individuals often do damage to others that they later regret. There was evidence that service to others helps individuals maintain their recovery. A survey of more than 3,000 people in recovery indicated that fulfilling important roles and being civically engaged, such as paying taxes, holding a job, and being a responsible parent and neighbor, became much more common after their substance use ended.

Recovery Defined

Developing Competencies for Recovery suggests nine essential recovery goals. These goals parallel the existential self-states of being, becoming, and beyond; Maslow's physiological needs, safety needs; as well as the needs for love and belonging, esteem, self-actualization, and self-transcendence; and the findings from the Life in Recovery Survey.

Recovery is *the ability to master addiction, live well, and do good* as evidenced by abstinence or harm reduction and relapse prevention; health, wellness, and well-being; and helping, service, and altruism. Recovery often begins in treatment or at a self-help meeting like AA or NA. Abstinence or harm reduction and relapse prevention are early, continuing recovery goals. Health, wellness, and well-being are personal growth goals that build on early recovery. Helping, service, and altruism are recovery goals that transcend the self.

Set these essential recovery goals, to:

- Attain abstinence.
- Maintain harm reduction.
- Prevent relapse.
- Promote health.
- Foster wellness.
- Experience well-being.
- Offer helping.
- Volunteer services.
- Do "the right thing."

See Table 5.1 and notice the parallel relationships among the existential self-states, Maslow's Hierarchy of Needs, the Life in Recovery findings, and the nine recovery goals. Descriptions of these nine essential goals follow in the sections Mastering Addiction, Living Well, and Doing Good.

Mastering Addiction

Abstinence or harm reduction and relapse prevention are early, continuing recovery goals.

Abstinence

Abstinence is the process of abstaining from addictive substances and/or behaviors. If an individual does not engage in the addictive behavior, either indefinitely or for a short time, that person is said to be abstinent or abstaining. Abstinence can be a personal recovery goal, or a program philosophy Abstinence is part of most 12-step facilitated treatment programs. Abstinence

Table 5.1 Parallel Self-States, Maslow's Needs, Life in Recovery, and Recovery Goals

Self-states	Maslow's Needs	Life in Recovery	Recovery Goals
Being	Physiological Needs Safety Needs	Abstinence	Abstinence Harm reduction Relapse prevention
Becoming	Love and Belonging Esteem	Personal Growth	Health Wellness Well-being
Beyond	Self-actualization Self-transcendence	Service to Others	Helping Service Altruism

is often the goal of choice for individuals with severe addictions. Abstinence is a healthy goal for pregnant women.

Abstinence is a challenge as it means **not** doing or having something that is wanted or enjoyable. People resent being told "you can't" drink, smoke, use, gamble, or game. The neurobiology of addiction describes the strength of the addictive process, especially its resistance to change. Yet, abstinence is the cornerstone of effective treatment for addiction and the beginning of recovery for many people with addiction.

Alcoholics Anonymous (AA), started in 1935, is an abstinence-based approach to recovery. AA-oriented treatment and recovery does not suit everyone with an addiction. The stigma of labeling oneself as an alcoholic or addict offends many people. Some people are uncomfortable with the spiritual nature of AA. Others find its framework too rigid, especially where complete abstinence is required.

Harm Reduction

"One size does not fit all" when it comes to treatment approaches and even recovery goals. While abstinence from substance use or other addictive behavior may be the best goal for many people, abstinence is an individual choice and should not be imposed or regarded as the only option. Programs have been developed to reduce the harm from addiction without requiring abstinence. The overall goal of harm reduction is to keep people alive, minimize adverse personal and social consequences from addiction and encourage positive changes in their lives.

Harm reduction is grounded on principles that aim to protect human rights and improve public health. Treating people who use drugs—along with their families and communities—with compassion and dignity is integral to harm reduction. Advocates of harm reduction believe when someone decides they want to use drugs more safely, they are saying that they care about whether they live or die and are taking the first step to end their addiction. Harm reduction helps people reduce harm while they fight their addiction, not silencing them, stigmatizing them, or pushing them into the shadows.

Harm-reduction views substance use and other addictive behaviors on a continuum from excess to abstinence. Excess is associated with high risks to health and well-being; risks decrease with abstinence. The goal of harm reduction is to help people with addiction move away from excessive use and excessive behaviors and in this way reduce the harmful consequences of their addictions.

Teens, college students, and other young adults, especially those who meet diagnostic criteria for mild to moderate addiction, are good candidates for harm reduction. Harm reduction is realistic for people who are highly resistant to abstinence: e.g., chronic intravenous drug users, and people who relapse repeatedly. Classic examples of harm reduction include the designated driver program, methadone maintenance programs, needle exchange services, safe legal injection sites, drinking and driving laws, responsible gambling policies, free condoms and, more recently, medication-assisted treatment (MAT).

According to the New York City health department, every four hours, someone in NYC dies from a drug overdose. In January 2022, NYC health officials announced a plan to install ten "public health vending machines" that would dispense sterile syringes, an anti-overdose medication, safe-sex kits, and other harm reduction supplies to help neighborhoods that have been hit hard by drug overdoses. All items in the vending machines will be free. As mentioned in Chapter 3, survey research from the Recovery Institute documents recovery from addiction. Harm reduction includes anything and everything that prevents overdose deaths, especially ODs from fentanyl use. Harm reduction helps people with addiction stay alive. Over time and with work, these individuals now have a chance to realize recovery.

Harm reduction includes policies, programs, and practices that try to minimize the negative health, social and legal impacts of addiction. Harm reduction policies and practices are informed by a strong body of evidence that shows interventions to be practical, feasible, effective, safe, and cost-effective in diverse social, cultural, and economic settings. Critics of harm reduction see the programs as encouraging drug use and keeping people addicted to drugs, yet research shows no increase in addictive behaviors (e.g., drug use). Harm reduction programs reduce the incidence of overdose deaths, HIV, hepatitis, tuberculosis, sexually transmitted infections (STI), unwanted pregnancies. Most harm reduction interventions are easy to implement and inexpensive, and all have a strong positive impact on individual and community health.

On December 8, 2021, the Substance Abuse Mental Health Services Administration (SAMHSA) announced a $30 million **harm reduction** grant funding opportunity to help address the nation's substance use and overdose epidemic. According to SAMHSA:

> The Substance Abuse and Mental Health Services Administration (SAMHSA) is now accepting applications for the first-ever SAMHSA Harm Reduction grant program and expects to issue $30 million in grant awards. This funding, authorized by the American Rescue Plan, will help increase access to a range of community harm reduction services and support harm reduction service providers as they work to help prevent overdose deaths and reduce health risks often associated with drug use. SAMHSA will accept applications from State, local, Tribal, and territorial governments, Tribal organizations, non-profit community-based organizations, and primary and behavioral health organizations.
>
> SAMHSA will distribute $10 million per year over the next three years. Grant recipients must use the funds to support harm reduction services. Harm reduction service providers will be asked to develop or expand evidence-based services that may include, but not be limited to the provision of sterile syringes, safe sex kits, prevention education about synthetic opioids

and other substances, overdose prevention kits including naloxone distribution, peer worker engagement, medical services, case management and referral to treatment. Warm handoffs that facilitate engagement in care and referrals to treatment for individuals seeking these support services are also critical components of this grant program. Harm reduction services will be trauma-informed and guided by harm reduction stakeholder groups and other community members.

(SAMHSA 2021b)

This unprecedented grant employs harm reduction strategies to combat opioid abuse, including funding for needle exchanges and fentanyl test strips. Funds will not be used for supervised injection sites, which have been the subject of litigation across the country. This funding, provided by the American Rescue Plan, will help increase access to a range of community harm reduction services, and it will support harm reduction service providers as they work to help prevent overdose deaths and reduce health risks often associated with drug use.

Relapse Prevention

Relapse is a return to addictive behavior (alcohol, drugs, gambling, gaming) after a period of abstinence or a deviation from harm reduction protocols. Relapse happens with a fair amount of certainty and predictability for many people with addiction. Relapse rates for people with addiction are similar, even lower, when compared with people who have chronic conditions such as hypertension or asthma. Even with treatment, an estimated 60% of people relapse at some point post-treatment. Relapse prevention is a major goal in early recovery.

Relapse prevention is the way addiction/recovery practitioners and recovering people identify risks for relapse, act early in the relapse process, and prevent relapse. In the 1980s, the landmark work of Terrance T. Gorski, G. Alan Marlatt, and their colleagues brought the science and art of relapse prevention front and center. Later, Rasmussen (2015) described internal and external risks for relapse.

GORSKI

Terrance T. Gorski is a recognized leader in relapse prevention training, consultation, and publication. In the introduction to *The Staying Sober Workbook*, Terrance T. Gorski describes relapse:

Relapse is a process that begins long before people start drinking or drugging. Most people return to alcohol or drug use because they experience a sequence of problems which cause them to become so dysfunctional in sobriety that a return to chemical use seems like a reasonable choice. The pathway into dysfunction includes changes in attitudes, thoughts, feelings, and behaviors. These changes are often referred to as "stinking thinking" or "building up to drink."

(Gorski, 1992, p. 5)

This relapse process is similar for gambling, gaming, and other addictive behaviors. Gorski went on to identify *The Phases and Warning Signs of Relapse* and describe post-acute withdrawal symptoms (PAWS) that can contribute to relapse.

MARLATT

G. Alan Marlatt and associates introduced a cognitive-behavioral approach for relapse prevention. According to Marlatt, 1. *immediate determinants* of relapse include high-risk situations, a person's coping skills, outcome expectancies, and the abstinence violation effect; and 2. *covert antecedents* such as lifestyle imbalances, urges, and cravings.

Marlatt also differentiated between a lapse, often called a slip by lay people, and a relapse. Both concepts are important to understand. A lapse is a return to addictive behavior for a short time with minimal negative consequences: one drink, one use, one lottery ticket, or a weekend food binge. With a relapse, addictive behavior continues over time with adverse consequences for self and others. Early intervention with a lapse is critical to arrest the addictive process. All too often people who lapse continue addictive behavior until the episode becomes a true relapse. Harmful consequences follow. Progression of the addictive process continues. See especially the books by Marlatt and others, *Relapse Prevention: Maintenance Strategies in the Treatment of Addictive Behaviors* (1985) and Witkiewitz and Marlatt, *Therapists Guide to Evidence-Based Relapse Prevention* (2007).

RASMUSSEN

Risks for relapse are legion. Craving, cross-addiction, complacency, noncompliance, and co-morbidity are internal risks for relapse. that originate in the self. External risks come from one's surroundings and include cues, circumstances, and crises. Short definitions of these risks follow.

Craving is an intense desire to repeat a pleasant experience often associated with drinking, using, gambling, or other addictive behavior. *Cross-addiction* is adding or replacing one's primary addictive substances or behavior with other addictive substances or behaviors. *Complacency* is a feeling of contentment, self-satisfaction, even smugness about recovery with a lack of interest or concern for recovery, evident in thoughts, feelings, and actions. *Non-compliance* means a person fails to adhere to treatment or recovery regimens.

Co-morbidity is the presence or effects of one or more additional diseases, disorders, or conditions beyond addiction. Estimates suggest that 40–60% of adults hospitalized with medical/surgical problems meet criteria for a substance-related or addictive-related diagnosis. Unrelieved acute and chronic pain invites addiction and increases risk for relapse. People living with physical disabilities are at increased risk for addiction and relapse. Trauma, including adverse childhood experiences (ACEs), intimate partner violence (IPV), and post-traumatic stress disorder (PTSD) increases risk for relapse. Dual disorders and personality disorders are mental health problems described and diagnoses using the *DSM-5*.

Cues are conditioned reminders of addiction that can trigger relapse; especially sights, sounds, or smells in thoughts or dreams associated with addiction. *Circumstances* include life events, daily hassles, and social situations that produce stress and thus increase risk for relapse. *Crises* are major personal, social, or natural events with a major impact on individuals and groups. Often people "rise to the occasion" when a crisis occurs: a fire, a tornado, a terror attack. However, following the crisis, they may experience PTSD and risk relapse. A prolonged crisis like the COVID-19 pandemic, entering its third year in 2022, witnessed an increased use of and relapse with substances and other addictive behaviors. Co-morbidity, especially major mental illness and suicide increased.

See *Ready, Set, Go! Addiction Management* by Sandra Rasmussen (2015), especially the three chapters on relapse, risks for relapse, and relapse prevention.

STAGES OF RELAPSE

Relapse is a gradual process with distinct stages. *Emotional relapse* occurs before an individual thinks about using or uses and is characterized by mood swings, negative feelings, restlessness, anxiety, depression, and even anger. Accompanying behaviors include self-isolation, poor eating or sleeping habits, and missing support meetings. The term *dry drunk* is a term one might hear at an AA meeting and means the uncomfortable symptoms and dysfunctional signs individuals experience before they drink, use, or gamble. *Mental relapse* exemplifies cognitive dissonance and ambiguity "to use or not to use." People often glamorize and fantasize about past use. Defense mechanisms that deny or minimize consequences of use kick in: "it wasn't that bad." Rationalization and justification loom large: "I just lost my job; I need to take the edge off." Accompanying behaviors include associating with people, places, and things where the person used. *Physical relapse* is using, such as going to a bar and drinking, finding a hidden stash and shooting up, or placing a sports bet and then another.

People in recovery often describe these stages as budding: building up to drink or drug. A bud precedes a full-blown flower. Caring friends at a support meeting who observe "emotional relapse" indicators, may ask the person "are you budding?"

RELAPSE PREVENTION DIRECTIVES

Books, especially workbooks, about relapse prevention abound. Recommended relapse prevention directives follow:

- **Identify triggers.** Triggers are internal or external factors that contribute to relapse. Know what people, places, and things triggers could trigger relapse. Avoid triggers or take an alternative course of action when confronted by a trigger.
- **Practice self-care.** Maintain a healthy diet, sleeping pattern, and exercise routine; mindfulness including meditation, breathing techniques, yoga, and grounding techniques can help. Note: Mindfulness-Based Relapse Prevention (MBRP) integrates techniques from Mindfulness-Based Stress Reduction (MBSR) and Mindfulness-Based Cognitive Therapy (MBCT).
- **HALT.** Do not get too hungry, angry, lonely, or tired. HALT helps reduce chances of relapse, especially useful to manage what Gorski called post-acute withdrawal symptoms (PAWS), a phenomenon that can contribute to relapse.
- **Play the tape through.** Visualize the adverse consequences of a relapse.
- **Seek support.** Recovery practitioners and mutual-self-help groups are well-equipped to help prevent relapse and address relapse when it occurs.
- **Accept help.** Relapse is a defining characteristic of addiction. Forgive yourself and return to recovery work.

Living Well

Health, wellness, and well-being are recovery goals that indicate personal growth.

Health

Health is a core recovery goal. According to the World Health Organization (WHO), "Health is a state of complete physical, mental and social well-being and not merely the absence of disease or infirmity."

People with addiction usually have one or more associated health issues, including cardiovascular disease, stroke, cancer, HIV/AIDS, hepatitis B and C, lung disease, and mental disorders. Tobacco smoke causes many cancers, methamphetamine causes severe dental problems known as meth mouth, and opioids lead to overdose and death. Drug use also increases the risk of contracting infections. HIV and hepatitis C occur from sharing injection equipment or from unsafe practices such as condom-less sex. Infection of the heart and its valves (endocarditis) and skin infection (cellulitis) occur after exposure to bacteria by injection drug users.

Addiction and mental illness often co-exist. In some cases, mental disorders such as anxiety, depression, or schizophrenia come before addiction. In other cases, addiction triggers or worsens mental health conditions. Some people with anxiety or depression may use alcohol or other drugs to alleviate symptoms. This self-medication may exacerbate their mental disorder in the long run and increase the risk of developing addiction. When compared to the general population, mortality and suicide rates are significantly elevated among individuals with gambling disorder.

Beyond the harmful health consequences for people with an addictive disorder, addiction causes serious health problems for others. Well-documented examples include the negative effects of drug use while pregnant or breastfeeding, the harmful effects of secondhand smoke, the increased spread of infectious diseases, and the higher risk of motor vehicle accidents to name a few.

Since 1980 and every decade thereafter the U.S. government has published *Healthy People*, science-based objectives with targets to monitor progress and motivate and focus action. *Healthy People 2030* identifies overarching health goals for U.S. citizens. Recovery will help people with addiction achieve health goals.

- Attain healthy, thriving lives and well-being, free of preventable disease, disability, injury, and premature death.
- Eliminate health disparities, achieve health equity, and attain health literacy to improve the health and well-being of all.
- Create social, physical, and economic environments that promote attaining full potential for health and well-being for all.
- Promote healthy development, healthy behaviors, and well-being across all life stages.
- Engage leadership, key constituents, and the public across multiple sectors to take action and design policies that improve the health and well-being of all.

(Levine 2021, p. 220)

Wellness

Wellness is a recovery goal. Wellness is more than health. Wellness is different from well-being. The Global Wellness Institute defines wellness as the active pursuit of activities, choices, and lifestyles that lead to a state of holistic health. The National Wellness Institute, under the leadership of Dr. Bill Hettler, sees wells as an active process through which people become aware of, and make choices toward, a more successful existence. Three tenets ground this concept.

- Wellness is a conscious, self-directed, and evolving process of achieving full potential.
- Wellness is multidimensional and holistic, encompassing lifestyle, mental and spiritual well-being, and the environment.
- Wellness is positive and affirming.

Wellness is multidimensional. Wellness models include at least six or more dimensions. Graphic illustrations of wellness usually depict a wheel or interacting, overlapping, interacting circles. Short examples of the dimensions of wellness from the National Institute of Wellness (NWI) and the Substance Abuse Mental Health Services Association (SAMSHA) follow.

THE SIX DIMENSIONS OF WELLNESS FROM THE NATIONAL INSTITUTE OF WELLNESS (NWI)

Occupational: The occupational dimension recognizes personal satisfaction and enrichment in one's life through work. At the center of occupational wellness is the premise that occupational development is related to one's attitude about one's work.

Physical: The physical dimension recognizes the need for regular physical activity. Physical development encourages learning about diet and nutrition while discouraging the use of tobacco, drugs, and excessive alcohol consumption.

Social: The social dimension encourages contributing to one's environment and community. It emphasizes the interdependence between others and nature.

Intellectual: The intellectual dimension recognizes one's creative, stimulating mental activities. A well person expands his or her knowledge and skills while discovering the potential for sharing his or her gifts with others.

Spiritual: The spiritual dimension recognizes our search for meaning and purpose in human existence. It includes the development of a deep appreciation for the depth and expanse of life and natural forces that exist in the universe.

Emotional: The emotional dimension recognizes awareness and acceptance of one's feelings. Emotional wellness includes the degree to which one feels positive and enthusiastic about oneself and life (Hettler 1976).

THE EIGHT DIMENSIONS OF WELLNESS FROM THE SUBSTANCE ABUSE MENTAL HEALTH SERVICES ADMINISTRATION (SAMHSA)

Emotional: coping effectively with life and creating satisfying relationships.

Financial: satisfaction with current and future financial situation.

Social: developing a sense of connection, belonging, and a well-developed support system.

Existential (spiritual): expanding our sense of purpose and meaning of life.

Career: personal satisfaction and enrichment derived from one's work.

Physical: recognizing the need for physical activity, diet, sleep, and nutrition.

Intellectual/Creative: recognizing creative abilities and finding ways to expand knowledge and skills.

Environmental: good health by occupying pleasant, stimulating environments that support well-being (SAMHSA n.d.).

Well-being

Well-being is a recovery goal. Well-being is a personal phenomenon, a public construct, and an idea with national and global applications.

WELL-BEING: A PERSONAL PHENOMENON

There is no single definition of well-being. Well-being is characterized by the presence of positive emotions and moods (e.g., contentment, happiness), the absence of negative emotions (e.g., depression, anxiety), satisfaction with life, fulfillment, and positive functioning. Terms used interchangeably with well-being include quality-of-life, life satisfaction, and happiness.

While we have objectives measure of health and wellness dimensions, because well-being is subjective, it is typically measured with self-reports. For example, the Quality-of-Life Inventory (QOL) examines satisfaction or dissatisfaction in 16 areas of life: health, self-esteem, goals and values, money, work play, learning, creativity, helping, love, friends, children, relatives, home, neighborhood, and community. Each indicator is defined, and respondents are asked to rate *importance* and *satisfaction* with the item (Frisch, 2013).

WELL-BEING: A PUBLIC HEALTH CONSTRUCT

The WHO defines QOL as *an individual's perception of their position in life in the context of the culture and value systems in which they live and in relation to their goals, expectations, standards, and concerns.* WHO developed a tool (available in over 40 languages) that measures six domains of quality-of-life:

1   Physical health
2   Psychological health
3   Level of independence
4   Social relationship
5   Environment
6   Spirituality/religion/personal beliefs

The Satisfaction with Life Scale (SWLS), developed by Ed Diener and colleagues in 1985 is a short five-item instrument designed to measure global cognitive judgments of satisfaction with one's life. The scale usually requires only about one minute to complete. The Authentic Happiness Inventory (AHI) is a 24-item multiple-choice questionnaire that samples feelings about self and life to determine happiness. It is part of a battery of tools available from the University of Pennsylvania Positive Psychology Program.

WELL-BEING: A NATIONAL INTEREST

Interest in and measurement of well-being is a public health priority in the United States. Public health scientists believe well-being integrates mental health (mind) and physical health (body) resulting in more holistic approaches to disease prevention and health promotion. Well-being is a valid population outcome measure beyond morbidity, mortality, and economic status that indicates how people perceive their life is going from their perspective. Well-being is an outcome that is meaningful to the public.

Advances in psychology, neuroscience, and measurement theory suggest that well-being can be measured with some degree of accuracy. Well-being can provide a common metric that can help policymakers shape and compare the effects of different policies (e.g., loss of green space might impact well-being more so than commercial development of an area). Measuring, tracking, and promoting well-being can be useful for multiple stakeholders involved in disease prevention and health promotion.

WELL-BEING: A GLOBAL INDICATOR

For many years, the gross domestic product (GDP), a monetary measure of the market value of all the final goods and services produced by a country in a specific time has been used to indicate the health of a country, monitor trends, and compare countries. Many countries have added measures of well-being and happiness to indicate their countries' health.

According to *The 2020 Social Progress Index*, Norway, Denmark, Finland, New Zealand receive "highest marks" for well-being. *The Social Progress Index*, based on the research of Nobel-prize-winning economists, goes beyond measures of GDP measures 50 dimensions of well-being with a focus on three levels of quality of life: basic human needs, foundations of well-being, and opportunity. The scorecard highlights each country's strengths and weaknesses compared to 15 peer countries with similar levels of GDP. The U.S. fell from 19th to 28th on the list. It ranked 91st in access to quality basic education and 97th for health care. American ranked #100 in discrimination against minorities. Note: The four top-ranked countries in the world on 50 dimensions of well-being are all run by women (reported in Forbes on September 11, 2020, Wittenberg-Cox 2020).

The World Happiness Report is a publication of the United Nations Sustainable Development Solutions Network. The survey asks straightforward, subjective questions of more than 1,000 people in each country:

> Imagine a ladder, with steps numbered from 0 at the bottom to 10 at the top. The top of the ladder represents the best possible life for you and the bottom of the ladder represents the worst possible life for you. On which step of the ladder would you say you personally feel you stand at this time?
>
> (Helliwell et al. 2022)

Economic and social factors are considered along with the survey (namely GDP per capita, social support, life expectancy, freedom to make life choices, generosity, and perceptions of corruption), but the focus is on how happy citizens say they are; not how happy statisticians think they should be.

As of March 2021, Finland had been ranked the happiest country in the world four times in a row. Rounding out the rest of the top ten are countries that have consistently ranked among the happiest.

1 Finland
2 Denmark
3 Switzerland
4 Iceland
5 Netherlands
6 Norway
7 Sweden
8 Luxembourg
9 New Zealand
10 Austria

(Reported in https://www.atlasandboots.com/, See also
https://www.unsdsn.org)

Doing Good

Helping, service, and altruism are recovery goals that transcend the self. An "attitude of gratitude" grounds doing good.

Helping

Helping others who have a substance-related or addictive problem supports the helper's recovery. Often this "helping" is through personal or online participation in recovery-based mutual self-help groups such as Alcoholics Anonymous (AA), Narcotics Anonymous (NA); SMART Recovery, Women for Sobriety, and LifeRing Secular Recovery, to name a few. Mutual self-help groups provide a forum and opportunity for individuals in recovery to connect with others who have similar experiences and goals, allowing them to build relationships within an addiction-free support network. The groups are usually free, anonymous, and easily accessible. Helping often begins by sharing one's experience, strength, and hope at a meeting. Helping others in recovery greatly benefits the helper. Helping is a way of saying thank you for recovery and the help received from peers and practitioners.

Helping is almost an expectation of members of 12-step groups. This declaration of responsibility was formally introduced by Bill W. at the fourth international AA Convention in Toronto in 1965. It states, "I am responsible. When anyone, anywhere, reaches out for help, I want the hand of AA always to be there. And for that: I am responsible."

Service

One of the sayings used by 12-Step groups is *you must give it away to keep it*. Service in recovery refers to work carried out for no financial reward or compensation. Service includes setting up a meeting hall and making the coffee, giving a ride to meetings for someone who has no license to drive, chairing a meeting, serving as a group officer, sponsorship, answering emails from people looking for recovery support, facilitating an online meeting, or maintaining a group's website.

Groups like AA could not function without the voluntary services provided by members. Meetings around the world are organized and maintained by volunteers. There is usually a collection at the end of each meeting, but this money is used to pay for meeting space, recovery materials, and refreshments. Service in recovery helps the giver as much as the receiver. The benefits of service in recovery are legion!

Hospitals, other treatment facilities, and especially prisons welcome service by recovering men and women. Service also includes attendance or presentation at an addiction/recovery conference or convention.

Altruism

Altruism is more than helping, more than service. Altruism is selfless, often an anonymous concern, compassion, and care for others, without personal benefit, and frequently at the expense of the giver. Altruism is the unselfish concern for other people: simply acting out of a concern for the well-being of other people, not because of obligation, duty, loyalty, or religious reasons.

Altruism is one aspect of what psychologists call prosocial behavior. Prosocial behavior is any action that benefits other people, no matter what the motive or how the giver benefits from the action. Though some believe that humans are fundamentally self-interested, and active addiction is certainly self-centered, recent research suggests that healthy people's first impulse is to cooperate rather than compete.

Evolutionary scientists speculate that altruism has such deep roots in human nature because helping and cooperation promote the survival of our species. Darwin believed "sympathy" and "benevolence," were social instincts. Today, neuroscience studies show that when people behave altruistically, their brains activate in regions that signal pleasure, like rewards from substance use or addictive behavior. Empathy encourages altruism.

Altruism manifests what Abraham Maslow described as "beyond self-actualization," as well as the highest stage of moral development, Universal Ethical Principles, identified by Lawrence Kohlberg. According to Matthieu Ricard, altruism is the power of compassion to change yourself and the world. Empathy encourages altruism.

While news stories often focus on grand cases of altruism, such as the heroic rescue of a drowning man from an icy river, altruism more often is a random act of kindness. Altruism reflects the 12th step of AA and NA: "Having had a spiritual awakening as the result of these steps, we tried to carry this message to alcoholics/addicts, and to practice these principles in all our affairs." Altruism is "doing the next right thing."

Remission and Recovery

Remission

Addiction practitioners who use the *Diagnostic Statistical Manual* (5th ed.) refer to remission rather than recovery. *DSM-5* criteria for remission from a substance use disorder (SUD) reflect duration (time) free from diagnostic criteria symptoms, excluding craving. Initial remission describes symptom-free time up to three months. Early remission is the period from three months to one year. Sustained remission from SUD is one to five years and stable remission is greater than five years.

Remission may be partial or full. Practitioners may specify "in a controlled environment" if the individual is living in a setting where access to substances is restricted. Today, many people with addiction receive medication-assisted treatment (MAT) that helps them control craving and this supports recovery.

Recovery is much more than remission. However, the terms used to describe remission categories are useful to understand the recovery continuum.

Initial Recovery (Up to Three Months)

Safe detoxification and a focus on abstinence or harm reduction are initial treatment/recovery goals. Recovery begins the day individuals with addiction stop drinking, using, or other addictive behavior or begin a medication-assisted treatment (MAT) program.

To "live one day at a time" is to focus on the present moment, and without worrying about the past or future. Recovering individuals may feel guilt and shame about their past addictive behaviors, and this can trigger use. Focusing on the future may increase doubts with fear of failure. The thought of lifetime sobriety can be overwhelming. There is a treatment facility in Philadelphia dedicated to serving low-income and homeless men and women and their families who are afflicted by addiction and HIV/AIDs called One Day A Time Recovery, Inc. (ODAAT).

Mutual self-help support groups stress one day at a time. The longer version of The Serenity Prayer, the unofficial mantra of many 12-step groups, emphasizes one day at a time.

> God, grant me the Serenity
> To accept the things I cannot change…
> Courage to change the things I can,
> And Wisdom to know the difference.
> Living one day at a time,
> Enjoying one moment at a time.

Daily meditations books for recovery abound. *Twenty-Four Hours a Day* is perhaps the best-selling daily meditation book. First published in the early 1950s, and with over nine million copies in print, the "little black book" offers daily thoughts, meditations, and prayers for living a clean and sober life. Many other publications offer daily support.

Day by Day Meditations for Recovering Addicts
Just for Today: Daily Meditations for Recovering Addicts
Each Day a New Beginning: Daily Meditations for Women
Touchstones: A Book of Daily Meditations for Men
Food for Thought: Daily Meditations for Overeaters
A Day at a Time Gamblers Anonymous

"One Day at a Time," a popular Country and Western-style Christian song, became best known among country fans when recorded by American country gospel singer Cristy Lane. The song is a theme song at many addictions treatment centers; it is especially popular with women.

Early Recovery (Three Months to One Year)

Addiction practitioners describe early remission as a period greater than 3 months but less than 12 months without meeting *DSM-5* substance use disorders criteria other than craving. Recovering men and women develop skills and use resources to continue abstinence or harm reduction and prevent relapse. Relapse prevention is a very important early recovery goal. Today, many treatment programs use medications to help patients manage craving.

Mutual support groups recognize and reinforce recovery, so very important in year one. Many AA and NA groups have a chip system. The White Chip, also known as the "Surrender Chip" is for anyone starting, or for anyone starting over in the program of Alcoholics Anonymous. Gamblers Anonymous gives out a "welcome" white key tag when a person attends a first GA meeting. Different colored chips and key tags are awarded at 30 days, 60 days, 90 days, 6 months, and 9 months. If recovering men and women belong to a home support group, there is usually a celebration with a cake and medallion to celebrate one year of recovery.

Sustained Recovery (One to Five Years)

Recovering men and women often report year two as "challenging." Marital relationships, parental responsibilities, and work expectations loom large. Health factors neglected during active addiction need to be addressed. During sustained recovery, men and women develop many dimensions of wellness and experience well-being. Mutual support groups award anniversary medallions (coins) for each year of recovery.

Stable Recovery (Greater than Five Years)

In 1996, George E. Vaillant, MD, author of the *Natural History of Alcoholism Revisited,* suggested that a five-year period of abstinence from alcohol is necessary to reduce the danger of relapse. Valliant likened recovery from alcoholism to recovery from cancer: an individual needs a set period of freedom from the disease to be considered "cured."

State monitoring programs for health practitioners with addiction are usually five years long. Program evaluation finds that the longer the monitoring program, the more effective for the practitioners and public safety.

According to NIDA, the length of abstinence is predictive of future sobriety; a person who remains sober for three years has increased chances of remaining sober. Although there is no guarantee of continuing recovery after three or five years of stable recovery, the likelihood of relapse decreases with time. Long-term recovery is most likely when there are strong community ties, participation in self-help groups, adherence to medication regimens for addiction and co-occurring mental health disorders, and management of general medical conditions. Serious adverse events like illness, a major loss, or catastrophic events like the COVID-19 pandemic increase risks for relapse.

There is much interest in studying the dimensions and dynamics of log-term recovery with the following paragraph that begins with See especially the work of the Recovery Institute in Boston, MA, and the research of Mark Gold, Warren Bickel, and Keith Humphreys on the neuroscience of long-term recovery. The *Life in Recovery* Survey found "life kept getting better as recovery progressed." Family and social life were better. Financial well-being improved with recovery. Legal problems that were highly prevalent in active addiction decreased as a function of recovery duration. Civic involvement increased.

Section I presented facts, concepts, principles, and theories about recovery goals, mastering addiction, living well, doing good, and remission and recovery. Continue recovery work in Section II with applications about the competency.

II

Section II suggests applications about recovery goals, mastering addiction, living well, doing good, and remission and recovery.

Recovery Goals

1   Three dominant recovery themes emerged from the Life in Recovery survey: abstinence, personal growth, and service to others. How would you describe life in recovery?

Mastering Addiction

2   **Abstinence** is an early, continuing recovery goal for many people with addiction. What does abstinence mean for you?
3   **Harm** reduction may be an early, continuing goal for some individuals with addiction. What does harm reduction mean to you?
4   **Relapse** prevention is an early, continuing goal for people with addiction. How can you reduce risks for relapse? Scaling is a way to assess risk for relapse. Use Table 5.2 to complete the Risk for Relapse Assessment that follows: 1 is very low risk and 5 is very high risk.

Living Well

5   **Health** is a recovery goal that indicates personal growth. A Health Improvement Plan supports a healthy lifestyle which in turn supports recovery. Use Table 5.3 to complete the Health Improvement Plan worksheet.
6   **Wellness** is a recovery goal that indicates personal growth. Assess, and perhaps affirm, your Eight Dimensions of Wellness. Use Table 5.4 and the following scale to rank your satisfaction with wellness.

1 = completely dissatisfied
2 = dissatisfied
3 = undecided/unsure
4 = satisfied
5 = completely satisfied

7 **Well-being** is a recovery goal that indicates personal growth. How do you experience well-being? What does quality-of-life mean for you?

Doing Good

8 **Helping.** Are you a good helper? Use Table 5.5 and the following scale to identify your helping characteristics. The higher the score the better: 40 and above reflects good change-readiness.

1 = Untrue of me
2 = Somewhat untrue of me
3 = Neutral
4 = Somewhat true of me
5 = True of me

9 **Service.** How do you serve others? Review the following ideas for service to your community. Add your own. Volunteer your time and effort with one or more of these community service ideas.

1 Reach out to a neighbor in need.
2 Perform an act of random kindness.
3 Mentor children at your local school. library, or neighborhood center.
4 Serve at a local soup kitchen or food bank.
5 Donate blood.
6 Volunteer at the local animal shelter, rescue group, or humane society.
7 Visit local volunteer websites.
8 Pick up trash along the road, at a local park, or along a river, stream, or lake.
9 Help build a home with Habitat for Humanity.
10
11
12
13
14
15

10 **Altruism.** Altruism is selfless, often an anonymous concern, compassion, and care for others, without personal benefit and frequently at the expense of the giver. Describe someone you consider altruistic.

Section II suggested applications about recovery goals, mastering addiction, living well, doing good, and remission and recovery. Complete Chapter 5 with evaluations of recovery work and competency development.

Table 5.2 Rasmussen Risks for Relapse

RISKS	SCALE				
Craving	1	2	3	4	5
Cross-addiction	1	2	3	4	5
Complacency	1	2	3	4	5
Non-compliance	1	2	3	4	5
Co-morbidity: Medical, Trauma, Dual Disorder, Personality Disorder (Please specify)	1	2	3	4	5
Cues	1	2	3	4	5
Circumstances: Life Events Daily Hassles Social Problems (Please specify)	1	2	3	4	
Crises (Please specify)					

Table 5.3 Health Improvement Plan

Healthy Factors	Begin	Continue	Improve
Exercise			
Nutrition and Diet	.		
Time in Nature			
Relationships			
Recreation			
Relaxation/Stress Management			
Religious/Spiritual Involvement			
Service to Others			

Table 5.4 Eight Dimensions of Wellness

WELLNESS	Meaning	1	2	3	4	5
Emotional	I am coping effectively with life and creating satisfying relationships.					
Financial	I am satisfied with current and future financial situations.					
Social	I am developing a sense of connection, belonging, and a well-developed support system.					
Spiritual	I am expanding my sense of purpose and meaning in life.					
Occupational	I derive personal satisfaction and enrichment derived from my work.					
Physical	I recognize the need for physical activity, diet, sleep, and nutrition.					
Intellectual	I recognize my creative abilities and am finding ways to expand my knowledge and skills.					
Environmental	I experience good health by occupying pleasant, stimulating environments that support well-being.					

Table 5.5 Characteristics of a Good Helper

Characteristics	Reflects Me
Genuine caring	1 2 3 4 5
Clear thinking	1 2 3 4 5
Common sense	1 2 3 4 5
Self-awareness	1 2 3 4 5
Warmth	1 2 3 4 5
Calm manner	1 2 3 4 5
Dependability	1 2 3 4 5
Nonjudgmental attitude	1 2 3 4 5
Positive attitude toward life	1 2 3 4 5
Flexibility	1 2 3 4 5
Sense of humor	1 2 3 4 5
Honesty	1 2 3 4 5
Self-confidence	1 2 3 4 5
Respect for others	1 2 3 4 5
Openness	1 2 3 4 5

III

Evaluate recovery work and competency development.

1 Evaluate recovery work with a short True/False Quiz and a review of the outcome, effort, process, and decisions of recovery work.

    a Quiz: Based on your learning from Chapter 5 "Set Recovery Goals," indicate whether each of the following statements is True (T) or False (F).

       1 T or F Goals are specific action plans with measurable steps and time-bound schedules.

       2 T or F *Being, becoming,* and *beyond* are three existential self-states that structure recovery goals.

       3 T or F Self-actualization is the highest level of functioning in Maslow's six-level Hierarchy of Needs.

       4 T or F Abstinence or harm reduction and relapse prevention are early, continuing recovery goals.

       5 T or F Harm reduction helps people prevent the harmful consequences of their addictions.

       6 T or F Health, wellness, and well-being as personal growth goals that build on early recovery.

       7 T or F Health is the absence of disease or infirmity.

       8 T or F Helping, service, and altruism are recovery goals that transcend self.

       9 T or F Remaining clean and sober for 90 days is considered stable recovery.

10   T or F   The Life in Recovery Survey found "life kept getting better as recovery progressed."

(True: 2, 4, 6, 7, 10. False: 1, 2, 5, 7, 9)

b   Outcome, Effort, Process, and Decisions

Examine the outcome, effort, process, and decisions of your recovery work in Chapter 5.

Outcome

Did you meet **objectives** for Chapter 5? Use Table 5.6 to review objectives and rank as:

Strongly disagree = 1
Disagree = 2
Undecided = 3
Agree = 4
Strongly agree = 5

Effort

Effort evaluation reviews the input or energy you invested in recovery work. Ask and answer the following questions.

- How hard did you work on Chapter 5?
- How much time did you dedicate to Chapter 5?
- What resources did you employ for Chapter 5 work?

Table 5.6 Objectives

Objectives	Rank
I define goals, objectives, and outcomes.	1, 2, 3, 4, 5
I acknowledge the contributions from existential self-states, Maslow's Hierarchy of Needs, and the Life in Recovery survey to the development of recovery goals.	1, 2, 3, 4, 5
I embrace recovery as *the ability to master addiction, live well, and do good.*	1, 2, 3, 4, 5
I recognize abstinence or harm reduction and relapse prevention as early, continuing recovery goals.	1, 2, 3, 4, 5
I welcome health, wellness, and well-being as personal growth goals that build on early recovery.	1, 2, 3, 4, 5
I affirm helping, service, and altruism as recovery goals that transcend self.	1, 2, 3, 4, 5
I know the characteristics of initial, early, sustained, and stable recovery.	1, 2, 3, 4, 5

Table 5.7 Process

Process	Yes or No	Comment
I read the narrative (Section I).		
I completed the applications (Section II).		
I evaluated recovery work and competency development (Section III).		

Process

Process evaluation is especially valuable when you want to improve outcome and increase the efficiency of your recovery work. Use Table 5.7 to evaluate process.

Decisions

Based on the evaluation of your recovery work from Chapter 5, decide to celebrate, continue, correct, or change your approach to recovery work. Reward yourself with a positive thought, feeling, or action. Keep doing what you are doing if "it works." Modify or adjust anything that is not working well. Plan and welcome change that supports your recovery work as you move on to Chapter 6. Ask and answer the following questions.

- Did you **celebrate** your recovery work from Chapter 5 Set Recovery Goals?
- Will you **continue** to approach recovery work in the same way in Chapter 6?
- Do you plan to **correct** your approach to recovery work in Chapter 6?
- Do you plan to **change** your approach to recovery work in Chapter 6?

2 Evaluate competency development using a KSA/Topic Matrix and a Rubric Review.

   a What knowledge, skills, and attitudes are you using to develop Competency 5 Set Recovery Goals. Document KSA examples in Table 5.8 KSA/Topic Matrix.

   b Evaluate the development of Competency 5 Set Recovery Goals with a Rubric Review. The chapter outline provides the criteria to evaluate competency development. Rank competency development on Table 5.9 as:

   - **Exceeds expectations:** Understands, applies, and evaluates competency criteria > 90% of the time.
   - **Meets expectations:** Understands, applies, and evaluates competency criteria 75% to 90% of the time.
   - **Needs improvement:** Understands, applies, and evaluates competency criteria < 75% of the time.

Table 5.8 KSA/Topic Matrix

Topics	Knowledge	Skills	Attitudes
Recovery Goals Goals, Objectives, and Outcome Being, Becoming, and Beyond Maslow's Hierarchy of Needs Life in Recovery Survey Recovery Defined			
Mastering Addiction Abstinence Harm Reduction Relapse Prevention			
Living Well Health Wellness Well-being			
Doing Good Helping Service Altruism			
Remission and Recovery Remission Initial Early Sustained Stable			

Table 5.9 Competency 5 Set Recovery Goals

Criteria	Exceeds Expectations 3	Meets Expectations 2	Needs Improvement 1
Recovery Goals Goals, Objectives, and Outcome Being, Becoming, and Beyond Maslow's Hierarchy of Needs Life in Recovery Survey Recovery Defined			
Mastering Addiction Abstinence Harm Reduction Relapse Prevention			
Living Well Health Wellness Well-being			
Doing Good Helping Service Altruism			
Remission and Recovery Remission Initial Early Sustained Stable			

Summary

Set recovery goals in Chapter 5. This chapter identified essential recovery goals. Topics that provided the organizing framework for the chapter included Recovery Goals, Mastering Addiction, Living Well, Doing Good, and Remission and Recovery. The chapter defined goals, objectives, and outcome. It acknowledged the contribution of existential self-states, Maslow's Hierarchy of Needs, and the Life in Recovery Survey to the development of recovery goals. It embraced recovery as the ability to master addiction, live well, and do good. The chapter recognized abstinence or harm reduction and relapse prevention as early continuing recovery goals. It welcomed health, wellness, and well-being as personal growth goals that build on early recovery. The chapter affirmed helping, service, and altruism as recovery goals that transcend self. It explained initial, early, sustained, and stable recovery. The chapter suggested applications—questions, worksheets, exercises, and projects—for the competency. Chapter 5 concluded with evaluations of recovery work and competency development.

6 Determine Motivation for Recovery

Sean has Low Motivation for Recovery

Sue W. (LICSW) works with families, teens, and children at the Fairview Behavioral Health Center. She is pleased to see a return appointment for Sean M. Sean was a highly motivated high school student with a promising soccer career ahead of him, complicated by some episodic pot use. Today, Sean appeared disheveled, restless, with impoverished speech. He minimized eye contact; his affect was flat. What a change! Slowly Sean told me about arrests over the summer with two drug-related felony convictions. Counseling is a requirement of his probation. He will not Captain the HS soccer team or even play. His plans for a college soccer scholarship are gone. "I checked out joining the air force, but the USAF is the most difficult branch of the military to join with a felony record. I am working part-time for Ted." I remembered Ted was his mother's boyfriend who owned a small manufacturing business in the area. Sean did not like Ted. "I have nothing more to lose, so I drink, smoke, and do a few "uppers." He seemed unaware or unconcerned of the consequences if he violates probation. I had Sean complete a Beck Depression Inventory (BDI-II). We scheduled an appointment for the same day, the same time next week. I gave Sean my on-call phone / text contact.

Purpose: This chapter considers three aspects of motivation: importance, confidence, and readiness.

Objectives

- Understand the dimensions and dynamics of motivation.
- Recognize three key motivation constructs: importance, confidence, and readiness.
- Use the Health Belief Model (HBM) and Motivational Interviewing (MI) to ascertain the importance of recovery.
- Enlist Self-Efficacy Concepts and Achievement-Motivation Theory to build confidence for recovery goal-achievement.
- Employ change concepts and the Stages of Change Model to assess readiness for recovery work.

DOI: 10.4324/9781003292944-6

Outline

Motivation

Importance

Beliefs
Commitment

Confidence

Self-Efficacy
Achievement Motivation

Readiness

Personality Traits
Courage to Change
ASAM Readiness to Change
Stages of Change

I

Determine motivation for recovery. Section I presents facts, concepts, principles, and theories about motivation and three motivation constructs: importance, confidence, and readiness.

Motivation

What are the dimensions and dynamics of motivation? Motivation is a biopsychosocial force people employ for recovery work, more specifically, to master addiction and to live well. Motivation is the push and pull initiatives and actions people use to meet recovery objectives and reach recovery goals. Lambert Decker identifies biological, psychological, and environmental sources of motivation. Activation, intensity, and persistence characterize motivation. Both internal and external factors provide the energy for motivation. The strength of motivation may be as important or even more so than its source. According to Decker motivation induces behavior, feelings, and cognition, like what we call knowledge, skills, and Attitudes (KSA).

We recognize three key motivation constructs: importance, confidence, and readiness. Motivation principles include beliefs, commitment, self-efficacy, achievement motivation, and change. By applying the principles of motivation, people can initiate self-change.

Importance

Beliefs about recovery and commitment to recovery indicate importance. Use the Health Belief Model (HBM) and Motivational Interviewing (MI) to ascertain the importance of recovery.

Beliefs

The Health Belief Model (HBM) was developed in the early 1950s by social scientists at the U.S. Public Health Service. The HBM suggests that individual beliefs about a potential or actual illness or disease, together with beliefs about the effectiveness of recommended health behavior, predict the likelihood of action. The course of action depends on the person's perceptions of the benefits and barriers related to the health behavior. Perceptions of susceptibility, severity, benefits, and barriers can vary. Cues to action and self-efficacy can change. Demographics influence the HBM process. See Figure 6.1, which is a depiction of the Health Belief Model.

Addiction/recovery practitioners have used the Health Belief Mode successfully to support behavior change with smoking and drinking. Today, the IIBM is being used with opioid addiction, specifically medication-assisted treatment (MAT).

A 2021 research report described a study that was conducted to determine the effect of education based on the health belief model on internet addiction status among university students. In this interventional study, two dormitories were divided into two groups of control and intervention in a completely

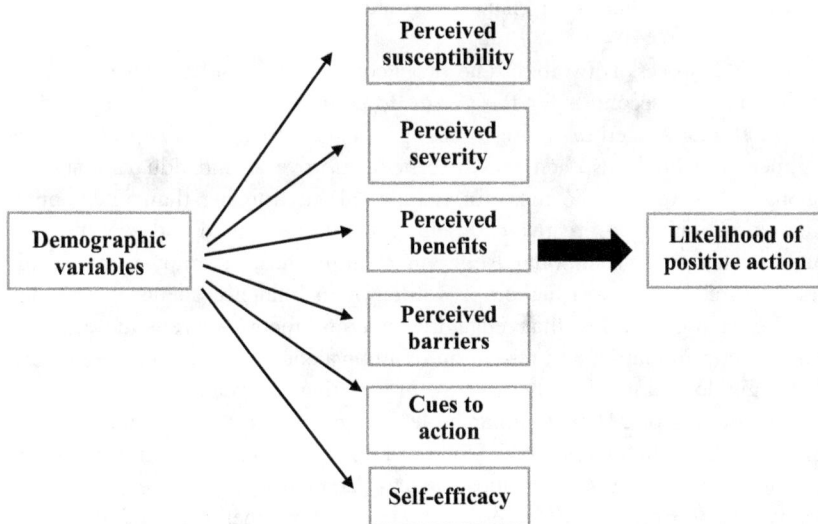

Figure 6.1 Health Belief Model

random manner using the random cluster sampling method from a total of eight dormitories. The results of this study show the effectiveness of educational intervention design based on the structures of the health belief model on reducing the frequency of internet addiction and adopting preventive behaviors (Ahmadi et al., 2021).

Commitment

Many people with addiction begin to develop competencies for recovery with the counselors who employ Motivation Interviewing (MI). MI is an empowering experience that emboldens people for recovery. MI is a counseling approach developed in part by clinical psychologists William R. Miller and Stephen Rollnick. See *Motivational Interviewing: Helping People Change* (2013). MI is a client-centered model of counseling, meaning that the focus is on figuring out what clients want, not what the counselor thinks is best for them. This requires high levels of empathy, reflective listening, and the ability to form a strong bond with the client. Several assumptions support the use of MI in addiction treatment and recovery work.

1   Ambivalence toward alcohol and drug abuse is a normal obstacle on the path to recovery.
2   People possess natural motivations and values that can help them overcome ambivalence.
3   The relationship between a therapist and client is a collaborative partnership.
4   An empathetic, supportive, and directive approach to counseling can establish conditions for change to occur.

The MI process is twofold. The first goal is to increase the person's motivation and the second is for the person to commit to change. As opposed to simply stating a need or desire to change, hearing themselves express a commitment out loud has been shown to help improve an individual's ability to change. The role of the therapist is more about listening than intervening. Compared with non-directive counseling, it is more focused and goal-directed and departs from traditional Rogerian client-centered therapy through this use of direction, in which therapists attempt to influence clients to consider making changes, rather than engaging in non-directive therapeutic exploration. The examination and resolution of ambivalence is a central purpose, and the counselor is intentionally directive in pursuing this goal.

The success of MI in treating addiction, especially alcohol, is well-documented. MI is often combined or followed up with other interventions, such as cognitive therapy, support groups such as Alcoholics Anonymous, and stress management training. MI is now being used for other types of addiction, especially gambling disorder and eating disorders, with mental illness and behavioral issues. In 2008, Miller and Rollnick simplified the principles of MI so that they could be applied by practitioners in many health care settings, especially in primary care.

MI is an addiction/recovery approach of choice when people with addiction lack motivation for change, present with a pattern of relapse, or when other techniques have failed. MI promotes commitment to change and recovery (Psychology Today n.d.).

Confidence

Confidence is the experience and expression of self-efficacy and achievement motivation. Enlist Self-Efficacy Concepts and Achievement-Motivation Theory to build confidence for recovery goal-achievement.

Self-Efficacy

Remember the children's book *The Little Engine That Could*. When other engines refuse to rescue the stranded train full of toys and food for good boys and girls, Little Blue responds *"I think I can, I think I can, I think I can."* The engine overcomes insurmountable odds and pulls the train up the towering mountain to the other side: a true case study in self-efficacy. Self-efficacy is an important part of the social-cognitive theory of personality developed by the psychologist Albert Bandura.

Self-efficacy is the idea that people can achieve and succeed at what they do: that is, be effective. Self-efficacy is confidence plus certainty in one's efficacy: the power to produce an effect. Self-efficacy is the perception of one's own ability to reach a goal. It is the belief in one's agency: an affirmation of ability and the strength of that belief. Self-efficacy is the belief of personal capability to perform specific actions: e.g., to reach recovery goals. Self-efficacy beliefs determine how people feel, think, and motivate themselves and their behavior. Such beliefs produce these diverse effects through four major processes: cognitive, motivational, affective, and selection processes.

People develop self-efficacy through mastery experiences, social modeling, social persuasion, and psychological responses to physiological states. Self-efficacy regulates functioning through cognitive, motivational, affective, and selective processes. People with a weak sense of self-efficacy experience and exhibit powerlessness. People with a strong sense of self-efficacy embody and express empowerment.

Self-efficacy is a key component of the Chronic Disease Self-Management Program (CDSMP) developed by Stanford University and described in Chapter 5 "Develop a Strategic Recovery Plan." Higher self-efficacy is linked to less frequent episodes of binge drinking, fewer instances of Marijuana use, and lower rates of relapse. In many studies of substance abuse treatment, self-efficacy has emerged as an important predictor of a desirable outcome, or as a mediator of positive treatment effects.

People with high self-efficacy approach recovery as a challenge they can master. They set realistic, but challenging goals for themselves, are committed to these goals and work very hard to reach them, even in the face of adversity. If they are unable to achieve an initial goal, they recognize this as a limitation then can overcome, and then try again. Self-efficacy is a key aspect of empowerment. People with high self-efficacy are empowered to develop competencies for recovery including mastering addiction, living well, and doing good.

Achievement Motivation

Simply stated, achievement motivation is an individual's need to meet realistic goals, receive feedback, and experience a sense of accomplishment. Researchers have studied achievement motivation concepts since the emergence of psychology as a scientific discipline in the late 1800s when William James speculated about the relationship between competence strivings and self-evaluation. Most of us are familiar with Maslow's Hierarchy of Needs and the order of their importance: physiological needs, safety needs, and the needs for belonging, self-esteem, and self-actualization, David McClelland built on this work in his 1961 book, *The Achieving Society*.

McClelland and colleagues' work on achievement motivation supports the idea that motivation is a key competency for recovery work. What is achievement motivation?

The term achievement motivation may be defined by independently considering the words "achievement" and "motivation." Achievement refers to competence (a condition or quality of effectiveness, ability, sufficiency, or success). Motivation refers to the energization (instigation) and direction (aim) of behavior. Thus, achievement motivation may be defined as the energization and direction of competence-relevant behavior or why and how people strive toward competence (success) and away from incompetence (failure).

McClelland identified three dominant needs that motivate behavior, regardless of our gender, culture, or age: a need for achievement, a need for affiliation, and a need for power. People will have different characteristics depending on their dominant motivator. According to McClelland, high achievers have strong needs to set and accomplish challenging goals, take calculated risks to accomplish their goals, and receive regular feedback on their progress and achievements. People motivated by achievement seek challenging, but not impossible, projects. They thrive on overcoming difficult problems or situations. They work very effectively either alone or with other high achievers. Achievement motivation is a widely used theory in the business/work world.

Many achievement motivation concepts support the idea that motivation is a key competency for recovery work. Some years ago, Andrew J. Elliott and Holly A. McGregor described three types of these achievement goals: a performance-approach goal, a performance-avoidance goal, and a mastery goal.

A performance-approach goal is focused on attaining competence relative to others, a performance-avoidance goal is focused on avoiding incompetence relative to others, and a mastery goal is focused on the development of competence itself and task mastery. Achievement motivation theory supports the development of competencies, especially the concept of mastery.

Readiness

Change is both the process and outcome of effective recovery work. Employ change concepts and the Stages of Change Model to assess readiness for recovery work. Personality traits, especially the courage to change, may predict change readiness. The American Society of Addiction Medicine (ASAM) identifies "readiness to change" as one of six dimensions of a multidimensional assessment. The Stages of Change Model also helps determine readiness for recovery work.

Traits that Predict Readiness to Change

Organizations, especially in the business world, often assess readiness to change when planning a major change. Personality traits associated with readiness to change include adaptability, adventurousness, confidence, drive, flexibility, passion, optimism, resilience, resourcefulness, and tolerance of ambiguity. Recovery is a major change.

Courage to Change

> God grant me the **serenity** to accept the things, I cannot change,
> **courage** to change the things I can,
> and **wisdom** to know the difference.

The Serenity Prayer is almost an unofficial mantra for people with addiction. The Prayer is attributed to the theologian Reinhold Niebuhr. According to a book written by Niebuhr's daughter Elisabeth Sifton, her father wrote the prayer in 1943 for a church service in rural New England. See *The Serenity Prayer: Faith and Politics in Times of Peace. Serenity Prayer: Faith and Politics in Times of Peace and War* (2003). Niebuhr devoted his life to social justice. He spoke out against apathy and political indifference in the classroom, pulpit, and print. Niebuhr tried to waken colleagues to the dangers that threatened America in the 20th century culminating in World War II. His words ring loud and clear today, whether applied to world crises, systemic racism, or addiction. The Serenity Prayer gives many men and women the serenity, courage, and wisdom to change.

American Society of Addiction Medicine (ASAM) Dimensions

ASAM suggests a holistic, biopsychosocial assessment to determine addiction severity, level of care placement, and intensity of service. Readiness to change is one of six dimensions of this multidimensional assessment. Assessment explores an individual's readiness and interest in changing. This dimension reflects the Stages of Change Model and Transtheoretical Theory advanced by James Prochaska and Carlo DiClemente.

Stages of Change

Developed in the 1980s, Stages of Change is a dominant model for behavioral health change. See the pioneering book. *Changing for Good: A Revolutionary Six-Stage Program for Overcoming Bad Habits and Moving Your Life Positively Forward.* Stages of Change is part of the Transtheoretical Model (TTM) of health psychology. The Stages of Change Model systematically and explicitly incorporates principles of motivational psychology and behavior change to produce internally motivated, immediate change. People use Stages of Change to determine readiness to change, i.e., to begin recovery work.

The Model describes six stages—Precontemplation, Contemplation, Preparation Action, Maintenance, and Relapse—and the behaviors associated with each stage. Health practitioners have developed strategies and techniques to address these behaviors and help people reach each stage. Prochaska and colleagues identified cognitive, affective, and behavioral processes people use to progress through the stages. People themselves recognize these stages and effect self-change: For example:

- *I am not ready to change.*
- *I am thinking of changing.*
- *I am ready to change.*
- *I am making a change.*
- *I am on track.*
- *Oops, I fell off the wagon.*

See Table 6.1 for an addiction example of Stages of Change.

Section I presented facts, concepts, principles, and theories about motivation and three motivation constructs: importance, confidence, and readiness. Continue recovery work in Section II with applications about the competency.

II

Section II suggests applications about motivation and three motivation constructs: importance, confidence, and readiness.

Motivation

1   Understand the dimensions and dynamics of motivation. "May the force be with you!" Motivation is a biopsychosocial force people employ for

Table 6.1 Stages of Change, Characteristics, and Addiction Example

Stages of Change	Characteristics: Behaviors Associated with Each Stage	Example: Ellen, a 24-year-Old Graduate Student Who Smokes
Pre-contemplation	Ignore a problem. Deny a problem. Maintain the status quo.	*I smoke a pack of Marlboro Lights daily. No problem. Why change?*
Contemplation	Identify a problem. Consider the possibility of change. Evaluate pros and cons of change. Question willingness to change.	*My boyfriend Josh says smoking is an addiction. I should quit, but right now I am studying for exams. Smoking "takes the edge off." I'm not sure I want to stop.*
Preparation	Decide to change. Motivate self to change. Develop a change plan. Ready self to change.	*I will quit smoking when I finish my exams. I can do it! I will use the Smoke-Free Plan from the Health Service; I will get the patch. I am ready to change.*
Action	Implement the change plan. Take steps to change. Revise change plan as needed. Begin the new behavior pattern.	*I have the plan, the patch, and no cigarettes. I am monitoring smoking thoughts, feelings, and actions every waking hour. I crave a cigarette in the morning, so I added a 30-minute run to my change plan. Hey, smoke-free is becoming a habit.*
Maintenance	Repeat the new behavior. Reward self for change. Integrate change into a lifestyle. Affirm change.	*WOW! No smoking for 6 months: one day at a time. I treated myself to a sapphire tennis bracelet with my cigarette money. A morning run is part of my life; I am eating wisely and sleeping well. School is great. Josh is proud of me. I did it!*
Relapse	Ignore indicators of relapse. Fail to manage stress. Remember fondly old behavior. Crave old behavior. Decrease supports of new behavior. Increase risks for the old behavior. Stop new behavior. Return to the old behavior.	*Everyone skips meals and sleeps less in graduate school. I don't have time to run every morning. Smoking takes the edge off; "how good it was." Josh will scold me but my new friends smoke. Let me put my smoke-free lifestyle on hold. "One pack of Marlboro Lights, please."*

recovery work. Think of some "ups and downs" or highs and lows in your recovery: e.g., a one-year medallion, a job promotion; a relapse, a divorce. Use Table 6.2 to examine what role motivation plays in your "ups" or "downs" in recovery.

Table 6.2 Motivation

Recovery	Motivation
"Ups"	
"Downs"	

Importance

Use the Health Belief Model (HBM) and Motivational Interviewing (MI) to ascertain the importance of recovery.

2 How *important* is your recovery? The Health Belief Model (HBM) suggests that individual beliefs about a potential or actual illness or disease, together with beliefs about the effectiveness of recommended health behaviors, predict the likelihood of action. Based on your beliefs about addiction and recovery, how likely are you to act to realize recovery?

    a This I believe about addiction:
    b This I believe about recovery:
    c I will act to realize recovery: yes, no, or maybe. Please comment.

3 Motivational Interviewing (MI) can help people commit to a difficult process of change. Commitment indicates the strength of motivation. To commit means to promise, pledge, or vow. What does it mean for you to commit to recovery?

Confidence

Enlist Self-Efficacy Concepts and Achievement-Motivation Theory to build confidence for recovery goal-achievement.

4 Self-efficacy is the belief you have the ability, competence, and likelihood of successfully accomplishing a task and producing a favorable outcome. Albert Bandura championed the concept of self-efficacy beginning in 1986. One of the best-known scales to measure self-efficacy is the General Self-Efficacy Scale (GSE). Matthias Jerusalem and Ralf Schwarzer developed the GSE in 1981. The scale is available in over 30 languages and has been used in many studies with thousands of participants.

General Self-Efficacy Scale (GSE)

Directions: Please respond to the following statements using these response categories: 1 = Not at all true 2 = Hardly true 3 = Moderately true 4 = Exactly true

5 How motivated are you for recovery-goal achievement? Select three recovery goals. Use Table 6.4 and the following scale to answer the importance, confidence, and readiness questions, with "one" being low and "five" being high.

Motivation for Recovery-Goal Achievement

Readiness

Employ change concepts and the Stages of Change Model to assess readiness for recovery work.

6 When planning change, organizations often assess individual readiness to change. Here are some of the traits that predict change readiness. Use Table 6.5 and the following scale, how well does each trait reflect you? The higher the score the better: 40 and above reflects good readiness to change.

1 = Untrue of me
2 = Somewhat untrue of me
3 = Neutral
4 = Somewhat true of me
5 = True of me

Table 6.3 General Self-Efficacy Scale

Statement	#
I can always manage to solve difficult problems if I try hard enough.	
If someone opposes me, I can find the means and ways to get what I want.	
It is easy for me to stick to my aims and accomplish my goals.	
I am confident that I could deal efficiently with unexpected events.	
Thanks to my resourcefulness, I know how to handle unforeseen situations.	
I can solve most problems if I invest the necessary effort.	
I can remain calm when facing difficulties because I can rely on my coping abilities.	
When I am confronted with a problem, I can usually find several solutions.	
If I am in trouble, I can usually think of a solution.	
I can usually handle whatever comes my way.	
TOTAL	

Source: Schwarzer, R., & Jerusalem, M. (1995). Generalized Self-Efficacy Scale. In J. Weinman, S. Wright, & M. Johnston, *Measures in Health Psychology: A User's Portfolio. Causal and Control Beliefs* (pp. 35–37). Windsor, UK: NFER-NELSON.

Scoring: Add the numbers to get your self-efficacy score. The higher the score, the greater your self-efficacy or confidence in your ability to successfully manage addiction and develop competencies for recovery. This score may change over time.

Table 6.4 Motivation for Recovery-Goal Achievement

Goals	Importance How important is the goal? 1 2 3 4 5	Confidence Can I reach the goal? 1 2 3 4 5	Readiness Am I ready to work toward goal achievement? 1 2 3 4 5

Table 6.5 Traits that Predict Readiness to Change

Trait	Reflects Me
Adaptability	1 2 3 4 5
Adventurousness	1 2 3 4 5
Confidence	1 2 3 4 5
Drive	1 2 3 4 5
Flexibility	1 2 3 4 5
Passion	1 2 3 4 5
Optimism	1 2 3 4 5
Resilience	1 2 3 4 5
Resourcefulness	1 2 3 4 5
Tolerance of Ambiguity	1 2 3 4 5

7   Write a short essay about your courage to change.
8   Use Table 6.6 to assess your readiness to change.

Section II suggested applications about motivation and three motivation constructs: importance, confidence, and readiness. Complete Chapter 6 with evaluations of recovery work and competency development in Section III.

III

Evaluate recovery work and competency development.

1   Evaluate recovery work with a short True/False Quiz and a review of the outcome, effort, process, and decisions of recovery work.

Table 6.6 Self-Assessment of Readiness to Change

Stages of Change	Statement	Yes/No
Precontemplation	I have no intention to change or act soon.	
Contemplation	I intend to change within the next 6 months.	
Preparation	I plan to act within the next month.	
Action	I am making changes in my behavior and way of life.	
Maintenance	I am working to continue change and prevent relapse.	
Relapse	I am re-grouping.	

Assessment:

Plan:

a   Quiz: Based on your learning from Chapter 6 Determine Motivation for Recovery, indicate whether each of the following statements is True (T) or False (F).

1   T or F   Motivation is a psychological force.
2   T or F   Importance, confidence, and readiness are three important aspects of motivation.
3   T or F   A commitment to change is a key part of the Health Belief Model (HBM).
4   T or F   The children's book *The Little Engine That Could* is an example of Motivational Interviewing (MI): "*I think I can, I think I can, I think I can.*"
5   T or F   People develop self-efficacy through mastery experiences, social modeling, social persuasion, and psychological responses to physiological states.
6   T or F   Self-efficacy is difficult to scale.
7   T or F   McClelland identified three dominant needs that motivate behavior: need for regulation, need for affiliation, and need for power.
8   T or F   "*Courage to change the things I can*" is part of the 12 Steps of Alcoholics Anonymous (AA).
9   T or F   Stages of Change is a dominant model for behavioral health change.

10   T or F   Personality traits are useful predictors of readiness to change.

(True: 2, 5, 9, 10. False: 1, 3, 4, 6, 7, 8)

b   Outcome, Effort, Process, and Decisions

Examine the outcome, effort, process, and decisions of your recovery work in Chapter 6.

Outcome

Did you meet **objectives** for Chapter 6? Use Table 6.7 to review objectives and rank as:

Strongly disagree = 1
Disagree = 2
Undecided = 3
Agree = 4
Strongly agree = 5

Effort

Effort evaluation reviews the input or energy you invested in recovery work. Ask and answer the following questions.

- How hard did you work on Chapter 6?
- How much time did you dedicate to Chapter 6?
- What resources did you employ for Chapter 6 work?

Process

Process evaluation is especially valuable when you want to improve outcome and increase the efficiency of your recovery work. Use Table 6.8 to evaluate process.

Table 6.7 Objectives

Objectives	Rank
I understand the dimensions and dynamics of motivation.	1, 2, 3, 4, 5
I recognize three key motivation constructs: importance, confidence, and readiness.	1, 2, 3, 4, 5
I use the Health Belief (HBM) and Motivational Interviewing (MI) to ascertain the importance of recovery.	1, 2, 3, 4, 5
I enlist Self-Efficacy Concepts and Achievement Motivation Theory to build confidence for recovery goal-achievement.	1, 2, 3, 4, 5
I employ change concepts and the Stages of Change Model to assess readiness for recovery work.	1, 2, 3, 4, 5

Table 6.8 Process

Process	Yes or No	Comment
I read the narrative (Section I).		
I completed the applications (Section II).		
I evaluated recovery work and competency development (Section III).		

Decisions

Based on the evaluation of your recovery work from Chapter 6 decide to celebrate, continue, correct, or change your approach to recovery work. Reward yourself with a positive thought, feeling, or action. Keep doing what you are doing if "it works." Modify or adjust anything that is not working well. Plan and welcome change that supports your recovery work as you move on to Chapter 7. Ask and answer the following questions.

- Did you **celebrate** your recovery work from Chapter 6 "Determine Motivation for Recovery"?
- Will you **continue** to approach recovery work in the same way in Chapter 7?
- Do you plan to **correct** your approach to recovery work in Chapter 7?
- Do you plan to **change** your approach to recovery work in Chapter 7?

2   Evaluate competency development using a KSA/Topic Matrix and a Rubric Review.

   a   What knowledge, skills, and attitudes are you using to develop Competency 6 Determine Motivation for Recovery. Document KSA examples in Table 6.9 KSA/Topic Matrix.

   b   Evaluate the development of Competency 6 Determine Motivation for Recovery with a Rubric Review. The chapter outline provides the criteria to evaluate competency development. Rank competency development on Table 6.10 as:

- **Exceeds expectations**. Understands, applies, and evaluates competency criteria > 90% of the time.
- **Meets expectations**: Understands, applies, and evaluates competency criteria 75% to 90% of the time.
- **Needs improvement**: Understands, applies, and evaluates competency criteria < 75% of the time.

Table 6.9 KSA/Topic Matrix

Topics	Knowledge	Skills	Attitudes
Motivation			
Importance Beliefs Commitment			
Confidence Self-Efficacy Achievement Motivation			
Readiness Personality Traits Courage to Change ASAM Readiness to Change Stages of Change			

Table 6.10 Competency 6 Determine Motivation for Recovery

Criteria	Exceeds Expectations 3	Meets Expectations 2	Needs Improvement 1
Motivation			
Importance Beliefs Commitment			
Confidence Self-Efficacy Achievement Motivation			
Readiness Personality Traits Courage to Change ASAM Readiness to Change Stages of Change			

Summary

Determine motivation for recovery in Chapter 6. This chapter considered three aspects of motivation: importance, confidence, and readiness. Topics that provided the organizing framework for the chapter included Motivation, Importance, Confidence, and Readiness. The chapter explained the dimensions and dynamics of motivation. It recognized three key motivation constructs: importance, confidence, and readiness. We used the Health Belief Model and Motivational Interviewing to ascertain the importance of recovery. The chapter enlisted Self-Efficacy Concepts and Achievement Motivation Theory to build confidence for recovery goal-achievement. It employed change concepts and the Stages of Change Model to assess readiness for recovery work. The chapter suggested applications—questions, worksheets, exercises, and projects—for the competency. Chapter 6 concluded with evaluations of recovery work and competency development.

7   Inventory Resources and Risks for Recovery

Deborah H. Identifies Resources and Risks for her Recovery

This is not a geographical cure. My name is Deborah H; I am a single 33-year-old software engineer. I am alcohol and drug-free for four years. My Bipolar I disorder is managed effectively. I received a job promotion and am moving cross-country with my parent company. I found an in-network psychiatrist who kept me on Abilify. I am now met with a mental health counselor to continue my overall recovery work. Together we reviewed my personal assets and liabilities. I have four years continuous recovery and reasonable stability of my bipolar disorder. I am highly motivated to grow in my recovery. Even though I planned the move and "feel ready" for the change, we identified personal, professional, and social stress and risks to manage. My apartment complex has a gym and pool. I am walking distance from a temple. I plan to participate in online recovery meetings until I am more comfortable around the city. The counselor suggested a focus on self-care and work as priority goals: "keep it simple." I scheduled sessions with the mental health counselor every two weeks for the next three months. I am cautiously optimistic about me, my recovery, and my future.

Purpose: This chapter catalogs personal, social, professional, and support factors that help or hinder recovery.

Objectives

- Identify personal assets and liabilities for recovery including age, sex, gender, race, ethnicity, and self.
- Determine social capital and deficits for recovery from family and friends, community, society, and culture.
- Acknowledge the professional services and limitations of providers, practitioners, and Recovery Oriented Systems of Care for recovery.
- Recognize mutual self-help groups, peer-based support, the Office of Recovery, and recovery residencies as effective support services for recovery.

DOI: 10.4324/9781003292944-7

Outline

Personal Assets and Liabilities

Age
Sex and Gender
Race and Ethnicity
Self

Social Capital and Deficits

Family and Friends
Community
Society
Culture

Professional Services and Limitations

Providers and Practitioners
Recovery-Oriented Systems of Care (ROSC)

Support Services and Scarcities

Mutual Self-Help Groups
Peer-Based Support
Office of Recovery
Recovery Residencies

I

Inventory resources and risks for recovery. Section I presents facts, concepts, principles, and theories about personal assets and liabilities, social capital and deficits, professional services and limitations, and support services and scarcities.

Personal Assets and Liabilities

Age

Is age an asset or liability for recovery? We know that addiction affects people across the life span. Smoking, drinking, or misuse of other drugs can harm the developing fetus and have life-long harmful effects on the child. Children living with parents or other caregivers who misuse substances may experience neglect or abuse.

The teen brain is especially vulnerable to the adverse effects of drugs; learning and memory are compromised. Teens are more apt to binge drink or engage in "pharm" or Skittles parties. The dangers are legion: driving while impaired, violent behavior, and unsafe sex to name a few. The younger the age individuals begin substance use, the more likely they will develop an addiction. Illicit drug use is more common with early-onset use.

The lifestyles of many young adults are rife with substance abuse and other additive problems including gambling, binge eating, compulsive shopping, internet addiction, as well as sex and love addictions. Addiction contributes to dysfunctional relationships and thwarted careers for many young men and women. Substance abuse, as well as other addictive disorders, exact a heavy toll on middle-aged adults, including job and career losses, financial and legal problems, divorce, and alienation from children. For older adults, life events such as retirement, death of a spouse, and chronic health problem invite problem drinking and abuse of prescription medications. Prescriptions for pain, anxiety, and sleep are common, and the risk for addiction is high Gambling has increased in older adults.

Health across the age span helps prevent substance misuse and promotes positive mental health. Healthy pregnancies contribute to a healthy start to life. Family, home, and neighborhoods free from addiction foster safe, sound development When teens have a healthy sense of self, positive peers, supportive parents, and full life, they have less need to misuse drugs or engage in excessive addictive behaviors. Young adults who further their education, pursue a career, and develop meaningful relationships can manifest a fulfilling addiction-free lifestyle. Adults who have learned to manage the challenges of family, work, and community rarely succumb to addiction. Older adults with friends, family, and social supports who have learned to manage their medications wisely remain addiction-free.

Sex and Gender

Is recovery different for men and women? Sex refers to biological differences between males and females while gender reflects social roles and concepts of self that individuals develop, often called gender identity. Both biology and sociology determine addiction and influence recovery.

Historically, drinking, smoking, using, gambling, and other thrill-seeking behaviors were associated with men and male lifestyles. Addictive behavior by women was less visible and less acceptable. Women were prescribed and abused pills. Today there are fewer differences between men and women in their drinking, gambling, and misuse of prescription drugs. Yet, the different effects of substance use and other addictive behaviors are noteworthy and their impact on recovery is great.

Because women typically weigh less than men, alcohol tends to have a greater effect on the female body. Women are more likely to develop alcohol-related disease and damage, even if they abused alcohol for a shorter time. The rate of death from alcohol use disorder (AUD) is 50% to 100% higher for women than men (including suicide, alcohol-related accidents, heart and liver disease, and stroke). See Table 7.1 and the comparison by Harvard Medical School of addiction susceptibility, recovery, and risk of relapse between men and women.

For decades, addiction research studied men only This male bias in research was also true for medical and pharmaceutical research. Even research animals like mice were male. In the 1990s, several U.S. organizations instituted requirements for the inclusion of women as study participants. Research demonstrates some differences in addiction and recovery between men and women.

Race and Ethnicity

What do race and ethnicity have to do with addiction and recovery? It is important to separate fact from fiction when we examine race, ethnicity, addiction, and recovery. Race describes physical traits an individual inherits, while ethnicity refers to cultural identity that is acquired through social learning. Ethnicity is shaped by the language, cultural attitudes, values, religion, customs, beliefs, and experiences of a group with which a person identifies. Ethnicity influences thoughts, feelings, and actions about addiction, treatment, and recovery; for example, the belief that addiction is a sin versus addiction is a disease.

We accept as a fact that "addiction runs in families." Scientists estimate that genetic factors account for 40 to 60% of a person's risk to develop an

Table 7.1 Susceptibility, Recovery, and Risk of Relapse for Men and Women

	Men	*Women*
Susceptibility	Men are more likely to become addicts. Men are more likely to abuse substances due to peer pressure or to be part of a group.	Women are more likely to transition from substance abuse to substance dependence and addiction (i.e., telescoping) and do so at a faster pace. Women are more likely to self-medicate with illicit substances.
Recovery	Men are more likely to "stabilize" substance abuse at lower doses than women. Men are more likely to experience more intense symptoms of alcohol withdrawal than women.	Women are more likely to suffer substance abuse side effects (like liver damage) and overdose.
Risk of Relapse	The risk of relapse for men is less likely (i.e., longer periods of abstinence).	Women are more likely to experience intense cravings and relapse.

Source: https://www.addictioncenter.com/addiction/differences-men-women/

addiction. More than one in three people with East Asian heritage (Chinese, Japanese and Korean) experience facial flushing when drinking beer, wine, or spirits. In Asian populations, flushing is due to an inherited deficiency in one of the enzymes involved in the breakdown of alcohol: aldehyde dehydrogenase. This type of reaction is very rare, but not unknown, in other ethnic groups.

Yet beyond familial vulnerability and the Asian flush, few racial factors determine addiction and influence recovery. Gross social inequities in education, employment, housing, and healthcare increase addiction prevalence in many U.S. sub-populations. Access to addiction treatment and treatment completion are lower for minority populations. However, there was a "reverse of fortunes" with the recent opioid crisis, labeled by some the white person's disease. White individuals were prescribed opioids in greater amounts than black/brown populations.

The frameworks of *Healthy People 2020* and *Healthy People 2030* underscore the continued focus on population disparities, including those categorized by race/ethnicity, socioeconomic status, gender, age, disability status, sexual orientation, and geographic location.

Statistics reflect both the biology and sociology of race, ethnicity, and addiction. According to the 2019 *U.S. National Survey on Drug Use and Health*, 7.7% of the U.S. population, some 19.3 million people aged 18 or older, had a substance use disorder (SUD). In addition, 3.8%, some 9.5 million people aged 18 or older, had both a SUD and a mental illness (MI). See Table 7.2 to examine SUD and MI sub-populations.

Self

Many of us are familiar with the Pogo cartoon "We have met the enemy and he is us." Beyond age, sex and gender, race and ethnicity, "am I my worst enemy?" Self is the entire person of an individual, the unity of elements (physical, mental, emotional, and spiritual) that constitutes individuality and contributes to identity as a person. Elements of self are:

Table 7.2 SUD and MI by Sub-Populations

Sub-Population	SUD	SUD and MI	MI
General	7.7%	3.8%	20.6%
American Indian/ Alaskan Native	10.2%	3.8%	18.7%
African American	7.6%	3.2%	17.3%
Asian and Native Hawaiian	4.8%	2.1%	14.5%
Hispanic, Latino, Spanish Origin	7.0%	3.4%	18.0%

- Physical: body structure and function.
- Mental: thoughts and perceptions.
- Emotional: feelings, the range of emotions.
- Spiritual: beliefs and practices related to life, purpose, meaning, Higher Power; virtues and values.

Bio-psycho-social theory, holistic health, and developmental theories, especially the contributions of Erik Erikson, Jean Piaget, and Lawrence Kohlberg ground our understanding of self. The concepts of self-care, self-worth, self-in relation, and self-efficacy further our appreciation of self.

Erikson's theory of psychosocial development informs both addiction and recovery. Failure to negotiate psychosocial developmental stages in a timely and complete manner increases individual vulnerability for addiction and elevates the risk for relapse. Many manifestations of active addiction reflect unhealthy psychosocial development: mistrust, shame, doubt, guilt, inferiority, role confusion, isolation, stagnation, and despair. Rarely do individuals in active addiction experience a developmental stage fully or complete it successfully.

On the other hand, navigating Erikson's psychosocial stages in an age-appropriate manner promotes the development of a healthy self and helps protect individuals from addiction and relapse. Healthy psychosocial development characterizes recovery. Individuals in recovery experience and express healthy psychosocial development as evidenced by trust, autonomy, initiative, industry, identity, intimacy, generativity, and ego integrity.

The strengths identified by Erikson for each stage suggest the values that men and women often compromise or lose in active addiction but regain in recovery. Virtues such as hope, will, purpose, competence, fidelity, love, care, and wisdom distinguish recovery: the ability to master addiction, live well, and do good.

Social Capital and Deficits

Social environment includes friends and family, community, society, and culture. Home and community are two of the four recovery dimensions advanced by the Substance Abuse Mental Health Services Administration (SAMHSA), underscoring the importance of the social environment.

1   Recovery is supported by peers and allies. Mutual support and mutual aid groups, including the sharing of experiential knowledge and skills, as well as social learning, play an invaluable role in recovery.
2   Recovery is supported through relationships and social networks. An important factor in the recovery process is the presence and involvement of people who believe in the person's ability to recover; who offer hope, support, and encouragement; and who also suggest strategies and resources for change.

3 Recovery involves individual, family, and community strengths and responsibility. Individuals, families, and communities have strengths and resources that serve as a foundation for recovery.
4 Recovery is culturally based and influenced. Culture and cultural background in all its diverse representations, including values, traditions, and beliefs are keys in determining a person's journey and unique pathway to recovery.

Family and Friends

We are social. Interpersonal stress can trigger self-medication with alcohol, other drugs, or an escape to the casino. Substance use and other addictive behavior harm family and friends.

When there is addiction in the family, life often revolves around the addicted person. Rules become rigid, unrealistic, and difficult to keep. When children live in homes with active addiction, they often adapt to family dysfunction by playing certain roles: hero, scapegoat, lost child, or mascot. Role reversal among spouses is stressful. Losses and damage to families because of addiction include:

- Trust: the first casualty in a family with addiction.
- Respect: usually lost when the addiction surfaces.
- Relationships: difficult without trust and respect.
- Employment: underemployment, unemployment.
- Financial: family security threatened or lost.
- Reputations: difficult to protect as the addiction problem and the person's life become more public outside the family.

Enabling includes all actions by family or friends that prevent people who drink, use, or gamble from experiencing the full impact of the negative consequences of their addiction. Codependency describes a pattern of unhealthy behavior family and friends may develop to survive the stress caused by a loved one's drinking, using, or gambling. Organizations like Al-Anon emphasize self-care for family and friends.

Family and friends may help or hinder recovery. When damage from addiction to family and friends is great, it is difficult to support recovery: often slow, one day at a time. Parallel treatment and recovery by family and friends increase the likelihood of active support for the recovering person. Losses and damage to everyone can be reversed slowly, "if we work for them."

Community

School, work, church, and play are four examples of community surroundings that impact addiction and recovery.

School: Active addiction in teens and young adults greatly compromises education. Not surprisingly, truancy, underachievement, failure, dropout, and many unfulfilled dreams are some of the many consequences. Defense mechanisms abound with a high external locus of control. An immediate reward, be it from a substance, sex, gambling, fighting, shoplifting, or other crime, greatly outweighs the importance of classroom structure and discipline. Rarely do teens and young adults consumed by active addiction engage in meaningful educational age/stage-appropriate educational goals. Beginning or completing school are recovery goals for many men and women.

Work: There are fewer opportunities for meaningful work for men and women who abuse substances or engage in other addictive behaviors, often a consequence of poor education. When employed, these individuals usually exhibit poor performance on the job and often poor attendance: a major reason for job termination. Under-employment and unemployment have major financial, emotional, and social implications for the individual and the family. Meaningful employment with career advancement reflects recovery.

Church: Often men and women describe a loss of values as their addiction progresses. Lying is a means to an end; stealing and other illegal acts may be necessary to support one's addiction. Feelings of helplessness, hopelessness, and desperation may develop, coupled with suicide ideas, threats, plans, and attempts. Anger at organized religion may surface: "God, where were you when I needed you?" Addicts describe overwhelming experiences of shame and guilt directly related to their addictive lifestyle and the many adverse consequences for themselves and family. Some individuals and groups consider addiction as morally wrong, even a sin. Return to organized religion may be part of the recovery experience. Many recovery people describe themselves as "spiritual" rather than "religious." Spirituality is part of 12-step programs. Celebrate Recovery is a Christ-centered, 12-step recovery program for anyone struggling with hurt, pain, or addiction of any kind.

Play: As addiction develops and consumes individuals, interest, and participation in sports, arts, recreation for self, with friends and family disappear Drinking or doing drugs "is" the party. Family vacations are at casinos, on cruises, or include settings with gambling. The ability to play vanishes well as its importance for a balanced healthy lifestyle and well-being. The ability to live well as evidenced by health, wellness, and well-being includes play. People in recovery play well!

Society

It is doubtful that men and women in active addiction, who are not accountable and responsible for themselves as teens, young adults, parents, employees, can fulfill social roles as friendly neighbors or good citizens. These important social roles harm the individual and society itself, not to mention the financial burdens addiction places on society. The social costs of addiction are staggering! Recovering men and women become responsible parents, good neighbors and active citizens. While there is still a strong history of anonymity among people with addiction, more recovering people are "going public" with their addiction and recovery. In the 1970s, First Lady Betty Ford raised awareness of addiction she announced her long-running battle with alcoholism and substance abuse.

Notable celebrities in recovery meet criteria for HFAs: high functioning alcoholics or high functioning addicts: Elton John, Jaime Lee Curtis, Drew Barrymore, and Olympic gold medalist swimmer Michael Phelps to name a few. CC Sabathia played 19 seasons of Major League Baseball, He was Rookie of the Year, Cy Young Award winner, World Series champion, and a six-time All-Star. In his recent book *Till the End*, he describes his life as a "disciplined drunk." For most of his playing career, Sabathia battled alcoholism, even as he soared to the top of his game. In 2015, he entered rehab and today CC says he is in the best mental and physical shape of his life. Sadly, when HFAs seek help, addiction is usually severe. Every year, celebrities die tragic, often premature. deaths from addiction.

In January 2021, members of the recovery community congratulated both Mayor Marty Walsh and U.S. Representative Deb Haaland, when nominated by President-elect Biden to cabinet-level positions in the new Administration. Both Walsh and Haaland are public figures who are open about their long-term recovery from substance use disorders.

Culture

According to SAMHSA, recovery is culturally based and influenced. Larry D. Purnell defines culture as the totality of socially transmitted behavioral patterns, arts, beliefs, values, customs, lifeways, and all other products of human work and thought characteristic of a population of people that guide their worldview and decision-making. Given this definition, we can readily see the powerful influence of culture on individual and collective beliefs and practices about drinking, gambling, eating, sex, and other behaviors that become addictive. Less obvious, but equally important, is the influence of culture on treatment and recovery.

Professional Services and Limitations

Providers and Practitioners

Traditional addiction treatment focuses on safe withdrawal with abstinence as a goal. In the 1980s, relapse prevention was added as a treatment goal. With the advent Medication-Assisted Treatment (MAT), harm reduction became a recognized treatment goal. Providers and professionals who embrace a 12-step philosophy may introduce patients to recovery and attending AA or NA as a part of treatment.

As reported, 90% of individuals with SUD diagnoses receive no treatment. Access to treatment and failure to complete treatment is limited for minority populations. There is little consensus among addiction providers and professionals about what constitutes "best treatment." Addiction treatment per se has become "big business." Although addiction medicine and addiction studies are recognized specialties, with the Affordable Care Act in 2010, health practitioners in general practice began to offer screening and early intervention services to people with addiction. Yet, *The National Survey on Drug Use and Health* (SAMHSA 2019) reported self-help groups provided more treatment for substance use than formal treatment locations. See the section that follows about Mutual Self-Help Groups.

Recovery-Oriented Systems of Care (ROSC)

About ten years ago, addiction recovery visionaries began working together to develop what we now call Recovery Oriented Systems of Care (ROSC). A ROSC is a coordinated network of community-based services and supports that is person-centered and builds on the strengths and resiliencies of individuals, families, and communities to achieve abstinence and improved health, wellness, and quality of life for those with or at risk of alcohol and drug problems.

We often think of recovery as activities after formal treatment. However, recovery-oriented activities and approaches offer a full continuum of care. A ROSC creates an infrastructure, a system of care with the resources to e address the full range of substance use problems within communities. The ROSC offers a continuum of substance use disorder care (prevention, early intervention, treatment, continuing care, and recovery) in partnership with other disciplines, such as mental health and primary care. ROSC services are individualized, person-centered, and strength-based. ROSC provides individuals and families with options with which to make informed decisions regarding their care. Services are designed to be accessible, welcoming, and easy to navigate. A ROSC involves people, their families, and their community in recovery, especially access to and quality of services.

Support Services and Scarcities

Recovering men and women offer peer-based services to individuals with addiction through mutual self-help groups, as recovery coaches, or in recovery residencies.

Mutual Self-Help Groups

Mutual self-help groups organizations are free, peer-led, non-professional organizations where recovering members share their experience, strength, and hope about addiction, relapse, and recovery.

Alcoholics Anonymous (AA) began in 1935 when Bill W. and Dr. Bob, two "hopeless alcoholics" shared their drinking experiences and hope for change with each other. Today, there are hundreds of self-help groups around the world: groups that have a 12-step focus like Alcoholics Anonymous (AA),

Narcotics Anonymous (NA), and Gamblers' Anonymous (GA); secular groups such as SMART Recovery, Women for Sobriety (WFS), and Life-Ring; and faith-based religious groups like Celebrate Recovery. There are parallel organizations like Al-Anon for the family and friends of the "alcoholic."

In 2020, AA estimated worldwide active membership of 2,138,201 individuals with 129,760 groups. Mutual self-help meetings abound in the community and online.

Most of the groups offer online services and meetings, especially valuable during the COVID pandemic. *In The Rooms*, a free online recovery tool that embraces multiple pathways to recovery, including all 12-step, non-12-step, wellness, and mental health modalities, offers many weekly online meetings for those recovering from addiction and related issues.

According to the American Society of Addiction Medicine, recovery groups such AA, NA, GA, or Smart Recovery do not constitute formal treatment programs. However, clinicians see the value of such groups as a lifelong support system and believe that an individual's chances of a successful outcome are significantly enhanced by involvement in recovery groups. Some providers embrace a twelve-step approach to treatment. Other programs may introduce clients to mutual self-help groups. Attending mutual self-help groups may be a recommended part of treatment at all levels of care.

The National Survey on Drug Use and Health (2019) reported self-help groups provided more treatment for substance use than any other formal treatment location. Participating in a mutual support group reinforces and extends the benefits of professional treatment and provides much-needed support for individuals beginning recovery and continuing recovery.

Peer-Based Support

Why the recent interest in peer recovery support services and peer recovery coaches? States and organizations are now scrambling to offer training and certification for peer support specialists and recovery coaches.

In the heyday of addiction treatment, recovering men and women provided counseling for individuals in the throes of active addiction. Training and education became required for counselors with state and national certification and licensing to follow. Today, people earn undergraduate and graduate degrees in addiction studies. Addiction medicine is a recognized specialty. Yet, one wonders if professionalization and the business of addiction have diminished the emphasis on recovery and contributed to the high incidence of relapse.

Peer support workers are people who have been successful in the recovery process who help others experiencing similar situations. Through shared understanding, respect, and mutual empowerment, peer support workers help people become and stay engaged in the recovery process and reduce the likelihood of relapse. Peer support services can effectively extend the reach of treatment beyond the clinical setting into the everyday environment of those seeking a successful, sustained recovery process.

Peer-based recovery support provides person-centered and strength-based supports to help people with addiction begin and maintain recovery, especially long-term recovery. Peer-based recovery helps people with addiction build recovery capital, i.e., develop internal resources and identify external resources to master addiction, live well, and do good.

Recovery coaches are paid paraprofessionals who bring their lived experience of recovery, together with training and supervision, to a treatment or recovery setting. Peer recovery coaches work in a range of settings, including recovery community centers, recovery residences, drug courts, and other criminal justice settings, hospital emergency departments, child welfare agencies, homeless shelters, and behavioral health and primary care settings. Recovery coaches are key staff in Recovery Oriented Systems of Care (ROSC) and Medication-Assisted Treatment (MAT) programs.

The Substance Abuse Mental Health Services Administration (SAMHSA) affirms recovery-oriented care and recovery support systems help people with mental and substance use disorders manage their conditions successfully. To that end, SAMHSA *developed Core Competencies for Peer Workers in Behavioral Health Services – 2018.* Core competencies are the capacity to easily perform a role or function. They are often described as clusters of the knowledge, skills, and attitudes a person needs to have to successfully perform a role or job. Training, mentoring, and supervision can help people develop core competencies.

Core competencies for peer workers reflect certain foundational principles identified by members of the mental health consumer and substance use disorder recovery communities. These are:

- **Recovery-oriented:** Peer workers hold out hope to those they serve, partnering with them to envision and achieve a meaningful and purposeful life. Peer workers help those they serve to identify and build on strengths and empower them to choose for themselves, recognizing that there are multiple pathways to recovery.
- **Person-centered:** Peer recovery support services are always directed by the person participating in services. Peer recovery support is personalized to align with the specific hopes, goals, and preferences of the people served and to respond to specific needs the people have identified to the peer worker.
- **Voluntary:** Peer workers are partners or consultants to those they serve. They do not dictate the types of services provided or the elements of recovery plans that will guide their work with peers. Participation in peer recovery support services is always contingent on peer choice.
- **Relationship-focused:** The relationship between the peer worker and the peer is the foundation on which peer recovery support services and support are provided. The relationship between the peer worker and peer is respectful, trusting, empathetic, collaborative, and mutual.
- **Trauma-informed:** Peer recovery support utilizes a strength-based framework that emphasizes physical, psychological, and emotional safety

and creates opportunities for survivors to rebuild a sense of control and empowerment.

Office of Recovery

On September 30, 2021, SAMHSA launched the Office of Recovery. Growing and expanding recovery support services nationwide is a core component of the new office. As stated in Chapter 3, SAMHSA believes:

> Recovery is enhanced by peer-delivered services. These peer support services have proven to be effective as the support, outreach and engagement with new networks help sustain recovery over the long term. Peer services are critical, given the significant workforce shortages in behavioral health. SAMHSA's new Office of Recovery will promote the involvement of people with lived experience throughout agency and stakeholder activities, foster relationships with internal and external organizations in the mental health and addiction recovery fields and identify health disparities in high-risk and vulnerable populations to ensure equity for support services across the Nation.
>
> (SAMHSA 2021a)

Recovery Residencies

"First things first" has been a core AA slogan since its inception. Sobriety first! Yet, recovery residencies, once thought to help individuals with addiction maintain recovery after treatment, are now recognized as an important "first" support, especially in early treatment. Therapeutic communities (TCs) are a common form of long-term residential treatment for substance use disorders (SUDs). Residential treatment for SUDs emerged in the late 1950s out of the self-help recovery movement. Recovery residences provide a sober living environment and a readily available community of recovery-related social support.

Recovery homes vary in level of structure and program elements. Most recovery residencies are small with six to eight residents of the same gender. Length of stay varies, often several months or more, if individuals follow the rules. A sober house, like the Oxford Houses, is a peer-run. Some halfway houses are monitored by a House Manager or Senior Resident. Other recovery residencies employ certified staff, case managers, and facility managers. Here residents receive recovery support, life skills training, and clinical services, usually in the community. Addiction treatment providers and ROSC may operate a recovery residency as a step-down service, a step-out transition into the community. Residents receive clinical services on-site or in conjunction with the facility operating the residence.

Recovery residences are a key component of long-term, successful sobriety; however, quality can vary greatly, and some do more harm than good. Quality recovery residences must be treated as part of the continuum of care.

Section I presented facts, concepts, principles, and theories about personal assets and liabilities, social capital and deficits, professional services and limitations, and support services and scarcities. Continue recovery work in Section II with applications to the competency.

II

Inventory resources and risks for recovery. Section II suggests applications about personal assets and liabilities, social capital and deficits, professional services and limitations, and support services and scarcities.

Personal Assets and Liabilities

1   Are individual factors assets or liabilities? Use Table 7.3 and check.
2   Are self-elements assets or liabilities? Use Table 7.4 and check.
3   Who am I?

    a   Ask and answer the question "who am I?" 20 times.

        1.
        2.
        3.
        4.
        5.
        6.
        7.
        8.
        9.
        10
        11.
        12.
        13.
        14.
        15.
        16.
        17.
        18,
        19.
        20.

Table 7.3 Individual Factors as Assets or Liabilities

	Asset	Liability
Age	_____	_____
Sex	_____	_____
Gender	_____	_____
Race	_____	_____
Ethnicity	_____	_____

Table 7.4 Self-Elements as Assets or Liabilities

	Asset	Liability
Physical	_____	_____
Mental	_____	_____
Emotional	_____	_____
Spiritual	_____	_____

b   Review answers and comment on the rank order of responses.

c   How is recovery reflected in the 20 replies?

Social Capital and Deficits

4   Identify resources for recovery from family and friends.

a   resources for recovery from family:

b   resources for recovery from friends:

5   Identify risks for recovery from family and friends.

a   risks for recovery from family:

b   risks for recovery from friends:

6   Use Table 7.5 to enter the name of a current of a former Provider or Professional. Indicate the frequency with which recovery was part of your service experience.

Table 7.5 Health Provider Recovery Experience

Recovery Indicator	Name of Provider or Professional	Name of Provider or Professional	Name of Provider or Professional
Abstinence			
Harm Reduction			
Relapse Prevention			
Health			
Wellness			
Well-being			
Helping			
Service			
Altruism			
TOTAL			

    5 = Always
    4 = Often
    3 = Sometimes
    2 = Rarely
    1 = Never

7   Describe your experience with mutual self-help groups.

Section II suggested applications about personal assets and liabilities, social capital and deficits, professional services and limitations, and support services and scarcities. Complete Chapter 7 with evaluations of recovery work and competency development in Section III.

III

Evaluate recovery work and competency development.

1   Evaluate recovery work with a short True/False Quiz and a review of the outcome, effort, process, and decisions of recovery work.

    a   Quiz: Based on your learning from Chapter 7 "Inventory Resources and Risks for Recovery," indicate whether each of the following statements is True (T) or False (F).

        1 T or F Personal assets and liabilities for recovery including age, sex, gender, race, ethnicity, and self.
        2 T or F Social capital and deficits for recovery come from family and friends, community, society, and culture.
        3 T or F The older the age individuals begin substance use, the more likely they will develop an addiction.
        4 T or F Susceptibility for addiction, recovery, and risk for relapse, are different for men and women.
        5 T or F Enabling is a helpful way family or friends can prevent people who drink, use, or gamble from experiencing the full impact of the negative consequences of their addiction.
        6 T or F Codependency describes a pattern of healthy behavior family and friends may develop to survive the stress caused by a loved one's drinking, using, or gambling.
        7 T or F Recovery Systems of Care (ROSC) have been the foundation of addiction treatment since the 1930s.
        8 T or F Core competencies for peer workers are recovery-oriented, person-centered, relationship-focused, voluntary, and trauma-informed.
        9 T or F Mutual self-help groups organizations are free, peer-led, non-professional organizations where recovering members share their experience, strength, and hope about addiction, relapse, and recovery.

10 T or F Recovery residencies offer short-term support for people with addiction.

(True: 1, 2, 4, 8, 9. False: 3, 5, 6, 7, 10)

b   Outcome, Effort, Process, and Decisions

Examine the outcome, effort, process, and decision-making of your recovery work in Chapter 7.

Outcome

Did you meet **objectives** for Chapter 7? Use Table 7.6 to review objectives and rank as:

Strongly disagree = 1
Disagree = 2
Undecided = 3
Agree = 4
Strongly agree = 5

Effort

Effort evaluation reviews the input or energy you invested in recovery work. Ask and answer the following questions.

* How hard did you work on Chapter 7?
* How much time did you dedicate to Chapter 7?
* What resources did you employ for Chapter 7 work?

Process

Process evaluation is especially valuable when you want to improve outcome and increase the efficiency of your recovery work. Use Table 7.7 to evaluate process.

Table 7.6 Objectives

Objectives	Rank
I identify personal assets and liabilities for recovery including age, sex, gender, race, ethnicity, and self.	1, 2, 3, 4, 5
I determine social capital and deficits for recovery from family and friends, community, society, and culture.	1, 2, 3, 4, 5
I recognize the professional services and limitations of providers, practitioners, and Recovery Oriented Systems of Care (ROSC) for recovery.	1, 2, 3, 4, 5
I appreciate mutual self-help groups, peer-based support, the Office of Recovery, and recovery residencies as effective support services for recovery.	1, 2, 3, 4, 5

Table 7.7 Process

Process	Yes or No	Comment
I read the narrative (Section I).		
I completed the applications (Section II).		
I evaluated recovery work and competency development (Section III).		

Decisions

Based on the evaluation of your recovery work from Chapter 7, decide to celebrate, continue, correct, or change your approach to recovery work. Reward yourself with a positive thought, feeling, or action. Keep doing what you are doing if "it works." Modify or adjust anything that is not working well. Plan and welcome change that supports your recovery work as you move on to Chapter 8. Ask and answer the following questions.

- Did you **celebrate** your recovery work from Chapter 7 "Inventory Resources and Risks for Recovery"?
- Will you **continue** to approach recovery work in the same way in Chapter 8?
- Do you plan to **correct** your approach to recovery work in Chapter 8?
- Do you plan to **change** your approach to recovery work in Chapter 8?

2   Evaluate competency development using a KSA/Topic Matrix and a Rubric Review.

   a   What knowledge, skills, and attitudes are you using to develop Competency 7 Inventory Resources and Risks for Recovery. Document KSA examples in Table 7.8 KSA/Topic Matrix.

   b   Evaluate the development of Competency 7 Inventory Resources and Risks for Recovery with a Rubric Review. The chapter outline provides the criteria to evaluate competency development. Rank competency development on Table 7.9 as:

   - **Exceeds expectations**. Understands, applies, and evaluates competency criteria > 90% of the time.
   - **Meets expectations**: Understands, applies, and evaluates competency criteria 75% to 90% of the time.
   - **Needs improvement**: Understands, applies, and evaluates competency criteria < 75% of the time.

Table 7.8 KSA/Topic Matrix

Topics	Knowledge	Skills	Attitudes
Personal Assets and Liabilities Age Sex and Gender, Race and Ethnicity Self			
Social Capital and Deficits Family and Friends Community Society Culture			
Professional Services and Limitations Providers and Practitioners Recovery-Oriented Systems of Care (ROSC)			
Support Services and Scarcities Mutual Self-Help Groups Peer-Based Support Office of Recovery Recovery Residencies			

Table 7.9 Competency 7 Inventory Resources and Risks for Recovery

Criteria	Exceeds Expectations 3	Meets Expectations 2	Needs Improvement 1
Personal Assets and Liabilities Age Sex and Gender, Race and Ethnicity Self			
Social Capital and Deficits Family and Friends Community Society Culture			
Professional Services and Limitations Providers and Practitioners Recovery-Oriented Systems of Care (ROSC)			
Support Services and Scarcities Mutual Self-Help Groups Peer-Based Support Office of Recovery Recovery Residencies			

Summary

Inventory resources and risks for recovery in Chapter 7. This chapter cataloged personal, social, professional, and support factors that help or hinder recovery. Topics that provided the organizing framework for the chapter included Personal Assets and Liabilities, Social Capital and Deficits, Professional Services and Limitations, and Support Services and Scarcities. The chapter identified personal assets and liabilities for recovery including age, sex, gender, race, ethnicity, and self. It determined social capital and deficits for recovery from family and friends, community, society, and culture. The chapter acknowledged the professional services and limitations of providers, practitioners, and Recovery Oriented Systems of Care. We recognized mutual self-help groups, peer-based support, the Office of Recovery, and recovery residencies as effective support services for recovery. The chapter suggested applications—questions, worksheets, exercises, and projects—for the competency. Chapter 7 concluded with evaluations of recovery work and competency development.

8 Draft Recovery Objectives

Frank O. Develops SMART Recovery Objectives

This month's continuing education at our school focused on developing SMART objectives for our Weekly Lesson Plans. I learned that SMART Learning Objectives (SLO) are specific, measurable, attainable, relevant, and timely. SMART objectives promote student achievement and increase teacher effectiveness: a win/win situation. My name is Frank O. and I teach several different math classes to middle school students. I am reviewing current lessons plans with my coordinator and beginning to incorporate SMART objectives. Why not talk with my recovery coach at the medication-assisted treatment (MAT) program about developing a weekly recovery plan with SMART objectives?

Purpose: This chapter suggests a SMART way to draft recovery objectives.

Objectives

- Use the cognitive, affective, and psychomotor domains of learning to develop objectives.
- Consider the ASK model as an alternative to the KSA emphasis and order.
- Draft objectives that are specific, measurable, attainable, relevant, and time-based.
- Review Healthy People 2030 objectives for addiction, drug and alcohol use, and tobacco use.
- Examine examples of effective, efficient objectives.
- Practice writing SMART objectives.

Outline

Objectives

Cognitive Domain
Affective Domain
Psychomotor Domain

DOI: 10.4324/9781003292944-8

The ASK Model

SMART Objectives

Specific
Measurable
Attainable
Relevant
Timely

Healthy People 2030 Objectives

Examples of Recovery Objectives

I

Draft recovery objectives. Section I presents facts, concepts, principles, and theories about objectives, the ASK model, SMART objectives, Healthy People 2030 objectives, and examples of recovery.

Objectives

As described in Chapter 4, goals are broad declarations of future aspirations. Objectives are "thinking, feeling, and doing" ways people achieve goals. SMART objectives are specific, measurable, attainable, relevant, and timely action plans to reach goals. Outcomes are the final results of meeting objectives and reaching goals.

Cognitive, Affective, Psychomotor Domains

Some years ago, educators identified and described three learning domains. Benjamin Bloom and David Krathwohl at the University of Chicago developed the original **cognitive** and **affective** domains. Anita Harrow, Elizabeth J. Simpson, and Ravindra H. Dave followed with versions of a **psychomotor** domain. Functions within each domain are characterized by progressive levels of behaviors from simple to complex, a so-called taxonomy. For decades, educators, health practitioners, and business professionals have used the cognitive (knowledge), psychomotor (skills), and affective (attitudes) domains to develop objectives. Although the language is somewhat cumbersome, Taxonomy examples and revisions follow. See Boxes 8.1, 8.2, 8.3, 8.4, and Table 8.1.

Box 8.1 Taxonomy of the Cognitive Domain (Bloom)

Knowledge
Comprehension
Application
Analysis
Synthesis
Evaluation

Box 8.2 Bloom's Revised Taxonomy—Cognitive Domain

Remembering
Understanding
Applying
Analyzing
Evaluating
Creating

Box 8.3 Taxonomy of the Affective Domain (Krathwohl)

Receiving
Responding
Valuing
Organization
Characterization

Box 8.4 Revised Taxonomy—Affective Domain

Receiving Phenomena
Responding to Phenomena
Valuing
Organization
Internalizing Values (characterization)

See examples of objectives in the cognitive, affective, and psychomotor domains in Table 8.2. Notice the different types of learning among the three domains and the movement from simple to more complex expectations between Day 1 and Day 2 objectives.

Table 8.1 Taxonomy of the Psychomotor Domain

Harrow	Simpson	Dave
Reflex Movements	Perception	Imitation
Fundamental Movements	Set	Manipulation
Perceptual Abilities	Guided Response	Precision
Physical Abilities	Mechanism	Articulation
Skilled Movements	Complex Overt Response	Naturalization
Non-discursive Communication	Adaptation	
	Origination	

Table 8.2 A Recovery Wellness Retreat (RWR) for Men

Domains	Day 1 Objectives	Day 2 Objectives
Cognitive	Describe the eight Dimensions of Wellness suggested by SAMHSA.	Explain the contribution of wellness to recovery.
Affective	Listen to an RWR Leader tell his wellness story.	Share your Recovery Wellness plan with your small RWR group.
Psychomotor	Stroll the half-mile nature trail.	Jog the one-mile nature track.

Often the three learning domains are referred to as KSAs as in the definition of competency:

- **Knowledge:** cognitive or mental abilities used to retain and process information.
- **Skills:** physical abilities used to perform activities or tasks.
- **Attitudes:** feelings or emotions about someone or something.

The ASK Model

The ASK Model of learning alters the order and emphasis of the competency dimensions: knowledge, skills, and attitudes (KSA). James Nottingham, European coordinator for the international Community Designed Education network and co-founder of p4c.com international resource and collaboration website for philosophy for children, uses a sequence of attitudes, skills, and knowledge (ASK) in his teaching.

The Life Skills Coach, Shubha Rajan from India, believes knowledge accounts for only 15% of learning while skills and attitude together account for 85%. Attitude is even more critical than skills. Knowledge and skills can be acquired while attitude needs to be there internally or developed.

Consider the ASK model. Is the Knowledge, Skills, Attitudes (KSA) regimen "too western" or alien? Search the internet for more details about the ASK Model with teaching/learning examples and as a coaching approach.

- James Nottingham ASK Model
- Shubha Rajan ASK Model

SMART Objectives

SMART objectives are specific, measurable, attainable, relevant, and timely plans to reach goals. SMART objectives are effective and efficient ways to achieve goals. Peter Drucker, a strategy theorist, stressed the value of management by objectives (MBO), so widely used today in business, education, and health care. SMART is a mnemonic that reflects Drucker's management by objectives idea. The November 1981 issue of *Management Review* contained an article by George T. Doran called "There's a S.M.A.R.T. way to write management's goals and objectives." In general, the letters mean:

S = specific
M = measurable
A = attainable
R = relevant
T = timely

Specific objectives have a much greater chance of being accomplished than general statements. Is the objective exact, precise, detailed, explicit, definite, and unambiguous? **Measurable** objectives use criteria to measure progress and results: i.e., to monitor progress toward goal achievement and evaluate outcome, effort, and process. Is the objective quantifiable, assessable, computable, calculable, determinate, and reasonable? **Attainable** objectives map out a clear path to reach goals. Is the objective possible, achievable, realistic, reasonable, manageable, and within reach? **Relevant** objectives target the desired goals. Is the objective pertinent, applicable, germane, related, appropriate, significant, and important? **Timely** objectives have a completion endpoint. Is the objective timely, time-based? Does the objective include dates and times?

Healthy People 2030 Objectives

Visit https://health.gov/healthypeople. The Healthy People 2030 website is an excellent case study for learning more about drafting objectives: especially kinds, characteristics, and categories of objectives that can help draft recovery objectives.

Core, Developmental, or Research Objectives

Healthy People 2030 includes 355 core—or measurable—objectives as well as developmental and research objectives. Most Healthy People 2030 objectives are core, or measurable, objectives that are associated with targets for the decade. Core objectives reflect high-priority public health issues and are associated with evidence-based interventions. Core objectives have valid, reliable, nationally representative data, including baseline data from no earlier than 2015. If applicable, they have a measure of variability. Data will be provided for core objectives for at least three time periods throughout the decade. Developmental objectives represent high-priority public health issues that are associated with evidence-based interventions but do not yet have reliable baseline data. Research objectives represent public health issues with high health or economic burden or significant disparities between population groups. Research objectives are not yet associated with evidence-based interventions.

Leading Health Indicators, Social Determinants of Health, and Overall Health and Well-Being Measures

Leading Health Indicators (LHIs) are a small subset of high-priority objectives selected to drive action toward improving health and well-being. Healthy People 2030 includes objectives that highlight how personal, social, economic, and environmental factors can impact people's health. Overall Health and Well-Being Measures (OHMs) are broad, global outcome measures that help people assess progress toward achieving the Healthy People 2030 vision.

Health Conditions, Health Behavior, Populations, Settings and Systems

Healthy People 2030 has four categories of objectives: Health Conditions, Health Behavior, Populations, Settings and Systems. Health Conditions include addiction as well as mental illness and mental disorders. Health Behavior includes drug and alcohol use and tobacco use. These topics may be cross-listed in the Populations category with adolescents and drug and alcohol use or brief alcohol intervention in primary care in Settings and Systems.

The objective list often notes whether the problem the objective is addressing is improving, getting worse, or whether there is little or no detectable change. The site links readers to information about changes from 2020, current data, and tools for action for the specific objective.

Most objectives begin with wording to "increase" or "reduce." Lists of objectives from Healthy People 2030 for addiction, drug and alcohol use, and tobacco use follow. See how objectives support the goals. How SMART are the objectives?

Addiction

Goal: Reduce drug and alcohol addiction.

OBJECTIVES

Increase the rate of people with an opioid use disorder getting medications for addiction treatment.
Reduce the proportion of people who had opioid use disorder in the past year.
Increase the number of admissions to substance use treatment for injection drug use.
Increase the proportion of people who get a referral for substance use treatment after an emergency department visit.

Reduce the proportion of people who had marijuana use disorder in the past year.
Reduce the proportion of people who had alcohol use disorder in the past year.
Increase the proportion of people with a substance use disorder who got treatment in the past year.
Reduce the proportion of people who had drug use disorder in the past year.
Reduce current use of smokeless tobacco products among adolescents
Reduce the proportion of adults who used drugs in the past month.
Reduce current e-cigarette use in adolescents.
Reduce the proportion of adolescents who used drugs in the past month
Reduce the proportion of people who had marijuana use disorder in the past year.
Reduce the proportion of people who had alcohol use disorder in the past year.
Increase the proportion of people with a substance use disorder who got treatment in the past year.
Reduce the proportion of people who had drug use disorder in the past year.

Drug and Alcohol Use

Goal: Reduce misuse of drugs and alcohol.

OBJECTIVES

Reduce the proportion of adults who used drugs in the past month.
Reduce the proportion of adults who use marijuana daily or almost daily.
Reduce the proportion of people aged 21 years and over who engaged in binge drinking in the past month.
Reduce the proportion of motor vehicle crash deaths that involve a drunk driver.
Reduce the proportion of people who misused prescription drugs in the past year.
Reduce the proportion of people who used heroin in the past year.
Reduce the proportion of people who started using heroin in the past year.
Reduce cirrhosis death.
Reduce drug overdose deaths.
Reduce the proportion of adolescents who drank alcohol in the past month.
Reduce the proportion of adolescents who used drugs in the past month.
Reduce the proportion of adolescents who used marijuana in the past month.
Reduce the proportion of people under 21 years who engaged in binge drinking in the past month.
Increase the proportion of adolescents who think substance abuse is a risk.
Reduce the proportion of people who misused prescription opioids in the past year.
Reduce the proportion of people who started misusing prescription opioids in the past year.
Reduce emergency department visits related to nonmedical use of prescription opioids.
Reduce the rate of opioid-related emergency department visits.
Reduce the rate of acute hepatitis C.
Reduce overdose deaths involving opioids.

Reduce overdose deaths involving natural and semisynthetic opioids.
Reduce overdose deaths involving synthetic opioids other than methadone.
Reduce overdose deaths involving heroin.
Reduce overdose deaths involving methadone.
Reduce the proportion of lesbian, gay, or bisexual high school students who have used illicit drugs.
Reduce the proportion of transgender high school students who have used illicit drugs.
Increase the proportion of people with substance use and mental health disorders who get treatment for both.
Increase abstinence from alcohol among pregnant women.
Increase abstinence from illicit among pregnant women.
Reduce the proportion of women who use illicit opioids during pregnancy.

Tobacco Use

Note: as reported in Chapter 1, A troubling report in the January 13, 2022, Thursday Styles section of the *New York Times* titled "The Clouds of Smoke Return," reported that cigarettes, once shunned, have made a comeback among young people.

Goal: Reduce illness, disability, and death related to tobacco use and secondhand smoke.

OBJECTIVES

Reduce current cigarette smoking in adolescents.
Reduce current tobacco use in adolescents.
Reduce current use of flavored tobacco products in adolescents who use tobacco.
Reduce current use of smokeless tobacco products among adolescents.
Reduce current cigar smoking in adolescents.
Reduce current e-cigarette use in adolescents.
Eliminate cigarette smoking initiation in adolescents and young adults.
Reduce the proportion of adolescents exposed to tobacco marketing.
Reduce current tobacco use in adults.
Increase Medicaid coverage of evidence-based treatment to help people quit using tobacco.
Eliminate policies in states, territories, and DC that preempt local tobacco control policies.
Increase the number of states, territories, and DC that raise the minimum age for tobacco sales to 21 years.
Reduce current cigarette, cigar, and pipe smoking in adults.
Increase the national average tax on cigarettes.
Increase the proportion of adults who get advice to quit smoking from a health care provider.
Increase past-year attempts to quit smoking in adults.

Increase successful quit attempts in pregnant women who smoke.

Increase the proportion of oral and pharyngeal cancers detected in the earliest stage.

Increase use of smoking cessation counseling and medication in adults who smoke.

Reduce the lung cancer death rate.

Increase the proportion of adults who get screened for lung cancer.

Increase successful quit attempts in adults who smoke.

Increase the number of states, territories, and DC that prohibit smoking in worksites, restaurants, and bars.

Increase the proportion of smoke-free homes.

Reduce the proportion of people who do not smoke but are exposed to secondhand smoke.

Increase the number of states, territories, and DC that prohibit smoking in multiunit housing.

Increase the proportion of worksites with policies than ban indoor smoking.

Increase abstinence from cigarette smoking among pregnant women.

Examples of Recovery Objectives

1. Scenario: George has two years clean and sober. Alcohol and opioids (prescription or street) were his drugs of choice. He neglected to tell the dentist about his addiction history and recovery. George accepted a script for hydrocodone (Vicodin) following dental surgery. George called for a refill three days later.

Objective: Describe relapse with Vicodin to addiction counselor on Friday at 2 pm.

2. Scenario: Margaret described herself as a "lady drunk." When she passed out drunk at her eldest daughter's wedding two years ago, she agreed to treatment. Following detoxification, three residential programs, continuing bi-weekly counseling, and active AA, Maggie just received her two-year medallion.

Objective: Stand tall, breathe easily, and celebrate my youngest daughter's wedding on June 6th.

3. Scenario: Hank enjoyed hosting the holiday dinner for his extended family. Four years ago, he ate turkey with a group of men at a halfway house. Following a walk and talk with his brother, Hank decided to live well.

Objective: Develop a weekly wellness plan to begin January 1st.

4. Scenario: Jason completed a five-year Health Professional's Monitoring Program (HPMP). "My 'alcoholic lifestyle' is history; my dental practice is thriving; I'm back in the big bed." Jason is an active participant in community AA meetings and a recognized leader of the local Caduceus Group.

Objective: Serve as peer professional support for a new dentist in the monitoring program with weekly office visits.

5. Scenario: Bill and Angie enjoyed a 15th wedding anniversary at a favorite restaurant. Bill has been in recovery for 12 years. Life is good. Bill is running for town selectman.

Objective: Affirm recovery with expressions of gratitude daily at bedtime.

6. Scenario: Anne is an outpatient client at Riverside Medication Assistant Treatment (MAT) Program where she is being treated for an opioid use disorder (OUD). She is compliant with all aspects of the program. Anne acknowledges feelings of "doom and gloom," a "dark November of my soul."

Objective: Schedule a session with the mental health specialist at Riverside within the next ten days.

Section I presented facts, concepts, principles, and theories about objectives, the ASK model, SMART objectives, Healthy People 2030 objectives, and examples of recovery objectives. Continue recovery work in Section II with applications about the competency.

II

Draft recovery objectives. Section II suggests applications about objectives, the ASK model, SMART objectives, Healthy People 2030 objectives, and examples of recovery objectives.

Objectives

1   Cognitive, affective, and psychomotor domains of learning guide writing objectives. Use some of the suggested verbs associated with each learning domain in Box 8.5, Box 8.6, and Box 8.7 to draft six recovery objectives.

Box 8.5 Verbs for the Cognitive Domain

Remembering: define, describe, identify, know, label, list, match, name, outline, recall, recognize, reproduce, select, state.

Understanding: comprehend, convert, defend, distinguish, estimate, explain, extend, generalize, give an example, interpret, paraphrase, predict, rewrite, summarize, translate.

Applying: apply, change, compute, construct, demonstrate, discover, manipulate, modify, operate, predict, prepare, produce, relate, show, solve, use.

Analyzing: analyze, break down, compare, contrast, diagram, deconstruct, differentiate, discriminate, distinguish, identify, illustrate, infer, outline, relate, select, separate.

Evaluating: appraise, compare, conclude, contrast, criticize, critique, defend, describe, discriminate, evaluate, explain, interpret, justify, relate, summarize, support.

Creating: categorize, combine, compile, compose, create, devise, design, explain, generate, modify, organize, plan, rearrange, reconstruct, relate, reorganize, revise, rewrite, summarize, tell, write.

Example: Compare and contrast a recovery lifestyle with active addiction.

a   Cognitive Objective # 1.
b   Cognitive Objective # 2.

Box 8.6 Verbs for the Affective Domain

Receiving Phenomena: ask, choose, describe, follow, give, hold, identify, locate, name, point to, select, sit, erect, reply, use.
Responding to Phenomena: answer, aid, comply, conform, discuss, greet, help, label, perform, practice, present, read, recite, report, select, tell, write.
Valuing: complete, demonstrate, differentiate, explain, follow, form, initiate, invite, join, justify, propose, read, report, select, share, study, work.
Organization: adhere, alter, arrange, combine, compare, complete, defend, explain, formulate, generalize, identify, integrate, modify, order, organize, prepare, relate, synthesize.
Internalizing Values (Characterization): act, discriminate, display, influence, listen, modify, perform, practice, propose, qualify, question, revise, serve, solve, verify.

Example: Practice these principles in all our affairs (Narcotics Anonymous Step 12).

a   Affective Objective # 1.
b   Affective Objective # 2.

Box 8.7 Verbs for the Psychomotor Domain

Perception: choose, describe, detect, differentiate, distinguish, identify, isolate, relate, select.
Set: begin, display, explain, move, proceed, react, show, state, volunteer.
Guided Response: copy, trace, follow, react, reproduce, respond.
Mechanism: assemble, calibrate, construct, dismantle, display, fasten, fix, grind, heat, manipulate, measure, mend, mix, organize, sketch.
Complex Overt Response: The same verbs as Mechanism, but with an adverb or adjective that indicates more skillful performance.
Adaptation: adapt, alter, change, rearrange, reorganize, revise, vary.
Origination: arrange, build, combine, compose, construct, create, design, initiate, make, originate.

Example: Begin couples counseling.

a   Psychomotor Objective # 1.
b   Psychomotor Objective # 2.

The ASK Model

2 Compare the ASK Model with the KSA Competency Model

    a How important are attitudes when it comes to effective performance: e.g., developing competencies for recovery?

    b How important is knowledge when it comes to effective performance: e.g., developing competencies for recovery?

    c Could an integration of knowledge, skills, and attitudes be more important than their order of development?

SMART Objectives

Objectives are "thinking, feeling, and doing" ways people achieve goals. SMART objectives are specific, measurable, attainable, realistic, and timely action plans to reach goals.

3 Review essential recovery goals listed in Box 8.8.

Box 8.8 Essential Recovery Goals

Master Addiction

Abstinence
Harm Reduction
Relapse Prevention

Live Well

Health
Wellness
Well-being

Do Good

Helping
Service
Altruism

Use Table 8.3 to draft four SMART recovery objectives. How SMART is each objective?

Healthy People 2030 Objectives

4 Using some of the examples of objectives from Healthy People 2030, write an objective for addiction, drug and alcohol use, and tobacco use.

Table 8.3 SMART Objectives

Objective	S	M	A	R	T
1.					
2.					
3.					
4.					

    a   Addiction:
    b   Drug and alcohol use:
    c   Tobacco use:

Examples of Recovery Objectives

5   Practice, practice, and more practice. Draft two more recovery objectives.

Section II suggested applications about objectives, the ASK model, SMART objectives, Healthy People 2030 objectives, and examples of recovery objectives. Complete Chapter 8 with evaluations of recovery work and competency development in Section III.

III

Evaluate recovery work and competency development.

1   Evaluate recovery work with a short True/False Quiz and a review of the outcome, effort, process, and decisions of recovery work.

    a   Quiz: Based on your learning from Chapter 8 "Draft Recovery Objectives," indicate whether each of the following statements is True (T) or False (F).

        1 T or F   Objectives are "thinking, feeling, and doing" ways people achieve goals.
        2 T or F   Educators identified three cognitive, affective, and psychomotor learning domains.
        3 T or F   Comprehension is an affective function.
        4 T or F   Valuing is a cognitive function.
        5 T or F   The ASK Model of learning alters the order and emphasis of the competency dimensions: knowledge, skills, and attitudes (KSA).
        6 T or F   **S**MART objectives are sensible.
        7 T or F   S**M**ART objectives are measurable.
        8 T or F   SM**A**RT objectives are affirmative.

9   T or F   SMA**R**T objectives are rigorous.
10 T or F   SMA**R**T objectives are timely.

(True: 1, 2, 5, 7, 10. False: 3, 4, 6, 8, 9)

b   Outcome, Effort, Process, and Decisions

Examine the outcome, effort, process, and decisions of your recovery work in Chapter 8.

Outcome

Did you meet **objectives** for Chapter 8? Use Table 8.4 to review objectives and rank as:

Strongly disagree = 1
Disagree = 2
Undecided = 3
Agree = 4
Strongly agree = 5

Effort

Effort evaluation reviews the input or energy you invested in recovery work. Ask and answer the following questions.

- How hard did you work on Chapter 8?
- How much time did you dedicate to Chapter 8?
- What resources did you employ for Chapter 8 work?

Table 8.4 Objectives

Objectives	Rank
I use the cognitive, affective, and psychomotor domains of learning to develop objectives.	1, 2, 3, 4, 5
Consider the ASK Model as an alternative to the KSA emphasis and order.	1, 2, 3, 4, 5
I draft objectives that are specific, measurable, attainable, relevant, and timely.	1, 2, 3, 4, 5
I review Healthy People 2030 objectives for addiction, drug and alcohol use, and tobacco use.	1, 2. 3. 4. 5
I examine examples of effective, efficient recovery objectives.	1, 2, 3, 4, 5
I practice writing SMART objectives.	1, 2, 3, 4, 5

Table 8.5 Process

Process	Yes or No	Comment
I read the narrative (Section I).		
I completed the applications (Section II).		
I evaluated recovery work and competency development (Section III).		

Process

Process evaluation is especially valuable when you want to improve outcome and increase the efficiency of your recovery work. Use Table 8.5 to evaluate process.

Decisions

Based on the evaluation of your recovery work from Chapter 8, decide to celebrate, continue, correct, or change your approach to recovery work. Reward yourself with a positive thought, feeling, or action. Keep doing what you are doing if "it works." Modify or adjust anything that is not working well. Plan and welcome change that supports your recovery work as you move on to Chapter 9. Ask and answer the following questions.

- Did you **celebrate** your recovery work from Chapter 8 Draft Recovery Objectives?
- Will you **continue** to approach recovery work in the same way in Chapter 9?
- Do you plan to **correct** your approach to recovery work in Chapter 9?
- Do you plan to **change** your approach to recovery work in Chapter 9?

2   Evaluate competency development using a KSA/Topic Matrix and a Rubric Review.

  a   What knowledge, skills, and attitudes are you using to develop Competency 9 Draft Recovery Objectives. Document KSA examples in Table 8.6 KSA/Topic Matrix.

  b   Evaluate the development of Competency 8 Draft Recovery Objectives with a Rubric Review. The chapter outline provides the criteria to evaluate competency development. Rank competency development on Table 8.7 as:

  - **Exceeds expectations:** Understands, applies, and evaluates competency criteria > 90% of the time.
  - **Meets expectations:** Understands, applies, and evaluates competency criteria 75% to 90% of the time.
  - **Needs improvement:** Understands, applies, and evaluates competency criteria < 75% of the time.

Table 8.6 KSA/Topic Matrix

Topics	Knowledge	Skills	Attitudes
Objectives Cognitive Domain Affective Domain Psychomotor Domain			
Objectives Cognitive Domain Affective Domain Psychomotor Domain			
The ASK Model			
Healthy People 2030 Objectives			
Examples of Recovery Objectives			

Table 8.7 Competency 8 Draft Recovery Objectives

Criteria	Exceeds Expectations 3	Meets Expectations 2	Needs Improvement 1
Objectives Cognitive Domain Affective Domain Psychomotor Domain			
The ASK Model			
SMART Objectives Specific Measurable Attainable Relevant Timely			
Healthy People 2030 Objectives			
Examples of Recovery Objectives			

Summary

Draft recovery objectives in Chapter 8. This chapter suggested a SMART way to draft recovery objectives. Topics that provided the organizing framework for the chapter included Objectives, the ASK Model, SMART Objectives, Healthy People 2030 Objectives, and Examples of Recovery Objectives. The chapter used cognitive, affective, and psychomotor domains of learning to develop objectives. It considered the ASK model as an alternative to the KSA emphasis and order. We show how to draft objectives that are specific, measurable, attainable, relevant, and timely. It reviewed Health People 2030 objectives for addiction, drug and alcohol use, and tobacco use. It examined examples of effective, efficient objectives and urges practice writing SMART objectives. The chapter suggested applications—questions, worksheets, exercises, and projects—for the competency. Chapter 8 concluded with evaluations of recovery work and competency development.

9 Act for Recovery

Ben B. Acts to Reduce Harm from Gaming

Ruth and James B. contacted Dr. Mark D. (psychologist/addiction specialist) expressing worry and concern that their son Ben, a talented college Sophomore, is failing because of addictive gaming. Ben agreed to see Dr. Mark during spring break. According to Ben "gaming was fun during high school. I balanced my gaming as a freshman because college was new, busy, and satisfying. I liked my classes; I played in the orchestra; I had a great roommate. Things changed this year. My major classes are boring; I know the stuff. I live alone. Gaming is challenging, rewarding, and social. I am failing two courses in my major because I don't attend class or do the work. I know my parents are worried; I don't return their texts or calls. My sister seems to understand." Dr. Mark talks with Ben about harm reduction. Ben grasps the concept and is willing to try. Ben values a college education and does not want to disappoint his family. Together, Dr. Mark and Ben develop an action plan to manage his gaming. Act: Ben agrees not to game after 1 am. Habits; Ben will text/talk with his sister daily as she is a valuable support. Skills: Ben will return to orchestra as he is a skilled trumpet player and enjoys the socialization. Competencies: Ben will talk with his academic program advisor to address failing performance and seek approval to take some upper-division courses. Ben will check in with Dr. Mark by text or phone every two weeks to monitor progress.

Purpose: This chapter summons action for recovery, specifically acts, habits, skills, and competencies to meet recovery objectives.

Objectives

- Achieve recovery goals through action.
- Review action for recovery using the 12 Steps of Narcotics Anonymous and the SMART Recovery Program.
- Use concepts from behavioral psychology, behavioral therapies, and role theory to act for recovery.
- Develop an action hierarchy of acts, habits, skills, and competencies for recovery.
- Follow a four-step process to meet recovery objectives.

DOI: 10.4324/9781003292944-9

Outline

Recovery Goal Achievement Through Action

Into Action

12 Steps of Narcotics Anonymous
SMART Recovery
Behavioral Psychology and Behavioral Therapies
Role Theory

Action Hierarchy

Acts
Habits
Skills
Competencies

Four Steps to Meet Recovery Objectives

1 Review Objectives
2 Marshall Resources
3 Manage Risks
4 Initiate Actions

I

Act for recovery. Section I presents facts, concepts, principles, and theories about recovery goal achievement through action, "into action," an action hierarchy, and four steps to meet recovery objectives.

Recovery Goal Achievement Through Action

Action is the way people with addiction achieve goals:

- Attain abstinence.
- Maintain harm reduction.
- Prevent relapse.
- Promote health.
- Foster wellness.
- Experience well-being.
- Offer helping.
- Volunteer services.
- Do the right thing.

Into Action

12 Steps of Narcotics Anonymous

Into Action is the title of Chapter 6 in the *Alcoholics Anonymous* book. Action is central to 12-step programs and 12-step treatment approaches Notice the "action" in the 12 Steps from Narcotics Anonymous on Table 9.1.

The SMART Recovery Program

Founded in 1994, SMART Recovery (Self-Management and Recovery Training) helps individuals gain independence from addiction (substances or activities). SMART Recovery supports individuals who choose to abstain or are considering abstinence from any type of addictive behavior (substances or activities). SMART Recovery teaches how to change self-defeating thinking, emotions, and actions; and to work towards long-term satisfaction and quality of life.

SMART Recovery's approach to behavioral change is built around a 4-Point Program: (1) Building and maintaining the motivation to change. (2) Coping with urges to use. (3) Managing thoughts, feelings, and behaviors effectively without

Table 9.1 12 Steps of Narcotics Anonymous

1 We admitted that we were powerless over our addiction, that our lives had become unmanageable.
2 We came to believe that a Power greater than ourselves could restore us to sanity.
3 We made a decision to turn our will and our lives over to the care of God as we understood Him.
4 We made a searching and fearless moral inventory of ourselves.
5 We admitted to God, to ourselves, and to another human being the exact nature of our wrongs.
6 We were entirely ready to have God remove all these defects of character.
7 We humbly asked Him to remove our shortcomings.
8 We made a list of all persons we had harmed and became willing to make amends to them all.
9 We made direct amends to such people wherever possible except when to do so would injure them or others.
10 We continued to take personal inventory and when we were wrong promptly admitted it.
11 We sought through prayer and meditation to improve our conscious contact with God as we understood Him, praying only for knowledge of His will for us and the power to carry that out.
12 Having had a spiritual awakening as a result of these steps, we tried to carry this message to addicts and to practice these principles in all our affairs.

addictive behaviors. (4) Living a balanced, positive, and healthy life. More specifically, the SMART Recovery program and groups:

- Teach self-empowerment and self-reliance.
- Encourage individuals to recover and live satisfying lives.
- Suggest tools and techniques for self-directed change.
- Offer education meetings include open discussions.
- Advocate the appropriate use of prescribed medications and psychological treatments.
- Evolve as scientific knowledge of addiction recovery evolves.

SMART Recovery founders believe people find their individual paths to recovery. For some participants, that path may include 12-step programs like AA or NA, or other self-empowering groups such as Women for Sobriety, LifeRing Secular Recovery, Moderation Management, and Secular Organizations for Sobriety. Although the SMART Recovery approach differs from each of these approaches in various ways, it does not necessarily exclude them. SMART in Action was the title of the 25th anniversary of SMART Recovery in 2019.

Behavioral Psychology and Behavioral Therapies

Many principles of behavioral psychology and behavioral therapies are used in addiction treatment and recovery to change behavior and to maintain the change.

Beginning in the early 1900s and continuing strong today, behavioral psychology, sometimes called American psychology, holds that environment shapes behavior. Behavioral psychology studies, analyzes, quantifies, and seeks to change observable behavior. Psychologist John B. Watson built on the work of the famous Russian psychologist Ivan Pavlov. They developed what is known as classical conditioning. In the 1930s, B.F. Skinner developed operant conditioning, suggesting that behavior is controlled by reinforcement. Skinner advanced schedules of reinforcement that are still widely used today.

Clinical application of behavioral psychology followed, especially the use of behavior modification in the 1940s and 1950s. Behavior modification relies on many principles of behavioral psychology including reinforcement, punishment, extinction shaping, fading, and chaining. Later in the 1950s, American psychologist Albert Ellis created rational emotive behavior therapy (REBT). REBT is an action-oriented approach to managing cognitive, emotional, and behavioral disturbances. REBT influenced the development of cognitive-behavioral therapy (CBT) by Aaron Beck in the1960s (CBT), dialectical behavioral therapy (DBT) by Marsha Linehan in the 1970s, and acceptance and commitment therapy (ACT) by Steven C. Hayes in the 1980s. Key concepts from behavioral psychology that are used in behavioral therapies include systematic desensitization, exposure and response prevention, token economy, modeling, applied behavior analysis, and contingency management.

Role Theory

A role is a set of behaviors expected by others, implied by social norms, and often required by law. Roles serve as plans or blueprints for goals, tasks, and behavior, for example, as a mother, a teacher, a student. Sometimes roles ⋅ become labels, often with pejorative meanings. People often act in ways that exemplify these roles: a loser, a pervert; a diabetic, a cardiac; a moron, an idiot, a retard, a drunk, a lush, an alcoholic, an addict, or a junkie.

Individuals assume or adopt roles expected by others, then behave accordingly. Roles can become lifestyles: a healthy or unhealthy lifestyle, an addictive or recovering lifestyle.

- Cecil arrives an hour late for a mandatory session with his probation officer and announces "What do you expect, Joe. I am a teenager. At least I showed up."
- When asked by her mother about weekend plans with her husband, Joan replies "Just the same old same old. Frank heads to his mancave with a case of beer, a loaf of bread, a package of cold cuts, and his cell phone. Back-to-back sports with drinking, eating, and betting. He comes up to pee but says he plans to install a bathroom next year, but I doubt we will have enough money."
- Virginia gets up in the morning, lays out breakfast for the children, and catches the bus for work. She completes a satisfying day as a legal secretary and returns home. She finishes supper dishes, checks on the children doing homework, gives her partner a kiss on the cheek as she waits for a ride to keep a planned appointment with her recovery coach. "I'm just doing what is expected."
- Dan is coaching tackle football for his eight-year-old son and friends. After three years, Dan has his driver's license with full privileges back. He drove under the influence and crashed into another car, injuring the driver. Dan smiles with confidence and comments. "Good fathers are expected to coach their sons."

Action Hierarchy

Action is an essential part of strategic plans. Action may be a thought, feeling, or behavior. Like the psychomotor domain of learning and its range of behaviors from simple to complex, there is an action hierarchy of acts, habits, skills, competencies; see Figure 9.1. In contrast to many impulsive actions during active addiction, action for recovery is reasoned and planned. Master addiction! Individuals with addiction act to abstain or participate in a harm reduction program. Acts help prevent relapse. Habits reinforce recovery changes. Live well! Acts, habits, plus skills promote health, wellness, and well-being. Do good! People in long-term recovery develop competencies to help others, serve society, and "do the next right thing." While acts, habits, skills, and competencies help people with addiction achieve recovery goals, recovery, in turn, strengthens action for recovery.

Figure 9.1 Action Hierarchy

Acts

An act is a single here-and-now behavior. For example, Angie, a high school guidance counselor, signs a retirement card for Principal Jefferson Andrews: "I wish you and Jane health and happiness in your new Arizona home. Thank you for everything, especially approval of the Recovery Room, Angie." Acts that are part of a strategic recovery plan reflect "reasoned action" or "planned behavior." In the 1980s, Martin Fishbein and Icek Ajzen built on their original Theory of Reasoned Action (TRA) to develop the Theory of Planned Behavior (TPB). The TPB says an individual's intention predicts the likelihood of behavior at a specific time and place. The decision to engage in a particular behavior is based on the outcomes the individual expects from performing the behavior. Behavioral achievement depends on motivation (intention) and ability (behavioral control). The TPB predicts and explains a wide range of intentions and health behaviors.

Habits

A habit is a routine, automatic behavior that is repeated regularly and tends to occur subconsciously. Habits form without a person intending to acquire them. People also deliberately cultivate or eliminate habits, often part of goal achievement. Habits develop through learning and repetition, especially cues, associations, and reinforcement. It is harder to give up a habit the longer the behavior goes on.

Habits are efficient behaviors. For example, morning rituals largely consist of a variety of habits, like brushing teeth, taking a shower, making coffee, throwing a gym bag in the car, putting on a seat belt, and driving to work. Over time, the sequence of these behaviors becomes consistent, predictable, useful, desirable, and satisfying. See the book *The 7 Habits of Highly Effective People* by Stephen C. Covey, first published in 1989.

Addiction often begins with a habit: repeated substance use or addictive behavior. Addiction develops when a person is unable to go without the substance or the behavior, or activity. The person psychologically and physiologically needs the substance or behavior, despite knowing and experiencing harmful effects and adverse consequences.

Habits may be harmful or health-promoting. Habits play a big part in addiction and recovery. For example, for years Chuck instinctively reached for a cigarette after waking up. Daily drinking, weekend wipeouts, and a major motor vehicle accident led to Chuck's entry into a State Health Practitioners Monitoring Program. For several years, Chuck consciously reached for his iPhone and logged into the participant portal to see if he "tests today." Toxicology screening is part of his Recovery Monitoring Contract. Five years later, Chuck instinctively reaches for *Touchstones: A Book of Daily Meditations for Men* (Anonymous 1991) to start his day. On Monday night for over two years, Helen leaves the dinner table almost automatically. She drives to Joshua Baptist Church where she attends the 7:30 pm Experience, Strength, and Hope AA Discussion Meeting, her homegroup.

Skills

A skill is a learned ability to act with determined results with good execution often within a given amount of time, energy, or both. People develop a variety of skills: life skills, people skills, social skills, work skills. Sometimes work skills are described as hard or soft skills. Hard skills are related to specific technical knowledge and training while soft skills are personality traits such as leadership, communication, or time management. Soft skills are interpersonal or people skills. Both types of skills are necessary to successfully perform and advance in most jobs.

Skills that are repeated over time and with a high degree of effectiveness are often called skillsets. A skillset is the combination of knowledge, personal qualities, and abilities that a person develops through life and work. It typically combines two types of skills: soft skills and hard skills.

As active addiction progresses, the ability for skillful action diminishes, especially within the family and at work. With time and work, individuals develop skills for recovery. With recovery work, people develop skills, often lost during active addiction, for life and work.

Competencies

Competencies are clusters of related knowledge, skills, and attitudes (KSAs) that equip, enable, and empower a person to **act** effectively, usually with proficiency. A competency is more than an act, habit, or skill. *Developing Competencies for Recovery* suggests 12 core competencies people with addiction can develop to realize recovery. Notice the emphasis on action in each competency in Box 9.1.

Box 9.1 Action Competencies

- **Begin** recovery work
- **Face** addiction
- **Affirm** recovery
- **Develop** a strategic recovery plan
- **Set** recovery goals
- **Determine** motivation or recovery
- **Inventory** resources and risks for recovery
- **Draft** recovery objectives
- **Act** for recovery
- **Evaluate** recovery work and competency development
- **Record** recovery work and competency development
- **Construct** a recovery lifestyle.

Four Steps to Meet Recovery Objectives

Act for recovery. Four steps lead people with addiction into action to meet recovery objectives:

1 Review recovery objectives.
2 Marshall resources.
3 Manage risks.
4 Initiate action to meet recovery objectives.

1. Review Recovery Objectives

Review each recovery objective. Is the objective specific, measurable, attainable, relevant, and time-based? If "yes," move on to the next action step. If "no," try to modify the objective to meet SMART criteria. SMART objectives have a high likelihood of being met.

You may want to examine the objectives for addiction, drug and alcohol use, and tobacco use from Healthy People 2030. See Chapter 8 Draft Recovery Objectives, or visit the Healthy People 2030 website at https://health.gov/healthypeople.

2. Marshall Resources for Recovery

Check the Inventory of Resources for Recovery in Chapter 7. Marshall resources for recovery; more specifically:

- use personal assets including age, sex, gender, race, ethnicity, and self
- employ social capital from family and friends, community, society, and culture
- seek professional services from providers, practitioners, and Recovery Oriented Systems of Care (ROSC) for recovery if indicated
- engage mutual self-help groups, peer-based support, and recovery residencies

3. Manage Risks for Recovery

Check the Inventory of Risks for Recovery in Chapter 7. Manage risks for recovery. Try to:

- recognize personal liabilities associated with age, sex and gender, race and ethnicity, or self
- counter-balance social deficits from family and friend, community, society, and culture
- accept limitations of professional services from providers, practitioners, and Recovery Oriented Systems of Care (ROSC)
- acknowledge scarcities of mutual self-help groups, peer-based support, and recovery residencies.

4. Initiate Action to Meet Recovery Objectives

An initiative is an introductory act or first step that leads to action: something a person does. The initiative includes the readiness and ability to act. Personal initiative is an inner power, a spark that starts the action. Initiatives reflect energy, enterprise, independence, determination, and drive. Initiatives often present a new plan or process; initiatives provide a way and a direction to solve a problem or reach a goal. Initiatives are usually proactive in approach and persistent in the effort.

What does it mean to initiate action? According to the Department of Human Resources at the University of North Carolina initiating action means "Taking prompt action to accomplish objectives; taking action to achieve goals beyond what is required; being proactive." Key actions include the ability to:

- Respond quickly—Take immediate action when confronted with a problem or when made aware of a situation.
- Take independent action—Implement new ideas or potential solutions without prompting; do not wait for others to act or to request action.
- Go above and beyond—Take action that goes beyond job requirements to achieve objectives.

Why is initiating action so difficult? People with addiction rarely begin recovery now! They employ a host of defense mechanisms to avoid recovery. They deny, minimize, justify, rationalize, intellectualize, and explain to others and to themselves to continue addictive behavior. Remember the classic book (Johnson [1973]1990) and movie (Rogers 1975) *I'll Quit Tomorrow* by Vernon E. Johnson, Founder of the Johnson Institute, and the Johnson Intervention Model.

It is a challenge for people with addiction to take independent action. Until 2013, individuals with serious substance use disorders were diagnosed with alcohol and substance dependence. (DSM-IV-TR, 2000). Step 1 of the 12-step program states "We admitted we were powerless over our addiction." While we acknowledge the need for care by family and friends, treatment by providers and professionals, and support by peers, ultimately, an individual with addiction takes independent action to begin and continue recovery.

A counselor reported a client with addiction answered "more," when asked "what is your drug of choice" during a treatment intake. Diagnostic criteria for SUDs include language like "larger amounts, a great deal of time, recurrent use, continued use despite problems, continued use despite knowledge of problems, and tolerance." When behaviors such as gambling, sex, the internet, shopping, video games, food, exercise, work, tattoo, love, and porn become excessive they resemble addiction. Rarely, if ever, do we see people in early recovery "going the extra mile." Individuals required to attend three support meetings a week seldom attend four or five meetings. Yet, with mastery of addiction through abstinence or harm reduction and relapse prevention, people with addiction begin to experience health, wellness, and well-being. Long-term recovery becomes a way of life characterized by helping, service, and altruism. "More" recovery is good recovery.

Section I presented facts, concepts, principles, and theories about recovery goal achievement through action, "into action," an action hierarchy, and four steps to meet recovery objectives. Continue recovery work in Section II with applications about the competency.

II

Section II suggest applications about recovery goal achievement through action, "into action," an action hierarchy, and four steps to meet recovery objectives.

Recovery Goal Achievement Through Action

1   Achieve recovery goals through action. What does this mean?

Into Action

2   Describe the dynamics of recovery: the action!

Action Hierarchy

3   Explain each element of the action hierarchy of acts, habits, skills, and competencies.

- Acts
- Habits
- Skills
- Competencies

4   Compare and contract addictive and recovery actions in the two examples that follow, then record your application in Table 9.2.

Table 9.2 Addictive and Recovery Actions

Action Hierarchy		Addictive Actions	Recovery Actions
Acts			
Habits			
Skills			
Competencies			

  a   What were some addictive acts, habits, skills, even competencies? For example, "I could hold my liquor." "I knew my supplier." "I never shared needles."

  b   What are some recovery acts, habits, skills, and competencies? "I attend my recovery home group every Thursday night." "I end my day with a gratitude prayer." "My wife and I have a date night every two weeks."

Four Steps to Meet Recovery Objectives

5   Explain each of the four steps that lead people with addiction into action to meet recovery objectives:

- Review recovery objectives.
- Marshall resources for recovery.
- Manage risks for recovery.
- Initiate action to meet recovery objectives.

Section II suggested applications about recovery achievement through action, "into action," an action hierarchy, and four steps to meet recovery objectives. Complete Chapter 9 with evaluations of recovery work and competency development.

III

Evaluate recovery work and competency development.

1   Evaluate recovery work with a short True/False Quiz and a review of the outcome, effort, process, and decisions of recovery work.

  a   Quiz: Based on your learning from Chapter 9 Act for Recovery, indicate whether each of the following statements is True (T) or False (F).

     1   T or F   Action for recovery includes recovery acts, habits, skills, and competencies
     2   T or F   Action is central to 12-step programs and 12-step treatment approaches
     3   T or F   Humanistic psychology emphasizes action.
     4   T or F   Behavioral psychology and behavioral therapies guide action for change.

5 T or F An act is a single here-and-now behavior.
6 T or F Habits are usually bad.
7 T or F Hard skills are interpersonal or people skills.
8 T or F Soft skills are related to specific technical knowledge and training.
9 T or F Competencies are clusters of related knowledge, skills, and attitudes (KSAs) that equip, enable, and empower a person to **act** effectively, usually with proficiency.
10 T or F Two steps direct action for recovery: 1. Think, 2. Act.

(True: 1, 2, 4, 5, 9. False: 3, 6, 7, 8, 10)

b   Outcome, Effort, Process, and Decisions

Examine the outcome, effort, process, and decisions of your recovery work in Chapter 9.

Outcome

Did you meet **objectives** for Chapter 9? Use Table 9.3 to review objectives and rank as:

Strongly disagree = 1
Disagree = 2
Undecided = 3
Agree = 4
Strongly agree = 5

Effort

Effort evaluation reviews the input or energy you invested in recovery work. Ask and answer the following questions.

* How hard did you work on Chapter 9?
* How much time did you dedicate to Chapter 9?
* What resources did you employ for Chapter 9 work?

Table 9.3 Objectives

Objectives	Rank
I achieve recovery goals through action.	1. 2. 3. 4. 5
I review action for recovery using the NA 12 Steps and the SMART Recovery Program	1, 2, 3, 4, 5
Use concepts from behavioral psychology, behavioral therapies, and role theory to act for recovery.	1, 2, 3, 4, 5
I develop an action hierarchy of acts, habits, skills, and competencies for recovery.	1, 2, 3, 4, 5
I follow a 4-step process to meet recovery objectives.	1, 2, 3, 4, 5

Table 9.4 Process

Process	Yes or No	Comment
I read the narrative (Section I).		
I completed the applications (Section II).		
I evaluated recovery work and competency development (Section III).		

Process

Process evaluation is especially valuable when you want to improve outcome and increase the efficiency of your recovery work. Use Table 9.4 to evaluate process.

Decisions

Based on the evaluation of your recovery work from Chapter 9, decide to celebrate, continue, correct, or change your approach to recovery work. Reward yourself with a positive thought, feeling, or action. Keep doing what you are doing if "it works." Modify or adjust anything that is not working well. Plan and welcome change that supports your recovery work as you move on to Chapter 10. Ask and answer the following questions.

- Did you **celebrate** your recovery work from Chapter 9 Act for Recovery?
- Will you **continue** to approach recovery work in the same way in Chapter 10?
- Do you plan to **correct** your approach to recovery work in Chapter 10?
- Do you plan to **change** your approach to recovery work in Chapter 10?

2 Evaluate competency development using a KSA/Topic Matrix and a Rubric Review.

    a What knowledge, skills, and attitudes are you using to develop Competency 9 Act for Recovery? Document KSA examples in Table 9.5 KSA/Topic Matrix.

    b Outlines reflect competency dimensions and dynamics. Examine the criteria and your recovery work. Rank competency development on Table 9.6 as:

- **Exceeds expectations:** Criteria guide my understanding, application, and evaluation of recovery work > 90% of the time.
- **Meets expectations:** Criteria guide my understanding, application, and evaluation of recovery work 75% to 90% of the time.
- **Needs improvement:** Criteria guide my understanding, application, and evaluation of recovery work. < 75% of the time.

Table 9.5 KSA/Topic Matrix

Topics	Knowledge	Skills	Attitudes
Recovery Goal Achievement Through Action			
Into Action Steps of Narcotics Anonymous SMART Recovery Behavioral Psychology and Behavioral Therapies Role Theory			
Action Hierarchy Acts Habits Skills Competencies			
Four Steps to Meet Recovery Objectives 1 Review Objectives 2 Marshall Resources. 3 Manage Risks 4 Initiate Action			

Table 9.6 Competency 9 Act for Recovery

Criteria	Exceeds Expectations 3	Meets Expectations 2	Needs Improvement 1
Recovery Goal Achievement Through Action			
Into Action Steps of Narcotics Anonymous SMART Recovery Behavioral Psychology and Behavioral Therapies Role Theory			
Action Hierarchy Acts Habits Skills Competencies			
Four Steps to Meet Recovery Objectives 1 Review Objectives 2 Marshall Resources 3 Manage Risks 4 Initiate Action			

Summary

Act for recovery in Chapter 9. This chapter summoned action for recovery, specifically acts, habits, skills, and competencies to meet recovery objectives. Topics that provided the organizing framework for the chapter included Recovery Goal Achievement Through Action, Into Action, Action Hierarchy, and Four Steps to Meet Recovery Objectives. Achieve recovery goals through action. The chapter reviewed action for recovery using the 12 Steps of Narcotics Anonymous and the SMART Recovery Program. It used concepts from behavioral psychology, behavioral therapies, and role theory to act for recovery. The chapter developed an action hierarchy of acts, habits, skills, and competencies for recovery. It followed a four-step process to meet recovery objectives. The chapter suggested applications—questions, worksheets, exercises, and projects—for the competency. Chapter 9 concluded with evaluations of recovery work and competency development.

10 Evaluate Recovery Work and Competency Development

Ellen B. Evaluates her Recovery Work

My name is Ellen B., and I am an occupational therapist. I misused many prescription medications, complicated by alcohol. My attendance and work performance suffered, and I was terminated. Three years ago, I completed the State's Professional Assistance Program (PAP). I am back working as an OT at Grayson Children's Hospital. I just completed a self-evaluation of performance expectations. Today, my supervisor and I reviewed and evaluated my quality of work, the quantity of work, dependability, punctuality, and communication skills. I received "high marks" in many areas. I am going to suggest a Performance Appraisal of Recovery with my counselor, including my self-evaluation, her evaluation, and some goal setting.

Purpose: This chapter shows how to evaluate recovery work and competency development.

Objectives

- Review theories, models, and types of evaluation.
- Evaluate recovery work, especially outcome, effort, process, and decisions.
- Evaluate competency development with a KSA/Topic Matrix and a Rubric Review.

Outline

Theories, Models, and Types of Evaluation

Recovery Work

Outcome
Effort
Process
Decisions

DOI: 10.4324/9781003292944-10

Competency Development

KSA/Topic Matrix
Rubric Review

I

Evaluate recovery work and competency development. Section I presents facts, concepts, principles, and theories about evaluation, together with evaluations of recovery work and competency development.

Theories, Models, and Types of Evaluation

Evaluation involves collecting and analyzing information about activities, characteristics, and outcomes of a process or program. Evaluation helps people determine the value or worth of something like recovery work or competency development. Evaluation helps people make informed decisions whether to continue, improve, or change the process or program.

Theories, models, and concepts of evaluation abound. Some years ago, Edward A. Suchman proposed five criteria to evaluate the success or failure of a program: *effort, performance, adequacy of performance, efficiency*, and *process*. Avedis Donabedian suggested the categories of *structure, process*, and *outcome* to examine health services and evaluate the quality of care. The Donabedian model continues to be a dominant paradigm for assessing the quality of health care. Robert Schalock, the author of *Outcome-based Evaluation*, emphasized the measurement of results.

There are many types of evaluation. Michael Scriven introduced the concepts of formative and summative evaluation. Formative evaluation monitors a program at intervals while the program is going on. Formative evaluation helps people modify or improve the program, often with a mid-course correction of some fine-tuning of a program element. Summative evaluation determines the overall effectiveness of the program at some endpoint. In recovery work, this might one day, 30 days, or a year. Program stages or milestones invite summative evaluation.

This book uses outcome, effort, and process to evaluate recovery work. The book urges both formative and summative evaluation.

Recovery Work

Evaluate recovery work in an honest open, systematic, objective. complete, and evidenced-based way. Address outcome, effort, and process. This evaluation. grounds and guides decisions about recovery work. Section III of each chapter evaluates recovery work and competency development.

Outcome

Outcome evaluation examines the expectations, effects, and results of recovery work. Insofar as possible, outcome evaluation is evidence-based. In Section III, readers review and rank chapter objectives as outcome indicators. The Strategic

Recovery Plan includes questions "Did you meet recovery objectives?" and "Did you reach recovery goals?"

Effort

Effort evaluation reviews the input or energy you invested in recovery work. Ask and answer the following questions. How hard did you work? How much time did you dedicate to recovery work? What resources did you employ for recovery work?

Process

Process evaluation is especially valuable when you want to improve outcome, increase the efficiency of recovery work, change the Strategic Recovery Plan, or strengthen competency development. Evaluate chapter work as evidence of process. Did you read the chapter narrative (Section I)? Did you complete chapter applications (Section II)? Did you evaluate recovery work and competency development (Section III)?

Decisions

Based on evaluation of recovery work, decide to celebrate, continue, correct, or change recovery work. Reward yourself with a positive thought, feeling, or action. Keep doing what you are doing if "it works." Review your Strategic Recovery Plan. Modify or adjust anything that is not working well. Review the stages and process of change. Plan and welcome change that supports recovery work. Section III suggests the following questions to evaluate decisions.

- Did you **celebrate** your recovery work in this chapter?
- Will you **continue** to approach recovery work in the same way in the next chapter?
- Do you plan to **correct** your approach to recovery work in the next chapter?
- Do you plan to **change** your approach to recovery work in the next chapter?

Competency Development

Health professional students and most employees are familiar with performance reviews, performance evaluations, or performance appraisals. Sometimes these evaluations are competency-based. Like students and employees, people with addiction develop and use competencies. It is important to monitor and evaluate competency development.

Experiential Learning Theory (ELT) emphasizes learning by doing, an effective way to develop competencies for recovery. Dewey's philosophical pragmatism, Lewin's social psychology, and Piaget's cognitive developmental genetic epistemology inform Experiential Learning Theory. Experiential Learning Theory guides evaluation of competency development.

While goals are the WHAT of performance, competencies are the HOW. Core competencies are knowledge, skills, and attitudes shared by and expected of all members of a group. Individuals may develop specialized competencies commensurate with their respective roles or responsibilities. Specialized business competencies could reflect production, marketing, or sales expectations. People in recovery might focus on relapse, physical fitness, support for ex-offenders.

A rubric as a grid-type structure to evaluate performance is especially useful to evaluate competency development. Rubrics include criteria, levels of performance, scores, and descriptors. *Criteria* list the features of the competency being reviewed. *Levels of performance* describe gradations in competency performance, usually from high to low: e.g., exceeds expectations, meets expectations, or needs improvement. *Scores* are simple point values to rate each criterion and are often combined with the levels of performance; 3 > 2 > 1. *Descriptors* describe what competency performance looks like at each level. This book includes a Rubric Review of Competency Development at the end of each chapter, prefaced with the following directions.

Outlines reflect competency dimensions and dynamics. Examine the criteria and your recovery work. Rate competency development as:

- **Exceeds expectations:** Criteria guide my understanding, application, and evaluation of recovery work > 90% of the time.
- **Meets expectations:** Criteria guide my understanding, application, and evaluation of recovery work 75% to 90% of the time.
- **Needs improvement:** Criteria guide my understanding, application, and evaluation of recovery work. < 75% of the time.

Section I presented facts, concepts, principles, and theories about evaluation, together with evaluations of recovery work and competency development.

II

Section II suggests applications about evaluation, together with evaluations of recovery work and competency development.

Theories, Models, and Types of Evaluation

1   Formative evaluation helps people modify or improve the program, often with a mid-course correction of some fine-tuning of a program element. Describe a formative evaluation of your recovery work.
2   Summative evaluation determines the overall effectiveness of the program at some endpoint: one day, 30 days, or a year. Describe the endpoint of some recovery work.

Recovery Work

3   Use a current recovery experience, preferably one where you completed a Strategic Recovery Plan. Complete the Evaluate Recovery Worksheet in Table 10.1.

Competency Development

Developing competencies for recovery is a process of acquisition and application, the broadening and deepening of learning over time.

Table 10.1 Evaluate Recovery Work

Questions	Answers Yes/No or Comment	Decisions Celebrate, Continue, Correct, or Change
Outcome Did you meet recovery objectives? Did you reach recovery goals? Did you realize recovery?		
Effort How hard did you work? How much time did you dedicate to recovery work? What resources did you employ for recovery work?		
Process: Did you • begin recovery work? • face addiction? • affirm recovery? • develop a strategic recovery plan? • set recovery goals? • determine motivation for recovery? • inventory resources and risks for recovery? • draft recovery objectives? • act for recovery? • evaluate recovery work and competency development? • record recovery work and competency development? • construct a recovery lifestyle?		

4   Comment on the process—acquisition and application, broadening and deepening of learning.

5   Why is "over time" needed to develop competencies?

Section II suggested applications about evaluation and evaluations of recovery work, competency development. Complete Chapter 10 with evaluations of the recovery work and competency development.

III

Evaluate recovery work and competency development.

1   Evaluate recovery work with a short True/False Quiz and a review of the outcome, effort, process, and decisions of recovery work.

    a   Quiz: Based on your learning from Chapter 10 Evaluate Recovery Work and Competency Development, indicate whether each of the following statements is True (T) or False (F).

        1   T or F   Professionals evaluate recovery work for people with addiction.

2 T or F Evaluation helps people decide to continue, improve, or change a plan or program.
3 T or F Evaluation is a subjective process.
4 T or F There are few theories, models, and concepts of evaluation.
5 T or F Evaluation is part of a Strategic Recovery Plan.
6 T or F Summative evaluation helps people modify or improve a plan or program.
7 T or F Formative evaluation determines the overall effectiveness of a plan or program at some endpoint.
8 T or F "Did you meet recovery objectives" is an example of outcome evaluation.
9 T or F "How much time did you dedicate to recovery work" is an example of effort evaluation.
10 T or F Reviewing work steps is an example of process evaluation.

(True: 2, 5, 8, 9, 10. False: 1, 3, 4, 6, 7)

b Outcome, Effort, Process, and Decisions

Examine the outcome, effort, process, and decision-making of your recovery work.

Outcome

Did you meet **objectives** for Chapter 10? Use Table 10.2 to review objectives and rank as:

Strongly disagree = 1
Disagree = 2
Undecided = 3
Agree = 4
Strongly agree = 5

Effort

Effort evaluation reviews the input or energy you invested in recovery work. Ask and answer the following questions.

- How hard did you work on Chapter 10?
- How much time did you dedicate to Chapter 10?
- What resources did you employ for Chapter 10 work?

Table 10.2 Objectives

Objectives	Rank
I review theories, models, concepts, and types of evaluation.	1, 2, 3, 4, 5
I evaluate recovery work, especially outcome, effort, process, and decisions.	1, 2, 3, 4, 5
I evaluate competency development with a KSA/Topic Matrix and a Rubric Review.	1, 2, 3, 4, 5

Table 10.3 Process

Process	Yes or No	Comment
I read the narrative (Section I).		
I completed the applications (Section II).		
I evaluated my recovery work and competency development (Section III).		

Process

Process evaluation is especially valuable when you want to improve outcome and increase the efficiency of your recovery work. Use Table 10.3 to evaluate process.

Decisions

Based on the evaluation of your recovery work from Chapter 10, decide to celebrate, continue, correct, or change your approach to recovery work. Reward yourself with a positive thought, feeling, or action. Keep doing what you are doing if "it works." Modify or adjust anything that is not working well. Plan and welcome change that supports your recovery work as you move on to Chapter 11. Ask and answer the following questions.

- Did you **celebrate** your recovery work from Chapter 10 "Evaluate Recovery Work and Competency Development"?
- Will you **continue** to approach recovery work in the same way in Chapter 11?
- Do you plan to **correct** your approach to recovery work in Chapter 11?
- Do you plan to **change** your approach to recovery work in Chapter 11?

2   Evaluate competency development using a KSA/Topic Matrix and a Rubric Review.

    a   What knowledge, skills, and attitudes are you using to develop Competency 10 Evaluate Recovery Work and Competency Development? Document KSA examples in Table 10.4 KSA/Topic Matrix.

    b   Outlines reflect competency dimensions and dynamics. Examine the criteria and your recovery work. Rank competency development on Table 10.5 as:

- **Exceeds expectations:** Criteria guide my understanding, application, and evaluation of recovery work > 90% of the time.
- **Meets expectations:** Criteria guide my understanding, application, and evaluation of recovery work 75% to 90% of the time.
- **Needs improvement:** Criteria guide my understanding, application, and evaluation of recovery work. < 75% of the time.

Table 10.4 KSA/Topic Matrix

Topics	Knowledge	Skills	Attitudes
Theories, Models, and Types of Evaluation			
Recovery Work Outcome Effort Process Decisions			
Competency Development KSA/Topic Matrix Rubric Review			

Table 10.5 Competency 10 Evaluate Recovery Work and Competency Development

Criteria	Exceeds Expectations 3	Meets Expectations 2	Needs Improvement 1
Theories, Models, and Types of Evaluation			
Recovery Work Outcome Effort Process Decisions			
Competency Development KSA/Topic Matrix Rubric Review			

Summary

Evaluate recovery work and competency development in Chapter 10. This chapter showed how to evaluate recovery work and competency development. Topics that provided the organizing framework for the chapter included Theories, Models, and Types of Evaluation; Evaluation of Recovery Work; and Evaluation of Competency Development. The chapter reviewed theories, models, and types of evaluation. It showed how to evaluate recovery work, especially outcome, effort, process, and decisions. The chapter used a KSA/Topic Matrix and Rubric Review to evaluate competency development. The chapter suggested applications—questions, worksheets, exercises, and projects—for the competency. Chapter 10 concluded with evaluations of recovery work and competency development.

11 Record Recovery Work and Competency Development

Peggy G. Records and Submits Recovery Reports for Monitoring

Following a short tempestuous love affair with alcohol, Peggy G. began recovery. She became a nurse and then a pediatric nurse practitioner. Peggy had six years of rewarding recovery when she sustained multiple fractures from a hit-and-run motor vehicle accident. Pain management included use of opioids and Peggy became addicted. Peggy hopped and shopped for more meds and then bought street drugs, including Fentanyl. One day she ran into a grateful father and healthy son she had helped as a nurse. She remembered how satisfying life had been. Following a 90-day residential program for professionals, Peggy enrolled in the state Health Practitioners Monitoring Program, signing a 5-year contract. At a Caduceus Meeting, Peggy learned that about 50% of RNs completed the HPMP program. About half of the participants left the program or were dismissed, most often for non-compliance, including failure to submit reports in a timely way. Peggy read the detailed Orientation Handbook two times. Her Case Manager suggested a way to habitually log in daily to ascertain her schedule for toxicology testing. "I am responsible for a Monthly Participant Report and a Monthly 12-Step Attendance Report. I am also responsible to see that all provider and worksite reports are submitted on time. Record and submit! Record and submit! Record and submit!"

Purpose: This chapter explains why we record recovery work and competency development.

Objectives

- Document your work for Section II Applications and Section III Evaluations for all chapters.
- Record work on the Strategic Recovery Plan.
- Use the Recovery Worksheet.
- Explore recovery writing opportunities through workbooks, journals, and the 12 Steps.
- Acknowledges the federal laws health practitioners use to protect the personal health information (PHI) of individuals with addiction.

DOI: 10.4324/9781003292944-11

- Understand the risks and benefits of electronic medical records (EMR) and electronic health records (EHR).

Outline

Document Throughout the Book

Section II Applications
Section III Evaluation
A Strategic Recovery Plan
Recovery Work Evaluation

Writing Opportunities

Workbooks
Journals
The 12 Steps

Documentation by Health Practitioners

42 CFR Part 2 and HIPAA
Electronic Health Records (EHR)

I

Record recovery work and competency development. Section I presents facts, concepts, principles, and theories about expected documentation throughout the book, recovery writing opportunities, and documentation by health practitioners.

Document Throughout the Book

"Show your work and save it." Adults may remember math class when teachers required more than the right answer: "show your work." Today, with the increased use of computers, "save it" completes personal, social, and occupational work. These two directives apply to recovery work and competency development by people in recovery and health practitioners: "show your work and save it."

12 Competency Applications

Competencies for Recovery has 12 chapters, one for each competency. Each chapter has three sections. Section I presents facts, concepts, principles, and theories about the competency. Section II suggests applications of the competency in the form of questions, worksheets, exercises, and projects. In Section III, readers evaluate recovery work. by taking a short True/False Quiz and by reviewing the outcome, effort, process, and decisions of work. Readers use a KSA//Topic Matrix and a Rubric Review to evaluate competency development. Documentation of Section II applications and Section III evaluations is expected.

A Strategic Plan for Recovery

People in recovery and health practitioners can use the Strategic Recovery Plan introduced in Chapter 4 to record recovery work. The plan reflects the signature features of strategic plans. The plan also incorporates knowledge, skills, and attitudes from the competencies for recovery. Record recovery work in the Plan's sections for *goals, motivation, resources, risks, objectives, action,* and *evaluation.*

Recovery Work Evaluation

Record the information collected and analyzed to evaluate recovery work. Evaluation helps people in recovery and health practitioners appraise recovery work and decide "what's next." Use the Recovery Worksheet introduced in Chapter 10. Ask and answer questions about outcome, effort, and process in an honest, open, systematic, and complete way. Based on answers and comments, decide to celebrate recovery, continue, correct, or change your approach to recovery work.

Set up a paper and pencil or online journal to monitor competency development trends and progress. Note especially accomplishments in the application of KSA dimensions or any change in the empowerment dynamic. Keep a log of your Rubric Reviews. Aim for "exceeds expectations."

Writing Opportunities

Workbooks

Written applications are part of most addiction treatment programs and many recovery services. Workbooks about addiction, recovery, relapse prevention, and many related issues abound, including hundreds of online materials. Workbooks offer information about a great variety of addiction/recovery topics. Many workbooks emphasize skill development. Some workbooks address feelings.

An addiction professional or peer support staff may suggest resources to match your interests, needs, and recovery stage. The Hazelden Publications Catalog, available as a hard copy or online, is perhaps the best single source of addiction/recovery materials for reading, study, and writing. Conduct a general Google search by topic or visit an online store like Amazon, Barnes & Noble, or Hazelden. Search by grouping factors such as people, addiction, recovery work, and related issues. See Table 11.1 for examples.

Table 11.1 Self-Help Workbooks in Bookstores and Online

People	Addiction	Recovery Work	Related Issues
Men	Addiction	Treatment	Trauma
Women	Relapse	Recovery	Abuse
Children	Neurobiology	Abstinence	Guilt
Teens	Brain	Harm Reduction	Shame
Older Adults	Alcohol	Relapse Prevention	Anger
Family	Marijuana	12 Steps	Resentments
LGBTQ	Heroin	SMART Recovery	Anxiety
Ethnicity	Cocaine	Amends	Depression
Race	Methamphetamines	Forgiveness	PTSD
Disability	Prescriptions	Service	Pain
Immigrant Status	Gambling	Health	Co-dependency
Other	Gaming	Wellness	Enabling
	Pornography	Well-being	Mindfulness
	Binge Eating	Spirituality	Empowerment
	Other	Other	Other

There are many online sources for printable 12-step worksheets. The SMART Recovery Toolbox provides a variety of methods, worksheets, and exercises to help individuals self-manage their addiction recovery and their life. Self-help workbooks support recovery growth.

Journals

For centuries, children and teens, adult men and women have kept diaries, journals, notebooks, logs, records. Remember *The Diary of a Young Girl* by Anne Frank, *Conversations with Myself* by Nelson Mandela, *The Travels of Marco Polo*, or *Mark Twain's Notebooks and Journals*.

Many people in recovery write in a journal. Journals are an effective way to monitor recovery work. Recording thoughts, feelings, and actions help people regulate emotions, experience mindfulness, manage stress, clarify thinking, and review actions. Writing in a journal sharpens memory and develops disciplined habits. Journals reflect insight, progress, and goal achievement. Journals for recovery take many forms; entries may be daily, weekly, or episodic.

- Mary writes an affirmation in her journal every morning.
- Bill checks his physical, mental, emotional, social, and spiritual well-being daily using an online template.
- Joyce ends her day with an "attitude of gratitude" entry in her journal.
- Harold uses a Daily Planner to record recovery activities.
- As part of his probation, Todd keeps an Anger Management Journal where he records feelings, thoughts, and actions, at least weekly.
- Scott enters one cognitive strategy and one behavioral strategy for each recovery risk in his Relapse Prevention Journal.

- Ellen replaces negative thoughts with positive thoughts online during work lunch break.
- Helen records meals and snacks in My Food Diary.
- Bill logs workout and fitness daily on an excel worksheet.

12 Steps

There are many 12-step workbooks and printable 12-step worksheets. People working the steps may share their written work with a counselor, peer support staff, or a sponsor. Writing the first step is often part of addiction treatment. Many people in recovery write out the fifth Step and share this experience with a sponsor or clergy. Several other steps invite writing. See also Steps 4 and 8.

AA Steps

Step 1. We admitted we were powerless over alcohol—that our lives had become unmanageable.
Step 4. Made a searching and fearless moral inventory of ourselves.
Step 5. Humbly asked Him to remove our shortcomings.
Step 8: Made a list of all persons we had harmed and became willing to make amends to them all.

Documentation by Health Practitioners

42 CFR Part 2 and HIPAA

Health practitioners who provide addiction treatment and recovery services document their work. Basic documentation describes what was done, by whom, and what results occurred. Good documentation is factual, complete, current, and organized. Client records support the continuity of care and collaboration between and among health professionals. Case management and quality assurance require timely, accurate records. Sound documentation supports outcome evaluation. Documentation helps ensure consent and expectations. It is often the basis for billing. Accurate, timely documentation protects providers against complaints and lawsuits. Currency in understanding and practice of laws that protect personal health information (PHI) is mandatory for all health practitioners.

Two important federal laws protect this personal health information (PHI). In 1970, Congress passed the Comprehensive Alcohol Abuse and Alcoholism Prevention, Treatment, and Rehabilitation Act, part of which contained general rules establishing the confidentiality of alcohol abuse patient records. Today (1920) we have the Confidentiality of Substance Use Disorder Patient Records, 42 CFR Part 2 which regulates the disclosure and use of patient records that include information on substance use diagnoses or services. The Health Insurance Portability Accountability Act of 1996 (HIPAA) requires health care providers and organizations, as well as their business associates, to develop and follow procedures that ensure the confidentiality and security of protected health information (PHI) when it is transferred, received, handled, or shared. Because of the stigma still associated with a substance use disorder, 42 CFR Part 2 has stricter regulations about disclosure than HIPAA.

Electronic Health Records

Today, most health practitioners record their work on an electronic medical record (EMR) or electronic health record. An electronic medical record (EMR) is a digital version of the traditional paper-based medical record or chart for an individual. Electronic entries include information about client demographics, insurance, releases, followed by intake, assessment, diagnosis, treatment plan, the treatment itself, session and progress notes, concluding with referrals and/or a discharge plan. The EMR represents a medical record, usually within a single facility, such as a doctor's office or a clinic. Usually, EMRs are not shared outside of the provider's practice.

An Electronic Health Record (EHR) is a digital version of health information, a comprehensive report of an individual's overall health. EHRs contain information from all providers involved in a person's care. EHRs may include a range of data, such as demographics, personal statistics like age and weight, billing information medical history, medication and allergies, immunization status, laboratory test results, radiology images, and vital signs, EHRs are designed and managed to facilitate sharing of information among health care providers and organizations. Sharing health information fosters communication and promotes collaboration among a health care team. Mega data from many sources enhances research and greatly enhances research using this mega data. While the benefits of sharing health information are legion, health practitioners and consumers need to be fully aware of the policies, procedures, and practices that govern the security and use of PHI.

Section I presented facts, concepts, principles, and theories about expected documentation throughout the book, recovery writing opportunities, and documentation by health practitioners. Continue recovery work in Section II with applications about this competency.

II

Section II suggests applications about recovery writing opportunities, documentation by health practitioners, and expected documentation throughout the book.

Recovery Writing Applications

1   Keep a journal for one week. Write down thoughts, feelings, and actions about a recovery topic of interest and importance to you: e.g., craving, resentments, forgiveness, happiness, balance, empowerment, or spirituality.

Table 11.2 Strategic Recovery Plan

Strategic Recovery Plan
Name: **Date:**
Goal:

Motivation
Importance: 1–10 =
Confidence: 1–10 =
Readiness: 1–10 =

Objectives	Resources	Action	Risks / Evaluation
1		1	**Outcome** Did you meet each objective? Yes, or No Did you reach the goal? Yes, or No
.		.	**Effort** How hard did you work to meet objectives and reach the goal? Consider time and resources.
2		2	**Process** How useful was the Strategic Recovery Plan?
3		3	**Decisions** Celebrate: Continue: Correct:
4		4	Change:

Table 11.3 Recovery Worksheet

Competency	Yes, No Date	Comments
1. Begin recovery work. • narrative • applications • evaluation		
2. Face addiction. • narrative • applications • evaluation		
3. Affirm recovery. • narrative • applications • evaluation		
4. Develop a strategic recovery plan. • narrative • applications • evaluation		
5. Set recovery goals. • narrative • applications • evaluation		

Competency	Yes, No Date	Comments
6. Determine motivation for recovery. • narrative • applications • evaluation		
7. Inventory resources and risks for recovery. • narrative • applications • evaluation		
8. Draft recovery objectives. • narrative • applications • evaluation		
9. Act for recovery. • narrative • applications • evaluation		
10. Evaluate recovery work and competency development. • narrative • applications • evaluation		

Competency	Yes, No Date	Comments
11. Record recovery work and competency development. • narrative • applications • evaluation		
12. Construct a recovery lifestyle. • narrative • applications • evaluation		

Monday
Tuesday
Wednesday
Thursday
Friday
Saturday
Sunday

Documentation by Health Practitioners

2   How important are anonymity and confidentiality about addiction and recovery for you?

Experience:
Opinion:

Table 11.4 Recovery Evaluation Worksheet

Questions	Answers Yes/ No with Comment	Decisions: Celebrate Continue Correct Change
Outcome Did you meet recovery objectives? Did you reach recovery goals? Did you realize recovery?		
Effort How hard did you work? How much time did you dedicate to recovery work? What resources did you employ for recovery work?		
Process Did you: • begin recovery work? • face addiction? • affirm recovery? • develop a strategic recovery plan? • set recovery goals? • determine motivation or recovery? • inventory resources and risks for recovery? • draft recovery objectives? • act for recovery? • evaluate recovery work and competency development? • record recovery work and competency development? • construct a recovery lifestyle?		

3   How important are anonymity and confidentiality about addiction treatment and recovery services for you?

Experience:
Opinion:

Document Throughout the Book

4   Record on the Strategic Recovery Plan. See Table 11.2.
5   Complete the Recovery Worksheet. Use Table 11.3.
6   Complete the Recovery Evaluation Worksheet. Use Table 11.4.

III

Evaluate recovery work and competency development.

1   Evaluate recovery work with a short True/False Quiz and a review of the
outcome, effort, process, and decisions of recovery work.

    a   Quiz: Based on your learning from Chapter 11 "Record Recovery
Work and Competency Development," indicate whether each of the
following statements is True (T) or False (F).

        1   T or F   "Show your work and save it" has little relevance for
recovery work.

        2   T or F   The 12 steps emphasize action and require little if any
writing.

        3   T or F   Applications are an important part of recovery work.

        4   T or F   Journals require daily entries.

        5   T or F   Workbooks about addiction and recovery are difficult
to find.

        6   T or F   The Health Insurance Portability Accountability Act of
1996 (HIPAA) protects confidentiality when personal
health information (PHI) is transferred, received, handled,
or shared.

        7   T or F   The Confidentiality of Substance Use Disorder Patient
Records, 42 CFR Part 2 regulates the disclosure and use
of patient records that include information on substance
use diagnoses or services.

        8   T or F   Because of stigma associated with addiction, anonymity
and confidentiality are especially important for people
with addiction.

        9   T or F   An Electronic Medical Recovery (EMR) is a medical
record, usually within a single facility, such as a doctor's
office or a clinic.

(True: 3, 6, 7, 8, 9, 10. False: 1, 2, 4, 5)

    b   Outcome, Effort, Process, and Decisions

Table 11.5 Objectives

Objectives	Rank
I document work for Section II Applications and Section III Evaluations for all chapters.	1, 2, 3, 4, 5
I record work on the Strategic Recovery Plan.	1, 2, 3, 4, 5
I use the Evaluate Recovery Work form.	1, 2, 3, 4, 5
I explore recovery writing opportunities through workbooks, journals, and the 12 Steps.	1, 2, 3, 4, 5
I acknowledge the federal laws health practitioners use to protect the personal health information (PHI) of individuals with addiction.	1, 2, 3, 4, 5
I understand the risks and benefits of electronic medical records (EMR) and electronic health records (EHR).	1, 2, 3, 4, 5

Examine the outcome, effort, process, and decisions of your recovery work in Chapter 11.

Outcome

Did you meet **objectives** for Chapter 11? Use Table 11.5 to review objectives and rank as:

Strongly disagree = 1
Disagree = 2
Undecided = 3
Agree = 4
Strongly agree = 5

Effort

Effort evaluation reviews the input or energy you invested in recovery work. Ask and answer the following questions.

- How hard did you work on Chapter 11?
- How much time did you dedicate to Chapter 11?
- What resources did you employ for Chapter 11 work?

Process

Process evaluation is especially valuable when you want to improve outcome and increase the efficiency of your recovery work. Use Table 11.6 to evaluate the process.

Table 11.6 Process

Process	Yes or No	Comment
I read the narrative (Section I).		
I completed the applications (Section II).		
I evaluated recovery work and competency development (Section III).		

Decisions

Based on the evaluation of your recovery work and competency development from Chapter 11, decide to celebrate, continue, correct, or change your approach to recovery work. Reward yourself with a positive thought, feeling, or action. Keep doing what you are doing if "it works." Modify or adjust anything that is not working well. Plan and welcome change that supports your recovery work as you move on to Chapter 12. Ask and answer the following questions.

- Did you **celebrate** your recovery work from Chapter 11 "Record Recovery Work and Competency Development"?
- Will you **continue** to approach recovery work in the same way in Chapter 12?
- Do you plan to **correct** your approach to recovery work in Chapter 12?
- Do you plan to **change** your approach to recovery work in Chapter 12?

2 Evaluate competency development using a KSA/Topic Matrix and a Rubric Review.

 a What knowledge, skills, and attitudes are you using to develop Competency 11 Record Recovery Work and Competency Development. Document KSA examples in Table 11.7 KSA/Topic Matrix.

 b Outlines reflect competency dimensions and dynamics. Examine the criteria and your recovery work. Rank competency development on Table 11.8 as

 - **Exceeds expectations:** Criteria guide my understanding, application, and evaluation of recovery work > 90% of the time.
 - **Meets expectations:** Criteria guide my understanding, application, and evaluation of recovery work 75% to 90% of the time.
 - **Needs improvement:** Criteria guide my understanding, application, and evaluation of recovery work. < 75% of the time.

Table 11.7 KSA/Topic Matrix

Topics	Knowledge	Skills	Attitudes
Document Throughout the Book Section II Applications Section III Evaluation Strategic Recovery Plan Evaluation of Recovery Work Form			
Writing Opportunities Workbooks Journals The 12 Steps			
Documentation by Health Practitioners CFR Part 2 and HIPAA Electronic Health Records (EHR)			

Table 11.8 Competency 11 Record Recovery Work and Competency Development

Criteria	Exceeds Expectations 3	Meets Expectations 2	Needs Improvement 1
Document Throughout the Book Section II Applications Section III Evaluation Strategic Recovery Plan Evaluation of Recovery Work Form			
Writing Opportunities Workbooks Journals The 12 Steps			
Documentation by Health Practitioners CFR Part 2 and HIPAA Electronic Health Records (EHR)			

Summary

Record recovery work and competency development in Chapter 11. This chapter explained why "we show and save recovery work." Topics that provided the organizing framework for the chapter included *Developing Competencies for Recovery*, Writing Opportunities, and Documentation by Health Practitioners. The chapter reviewed documentation expectations for Section II applications and Section III evaluations for each chapter. It urged recording work on the Strategic Recovery Plan and using the Evaluate Recovery Work form. It explored recovery writing opportunities through workbooks, journals, and the 12 Steps. It acknowledged the federal laws health practitioners use to protect the personal health information of individuals with addiction, including the risks and benefits of electronic medical records and electronic health records. The chapter suggested applications—questions, worksheets, exercises, and projects—for the competency. Chapter 11 concluded with evaluations of recovery work and competency development.

12 Construct a Recovery Lifestyle

Mike and Melissa K. Construct a Recovery Lifestyle

Mike and Melissa K. constructed a recovery lifestyle. Both are abstinent from alcohol, pot, and misuse of psychotropic medications: Mike for seven years, Melissa for nine years. "Addiction was a living hell, but we didn't know it. We were high-functioning alcoholics/addicts (HFAs)." Mike was President and CEO of a Wealth Management Company. Melissa was a tenured college professor, teaching computer science. I had 15-year-old twins, Robert and Rachel; Melissa recalls "I saw a mental health counselor for advice about Mike's drinking, increasing anger, and volatile outburst. After her comprehensive assessment, she referred me to an Intensive Outpatient Program (IOP) to address my drinking. She suggested I return to work with her on what she called 'serious related issues'." Surprised? But I followed through. In the next five years, I got better physically, mentally, and spiritually. Home-life was a smoldering volcano with frequent eruptions followed by smoking wreckage. Rachel and I moved out of the house for three months, returning when Mike agreed to get help. He attended the noon AA meeting with me, expressing surprise at the stories some of the businessmen told. Someone he knew welcomed him. Mike mumbled something about "being there with me." Mike picks up the account. "I saw my primary care physician (PCP) the next day and because I was by now a heavy daily drinker, he wrote admission orders for hospital-based detoxification treatment. Upon discharge, I continued seeing an addiction psychologist weekly and began attending AA meetings: not the same ones Melissa frequented. We are living proof of 'how it works.' As Chapter 5 in the big book says, 'Rarely have we seen a person fail who has thoroughly followed our path.' The kids have had a tough time, especially Robbie. When he was 16 years old, he totaled a jeep we bought for him while drunk. He completed a vocational track in high school and is presently an apprentice in an EMT/Firefighter Program. We still worry about his drinking, drug use, and 'thrill-seeking personality.' He lives at home. Rachel is in college, away from home. She seems okay but has many of the cardinal characteristics of an adult child of alcoholics (ACOA). Fortunately, she is in therapy but does not talk too much about the sessions. Melissa and I continue our careers, with a balanced work week for ourselves, each other, the kids (when around), and the community. We are active in our respective AA home groups. Melissa is a volunteer mentor for foreign medical students at the hospital. I am running for a seat in the state House of Delegates. Life is good. Recovery works!"

Purpose: This chapter describes the construction of a recovery lifestyle.

DOI: 10.4324/9781003292944-12

Objectives

- Credit the Viennese psychiatrist Alfred Adler with the origin of the construct *lifestyle*.
- Note definitions and examples of lifestyle today.
- Examine construction as a concept and competency.
- Review frequently asked questions (FAQs) about constructing a recovery lifestyle.
- Recognize the parallel dimensions and dynamics of self-states, Maslow's needs, Life in Recovery, and recovery goals.
- Embrace *The Promises* of Alcoholics Anonymous.
- Attain milestones to construct a recovery lifestyle.

Outline

Lifestyle

Alfred Adler
Lifestyle Today

Construction

Concept
Competency

A Recovery Lifestyle

FAQs
Dimensions and Dynamics
The Promises

Milestones to Construct a Recovery Lifestyle

Acceptance
Action
Affirmation
Advocacy

I

Construct a recovery lifestyle. Section I presents facts, concepts, principles, and theories about lifestyle, construction, a recovery lifestyle, and milestones to construct a recovery lifestyle.

Lifestyle

Alfred Adler

Alfred Adler (1870–1937) was a leading Viennese psychiatrist who created the field of Individual Psychology. He emphasized a holistic approach to studying human cognition, behavior, and emotion. Adler is credited with the *construct* style of life and the term lifestyle.

Style of life is a personality feature that reflects the unity of an individual's way of thinking, feeling, and acting. It reflects a person's unique, unconscious, and characteristic way of responding to (or avoiding) the main tasks of daily living. Lifestyle is the total of the values, passions, knowledge, meaningful actions, and eccentricities that constitute the uniqueness of each individual. Lifestyle is the core schema of a person; it affects and is evident in everything the individual does, thinks, and perceives expressing itself in all behavior.

For Adler, there were four primary lifestyles; see Box 12.1. Three of them he said were "mistaken styles." These three "mistaken styles" resemble active addiction while the fourth lifestyle suggests recovery. Classical Adlerian psychotherapy attempts to dissolve the archaic styles of life such as active addiction and stimulate a more creative approach to living: a recovery lifestyle.

Box 12.1 Adlerian Primary Lifestyles

- **The ruling type:** aggressive, dominating people who have limited social interest or cultural perception.
- **The getting type:** dependent people who take rather than give.
- **The avoiding type:** people who try to escape life's problems with little socially constructive activity.
- **The socially useful type:** people with a great deal of social interest and activity.

Adler investigated the causes and treatment of substance use disorders, particularly "alcoholism and morphinism," which were serious social problems. Adler's work with addicts was significant since most other prominent psychiatrists gave little time or thought to this "widespread ill" of their times.

Although Adler developed a theory of Individual Psychology, he was the first psychiatrist to emphasize the importance of the social element of the individual. Adler brought psychiatry into the community. His theory and therapeutic approach influenced the child guidance movement, elementary education, parenting styles, and family therapy. Today, the Adler Institute is a small, professional group of like-minded individuals who study and apply his theory and practice. The *Manual for Lifestyle Assessment* by Dr. Bernard H. Schulman and Dr. Harold H. Mosak, first published in 1988, and now available as an eBook, describes in detail the theory and practice of Adlerian Lifestyle Assessment.

Lifestyle Today

Current definitions of lifestyle resemble the original construct Adler developed 100 years ago. For example:

- how a person or group lives
- the typical way of life of an individual, group, or culture
- the way a person lives including patterns of social relations, consumption, entertainment, and dress as well as attitudes, values, or world view
- the physical, psychological, social, and economic values, interests, opinions, and behaviors of a certain individual, group, or community
- the habits, attitudes, tastes, moral standards, economic level, that together constitute the mode of living of an individual or group
- spiritual elements of self together with the natural and social world of people places, and things.

Lifestyle embraces the individual and environment: the physical, mental, emotional, and spiritual elements of self together with the natural and social world of people places, and things. As such, lifestyle integrates the elements of self and surroundings. Lifestyle includes the habits, attitudes, tastes, moral standards, and economic level that constitute the mode of living of an individual or group we recognize as healthy lifestyles, unhealthy lifestyles, and alternatives.

Today, we recognize healthy lifestyles, unhealthy lifestyles, and alternative lifestyles. We notice the lifestyles of the rich and famous or the "royals." Diagnostic criteria from the *DSM-5* document well the features of an addictive lifestyle. Mastering addiction, living well, and doing good reflect a recovery lifestyle. "Old-timers" at 12-step meetings often suggest that people in recovery "remember when," or "keep the memory green." This does not mean dwelling on the past, especially one's active addiction and addictive lifestyle, but is an opportunity to learn from the past. Often men and men, who tell their stories at a recovery meeting, compare and contrast an addictive lifestyle with a recovery lifestyle.

Construction

Concept

Construction is a general term meaning the art and science to form objects, systems, or organizations. Construct is the verb: the act of building. The noun construction is both tangible like a structure or intangible like a theoretical framework.

Over the centuries people have constructed cathedrals, built trans-continental rail systems, and formed societies. Individuals construct reality. Men and women construct recovery lifestyles. For example, the book *The Social Construction of Reality* (1966) by Peter L. Berger and Thomas Luckmann was called the "fifth-most important sociological book of the 20th century" by the International Sociological

Association. Construction is the way individuals with addiction build a recovery lifestyle. Construction is a step-by-step process, often over a long time, for people to create and craft a way of life we call recovery.

Competency

Competencies reflect cognitive, affective, and psychomotor domains of learning. Chapter 8 shows how to use these domains to draft recovery objectives. Functions within each domain are characterized by progressive levels of behaviors from simple to complex, a so-called taxonomy. The highest levels of functioning from each domain describe well how to construct a recovery lifestyle. Use the action verbs to draft objectives to construct a recovery lifestyle; see Table 12.1.

A Recovery Lifestyle

Frequently Asked Questions (FAQs) About Constructing a Recovery Lifestyle

What is a recovery lifestyle?

A recovery lifestyle is a way of life characterized by abstinence or harm reduction and relapse prevention; health, wellness, and well-being, together with helping, service, and altruism.

Why do people with addiction construct a recovery lifestyle?

Addiction jeopardizes the health and well-being of individuals, families, communities, even society. Addiction causes impairment, disability, and death.

Who constructs a recovery lifestyle?

People with addiction who choose life, personal growth, and service to others construct a recovery lifestyle. "Rarely have we seen a person fail who has thoroughly followed our path." So, say the recovery men and women who wrote Chapter 5, "How it Works," in *Alcoholics Anonymous*.

Where do people with addiction build a recovery lifestyle?

Table 12.1 Action Verbs for a Recovery Lifestyle

Domain	Level	Verbs
Cognitive	Creating	categorize, combine, compile, compose, create, devise, design, explain, generate, modify, organize, plan, rearrange, reconstruct, relate, reorganize, revise, rewrite, summarize, tell, write
Affective	Internalizing Values (Characterization)	act, discriminate, display, influence, listen, modify, perform, practice, propose, qualify, question, revise, serve, solve, verify
Psychomotor	Origination	arrange, build, combine, compose, construct, create, design, initiate, make, originate

Recovery people build a recovery lifestyle anywhere and everywhere, using personal assets, social capital, professional services, and peer supports. Step 12 of AA, NA, and GA suggest that people with addiction "practice these principles in all our affairs."

When does recovery become a recovery lifestyle?

People with one–five years of sustained recovery demonstrate some of the characteristics of a recovery lifestyle. Most people with greater than five years of stable recovery are good candidates for a recovery lifestyle.

How do people with addiction construct a recovery lifestyle?

Consistent use of a competency-based strategic recovery plan over time helps people with addiction construct a recovery lifestyle.

Dimensions and Dynamics

Chapter 5, "Set Recovery Goals," recognized the parallel dimensions and dynamics of existential self-states, Maslow's Hierarchy of Needs, findings from the Life in Recovery survey, and nine basic recovery goals. Review these associations again in Table 12.2.

A recovery lifestyle reflects self-states, Maslow's needs, and Life in Recovery findings and manifests recovery goals.

The Promises

The AA Promises exemplify well a recovery lifestyle. The Promises are read at many AA Meetings and can be found in Chapter 6 "Into Action," on pages 83–84 of *Alcoholics Anonymous* (4th ed.).

If we are painstaking about this phase of our development, we will be amazed before we are halfway through. We are going to know a new freedom and a new happiness. We will not regret the past nor wish to shut the door on it. We will comprehend the word serenity and we will know peace. No matter how far down the scale we have gone, we will see how our experience can benefit others. That feeling of uselessness and self-pity will disappear. We will

Table 12.2 Parallel Self-States, Maslow's Needs, Life in Recovery, and Recovery Goals

Self-States	Maslow's Needs	Life in Recovery	Recovery Goals
Being	Physiological Needs Safety Needs	Abstinence	Abstinence Harm Reduction Relapse Prevention
Becoming	Love and Belonging Esteem	Personal Growth	Health Wellness Well-being
Beyond	Self-actualization Transcendence	Service to Others	Helping Service Altruism

lose interest in selfish things and gain interest in our fellows. Self-seeking will slip away. Our whole attitude and outlook upon life will change. Fear of people and of economic insecurity will leave us. We will intuitively know how to handle situations which used to baffle us. We will suddenly realize that God is doing for us what we could not do for ourselves.

Are these extravagant promises? We think not. They are being fulfilled among us—sometimes quickly, sometimes slowly. They will always materialize if we work for them.

(The excerpt from *Alcoholics Anonymous*, the Big Book, pages 83–84, is reprinted with permission of Alcoholics Anonymous World Services, Inc. ("A.A. W.S."). Permission to reprint this excerpt does not mean that A.A.W.S. has reviewed or approved the contents of this publication, or that A.A. necessarily agrees with the views expressed herein. A.A. is a program of recovery from alcoholism only—use of the 12 Steps in connection with programs and activities which are patterned after A.A., but which address other problems, or in any other non-A.A. context, does not imply otherwise.)

Milestones to Construct a Recovery Lifestyle

We identify four milestones or significant stages people with addiction attain to construct a recovery lifestyle: acceptance, action, affirmation, and advocacy.

Acceptance

Acceptance is a person's assent to the reality of a situation Acceptance means recognizing a condition, a circumstance, a process (often a negative or uncomfortable situation) as real. Acceptance is an honest acknowledgment, ownership of one's drinking, using, gambling, or addiction. Acceptance does not imply the person likes the situation. For example, Mary was recently diagnosed with Type 2 diabetes (T2D). "I am not thrilled with the diagnosis. I'm relieved I don't have cancer. I can learn to manage my diabetes and live well."

AA scholars suggest Step One reflects the principle of *acceptance*. "We admitted we were powerless over alcohol and that our lives had become unmanageable." See also the "Acceptance Prayer" on page 417 of the big book *Alcoholics Anonymous*, (4th ed.). On a lighter note, a dill pickle cannot turn back into a cucumber. Some AA members view *surrender* as a form of acceptance. Recovery stories describe the strength, peace, and serenity that comes when a "sick and suffering alcoholic stops struggling and surrenders to win."

Unfortunately, people with addiction have strong defense mechanisms that mitigate against acceptance; they deny, minimize, rationalize, justify, blame, project, intellectualize, explain, blame, generalize, avoid, and defy to protect their addictive lifestyle. Remember, the addictive process is strong! Acceptance is more than admission and surrender. Over time, individuals develop acceptance of their addiction. Acceptance is the first milestone to attain to construct a recovery lifestyle.

Action

Recovery is NOT a spectator sport. Bob A. remembers seeing a poster on the wall at an AA meeting that read "Do something! Lead, follow, or get out of the way."

Action is the process of doing something, especially when dealing with a problem or difficulty, typically to achieve an aim. An action is a thing done, a deed. Action also means accomplishing something, often over time.

Act for recovery is a core competency. In Chapter 9, we suggest an action hierarchy of acts, habits, skills, and competencies. As discussed, competencies are clusters of related knowledge, skills, and attitudes (KSAs) that equip, enable, and empower a person to **act** effectively, usually with proficiency. A recovery lifestyle reflects recovery goal achievement over time, usually greater than three–five years.

When an action elicits a desirable response (outcome), it is more likely to be repeated. Early recovery is a process of action and reward: one day at a day, for 30 days, 60 days, 90 days; even the first year. The addictive process is strong. Relapse characterizes the addiction cycle. It is often an uphill battle to stay abstinent or maintain a harm reduction program and in early recovery. A 90-day treatment program, medication-assisted treatment (MAT), counseling, peer support, recovery residencies, mutual self-help groups, together with understanding family and friends help people with addiction reach early recovery goals. Usually, people with addiction demonstrate sustained or stable recovery as a prelude to a recovery lifestyle. Over time, people with addiction act to meet recovery objectives and reach recovery goals. A recovery lifestyle is a dynamic way of life; see Box 12.2.

Box 12.2 A Recovery Lifestyle

Master Addiction

- maintain abstinence or
- continue harm reduction
- prevent relapse

Live Well

- promote health
- achieve wellness
- experience well-being

Do Good

- help others
- serve society
- do the right thing

Action is the second milestone people attain to construct a recovery lifestyle.

Affirmation

An affirmation is a statement or sign that something is true and valued; it is the act of saying YES or of showing that you mean yes. An affirmation is the opposite of denial. To *affirm* is to state, declare, announce, pronounce, assert, confirm, or verify with confidence that something is true and valued. For example, a person with addiction who constructs a recovery lifestyle would proclaim:

- YES to life!
- YES to personal growth!
- YES to service!

Affirmation is the third milestone people attain to construct a recovery lifestyle.

Advocacy

The moral model of addiction contributes to the stigma people with addiction experience and their practice of anonymity. Anonymity is the foundation of most 12-step programs. AA Tradition 12 states "Anonymity is the spiritual foundation of all our Traditions, ever reminding us to place principles before personalities." Federal laws like HIPAA protect personal health information (PHI); see especially 42 CFR Part 2, which regulates the disclosure and use of patient records that include information on substance use diagnoses or services.

Addiction treatment and recovery is often a private affair or at most a shared experience with addiction/recovery providers, peer support staff, mutual-self-help groups, together with family and close friends. Individuals with addiction can construct a recovery lifestyle through acceptance, action, and affirmation. Yet, many people in long-term recovery seek more than life and personal growth.

Thousands of people with long-term recovery accept Bill W.'s message, "I am responsible." The Responsibility Declaration was formally introduced there by Bill W. It states, "I am Responsible. When anyone, anywhere, reaches out for help, I want the hand of AA always to be there. And for that: I am responsible." Responsible recovery people may take a neighbor to an AA meeting, maintain a recovery website, or facilitate a weekly support meeting within a prison.

Advocacy is another way people in recovery transcend self through service. Perhaps the simplest and most well-known definition of advocacy is to defend or promote a cause. Advocacy is active, not passive: identify, influence, support, recommend, represent, defend, intervene, and change. Advocacy is the act of speaking on the behalf of or in support of another person, place, or thing. Advocates publicly express their interest in specific causes and take clear actions to support the positive advancement of those causes. In contrast to much addiction treatment and recovery which is anonymous, advocacy is public. Social, economic, or political institutions are often targets of advocacy.

FACES & VOICES OF RECOVERY

Faces & Voices of Recovery was founded in 2001 to provide a focus for a growing advocacy force among people in long-term recovery from addiction to alcohol and other drugs, their families, friends, and allies. Faces & Voices of Recovery is dedicated to organizing and mobilizing the over 23 million Americans in recovery from addiction to alcohol and other drugs, our families, friends, and allies into recovery community organizations and networks, to promote the right and resources for recovery through advocacy, education and demonstrating the power and proof of long-term recovery. Its Mission is to change the way addiction and recovery are understood and embraced through advocacy, education, and leadership. Faces & Voices of Recovery works hard to advocate for public policies and funding that support addiction recovery for all. See especially its Recovery Bill of Rights and the Life in Recovery Surveys.

THE NEW RECOVERY ADVOCACY MOVEMENT

Spearheaded by William White in the 1990s, the New Recovery Advocacy Movement (NRAM) is a social movement led by people in addiction recovery and their allies aimed at altering public and professional attitudes toward addiction recovery, promulgating recovery-focused policies and programs, and supporting efforts to break intergenerational cycles of addiction and related problems. The heart of the NRAM is a collaboration among local, national, and international Recovery Community Organizations (RCO). See also The Association of Recovery Community Organizations (ARCO) at Faces & Voices of Recovery.

SUBSTANCE ABUSE AND ADDICTION RECOVERY ALLIANCE (SAARA) OF VIRGINIA

The Substance Abuse and Addiction Recovery Alliance (SAARA) of Virginia is a grassroots Recovery Community Organization. "We transform communities through hope, education, and advocacy for addiction prevention, treatment, and recovery. All friends of recovery are invited and welcome to join us." Founded in 1997, The Substance Abuse and Addiction Recovery Alliance of Virginia (SAARA) is a statewide organization advocating for individuals and families affected by substance use disorder (SUD) and addiction. SAARA's core pillars are to Advocate, Educate and Support SUD and addiction communities. SAARA is committed to mobilizing supporters to work with legislators and other decision-makers to enhance our substance use disorder (SUD) and addiction system of care in Virginia. SAARA facilitates educational training for Peer Recovery Specialists and Community Supporters. SAARA provides Peer Recovery Support Services across the community. Note: The author was a founding member of Williamsburg, VA SAARA.

Advocacy is the fourth milestone people attain, especially when service becomes an important part of a recovery lifestyle.

SAMHSA OFFICE OF RECOVERY

On September 30, 2021, SAMHSA launched the Office of Recovery. SAMHSA identified recovery as a cross-cutting principle throughout SAMHSA's policies and programs. Growing and expanding recovery support services nationwide is a core component of the new office. According to SAMHSA, the Office of Recovery will promote the involvement of people with lived experience throughout agency and stakeholder activities, foster relationships with internal and external organizations in the mental health and addiction recovery fields, and identify health disparities in high-risk and vulnerable populations to ensure equity for support services across the Nation. Follow this initiative on the SAMHSA website.

Section I presented facts, concepts, principles, and theories about lifestyle, construction, a recovery lifestyle, and milestones to construct a recovery lifestyle.

Continue recovery work in Section II with applications about the competency.

II

Section II suggests applications about lifestyle, construction, a recovery lifestyle, and milestones to construct a recovery lifestyle.

Lifestyle

1   What is your understanding of lifestyle?
2   Describe the lifestyle of two people: one famous public person and another "regular" individual who meets classic and contemporary definitions of lifestyle.

    a   Lifestyle of a famous person:
    b   Lifestyle of a "regular" individual:

Construction

3   Describe something you have constructed: a playhouse for your children, perhaps an idea for a work project that originated with you.
4   Why does a recovery lifestyle require construction?

A Recovery Lifestyle

5   Answer the FAQs about a recovery lifestyle.

> **What** is a recovery lifestyle?
> **Why** do people with addiction construct a recovery lifestyle?
> **Who** constructs a recovery lifestyle?
> **Where** do people with addiction build a recovery lifestyle?
> **When** does recovery become a recovery lifestyle?
> **How** do people with addiction construct a recovery lifestyle?

6   Compare and contrast your answers to these FAQs with those given in the chapter.

The Promises of Alcoholics Anonymous

7   The Promises of Alcoholics Anonymous reflect recovery. Complete the following worksheet. Read each statement. Use a continuum scale of 1–5, with five being strongly agree and 1 being strongly disagree. Assess, and perhaps affirm, your recovery today on Table 12.3.

"Are these extravagant promises? We think not. They are being fulfilled for us sometimes quickly, sometimes slowly. They will always materialize if we work for them" (*Alcoholics Anonymous*, pp. 83–84).

Table 12.3 The Promises

The Promises *If we are painstaking about this phase of my development, we will be amazed before we are halfway through.*	Today
We are going to know a new freedom and a new happiness.	1 2 3 4 5
We will not regret the past nor wish to shut the door on it.	1 2 3 4 5
We will comprehend the word serenity and we will know peace.	1 2 3 4 5
No matter how far down the scale we have gone, we will see how our experience can benefit others.	1 2 3 4 5
That feeling of uselessness and self-pity will disappear.	1 2 3 4 5
We will lose interest in selfish things and gain interest in my fellows.	1 2 3 4 5
Self-seeking will slip away.	1 2 3 4 5
Our whole attitude and outlook upon life will change.	1 2 3 4 5
Fear of people and of economic insecurity will leave us.	1 2 3 4 5
We will intuitively know how to handle situations which used to baffle us.	1 2 3 4 5
We will suddenly realize that God is doing for us what we could not do for ourselves.	1 2 3 4 5

Milestones to Construct a Recovery Lifestyle

8 How have you accepted your addiction?
9 Comment on the statement, "Recovery is NOT a spectator sport."
10 How do you affirm your recovery?
11 How is advocacy part of your recovery?

Section II suggested applications about lifestyle, construction, a recovery lifestyle, and milestones to construct a recovery lifestyle. Complete Chapter 12 with evaluations of recovery work and competency development in Section III.

III

Evaluate recovery work and competency development.

1   Evaluate recovery work with a short True/False Quiz and a review of the outcome, effort, process, and decisions of recovery work.

    a   Quiz: Based on your learning from Chapter 12 "Construction a Recovery Lifestyle," indicate whether each of the following statements is True (T) or False (F).

        1   T or F   Bill W. is credited with the *construct* style of life and the term lifestyle.

        2   T or F   A recovery lifestyle is a way of life characterized by abstinence or harm reduction and relapse prevention; health, wellness, and well-being, together with helping, service, and altruism.

        3   T or F   Construction is the way individuals with addiction build a recovery lifestyle.

        4   T or F   Construction is a step-by-step process, often over a long time, people employ to create and craft a recovery way of life.

        5   T or F   Recovery people build a recovery lifestyle during treatment.

        6   T or F   People with 90 days clean and sober demonstrate a recovery lifestyle.

        7   T or F   Consistent use of a competency-based strategic recovery plan over time helps people with addiction construct a recovery lifestyle.

        8   T or F   A recovery lifestyle reflects self-states, Maslow's Hierarchy of Needs, Life in Recovery Survey findings, and recovery goals.

        9   T or F   The Promises of Alcoholics Anonymous (AA) exemplify well a recovery lifestyle.

      10   T or F   There are four milestones or significant stages people with addiction attain to construct a recovery lifestyle: acceptance, action, affirmation, and advocacy.

(True: 2, 3, 4, 7, 8, 9, 10. False: 1, 5, 6)

b   Outcome, Effort, Process, and Decisions

Examine the outcome, effort, process, and decisions of your recovery work in Chapter 12.

Outcome

Did you meet **objectives** for Chapter 12? Use Table 12.4 to review objectives and rank as:

Strongly disagree = 1
Disagree = 2
Undecided = 3
Agree = 4
Strongly agree = 5

Effort

Effort evaluation reviews the input or energy you invested in recovery work. Ask and answer the following questions.

- How hard did you work on Chapter 12?
- How much time did you dedicate to Chapter 12?
- What resources did you employ for Chapter 12 work?

Process

Process evaluation is especially valuable when you want to improve outcome and increase the efficiency of your recovery work. Use Table 12.5 to evaluate process.

Table 12.4 Objectives

Objectives	Rank
I credit the Viennese psychiatrist Alfred Adler with the origin of the construct *lifestyle*.	1, 2, 3, 4, 5
I note definitions and examples of lifestyle today.	1, 2, 3, 4, 5
I examine construction as a concept and competency.	1, 2, 3, 4, 5
I review frequently asked questions (FAQs) about constructing a recovery lifestyle…	1, 2, 3, 4, 5
I recognize the parallel dimensions and dynamics of self-states, Maslow's needs, Life in Recovery, and recovery goals.	1, 2, 3, 4, 5
I embrace *The Promises* of Alcoholics Anonymous.	1, 2, 3, 4, 5
I attain milestones to construct a recovery lifestyle.	1, 2, 3, 4, 5

Table 12.5 Process

Process	Yes or No	Comment
I read the narrative (Section I).		
I completed the applications (Section II).		
I evaluated recovery work and competency development (Section III).		

Decisions

Based on the evaluation of your recovery work from Chapter 12, decide to celebrate, continue, correct, or change your approach to recovery work. Reward yourself with a positive thought, feeling, or action. Keep doing what you are doing if "it works." Modify or adjust anything that is not working well. Plan and welcome change that supports your recovery work. Ask and answer the following questions.

- Did you **celebrate** your recovery work from Chapter 12 "Construct a Recovery Lifestyle"?
- Will you **continue** to approach recovery work in the same way?
- Do you plan to **correct** your approach to recovery work?
- Do you plan to **change** your approach to recovery work?

2   Evaluate competency development using a KSA/Topic Matrix and a Rubric Review.

    a   What knowledge, skills, and attitudes are you using to develop Competency 12 Construct a Recovery Lifestyle? Document KSA examples in Table 12.6 KSA/Topic Matrix.

    b   Outlines reflect competency dimensions and dynamics. Examine the criteria and your recovery work. Rank competency development on Table 12.7 KSA/Topic Matrix.

        - **Exceeds expectations:** Criteria guide my understanding, application, and evaluation of recovery work > 90% of the time.
        - **Meets expectations:** Criteria guide my understanding, application, and evaluation of recovery work 75% to 90% of the time.
        - **Needs improvement:** Criteria guide my understanding, application, and evaluation of recovery work. < 75% of the time.

Table 12.6 KSA/Topic Matrix

Topics	Knowledge	Skills	Attitudes
Lifestyle Alfred Adler Lifestyle Today			
Construction Concept Competency			
A Recovery Lifestyle FAQs Dimensions and Dynamics The Promises			
Milestones to Construct a Recovery Lifestyle Acceptance Action Affirmation Advocacy			

Table 12.7 Competency 12 Construct a Recovery Lifestyle

Criteria	Exceeds Expectations 3	Meets Expectations 2	Needs Improvement 1
Lifestyle Alfred Adler Lifestyle Today			
Construction Concept Competency			
A Recovery Lifestyle FAQs Dimensions and Dynamics The Promises			
Milestones to Construct a Recovery Lifestyle Acceptance Action Affirmation Advocacy			

Summary

Construct a recovery lifestyle in Chapter 12. This chapter proposed the construction of a recovery lifestyle. Topics that provided the organizing framework for the chapter included Lifestyle, Construction, A Recovery Lifestyle, and Milestones to Construct a Recovery Lifestyle. The chapter credited the Viennese psychiatrist Alfred Adler with the origin of the construct *lifestyle*. It noted definitions and examples of lifestyle today. The chapter examined construction as a concept and competency. It reviewed frequently asked questions about constructing a recovery lifestyle. It recognized the parallel dimensions and dynamics of self-states, Maslow's needs, Life in Recovery, and recovery goals. The chapter embraced *The Promises* of Alcoholics Anonymous. Acceptance, action, affirmation, and advocacy are milestones to construct a recovery lifestyle. The chapter suggested applications—questions, worksheets, exercises, and projects—for the competency. Chapter 12 concluded with evaluations of recovery work and competency development.

Resources for Recovery

Support Groups

Alcoholics Anonymous https://aa.org

Alcoholics Anonymous was founded in 1935 by Bill Wilson (known as Bill W.) and Robert Smith (known as Dr. Bob). AA is an international fellowship of men and women who want to do something about their drinking problem. It is nonprofessional, self-supporting, multiracial, apolitical, and available almost everywhere. There are no age or education requirements. This website includes a daily reflection, meeting lists, literature, videos, as well recovery resources, and news.

Narcotics Anonymous (NA) https://na.org

Narcotics Anonymous is a global, community-based organization with a multilingual and multicultural membership, founded in 1953, that provides literature, other produces, and meeting sites for men and women for whom drugs have become a major problem.

Gamblers Anonymous (GA) https://gamblersanonymous.org

Gamblers Anonymous is a fellowship of men and women who share their experience, strength, and hope with each other that they may solve their common problem and help others to recover from a gambling problem. The website connects individuals with meetings and hotlines to talk with someone "now."

Over Eaters Anonymous (OA) https://oa.org

Overeaters Anonymous is a twelve-step program founded in 1960 for people with problems related to food including, compulsive overeaters, binge eating, and individuals with diagnoses of feeding and eating disorders. The only requirement for memberships is a desire to stop eating compulsively. "We welcome everyone who feels they have an unhealthy relationship or problem

DOI: 10.4324/9781003292944-13

with food or body image. OA is a community of people who support each other to recover from compulsive eating and unhealthy food behavior."

Sexaholics Anonymous (SA) https://sa.org

Sexaholics Anonymous founded in 1979 is one of several twelve-step programs for compulsive sexual behavior based on the original twelve steps of Alcoholics Anonymous. SA takes its place among various twelve-step groups that seek recovery from sexual addiction: Sex Addicts Anonymous, Sex and Love Addicts Anonymous, Sexual Compulsives Anonymous, and Sexual Recovery Anonymous. Collectively these groups are referred to as "S" groups since all their acronyms begin with that letter: SA, SAA, SLAA, SCA, SRA.

On-Line Gamers Anonymous (OLGA) https://olganon.org

On-Line Gamers Anonymous®, founded in 2002, is a 12-step self-help group. Members share their experience, strength, and hope to help and support each other recover and heal from problems resulting from excessive video game playing (gaming disorder). "We know how powerful, cunning, baffling and destructive excessive video game playing can be, to some. It can be devastating to the real-world lives of gamers and those close to them. OLGA provides resources for open discussion, support, information, and professional referrals."

SMART Recovery https://smartrecovery.org

Self-Management and Recovery Training (SMART) is a global community of mutual support groups. At meetings, participants help one another resolve problems with any addiction (to drugs or alcohol or activities such as gambling or over-eating). Participants find and develop the power within themselves to change and lead fulfilling and balanced lives guided by a science-based, sensible 4-Point Program.

In the Rooms (ITR) https://intherooms.com

In the Rooms is a free global online recovery community that offers over 100 weekly online meetings for those recovering from addiction and related issues. In the Rooms embraces multiple pathways to recovery, including all 12 Step, Non-12 Step, Wellness, and Mental Health modalities. Through live meetings, discussion groups, and other tools, ITR offers people from around the world a way to connect and help each other along their recovery journeys.

Celebrate Recovery https://celebraterecovery.com

Celebrate Recovery is a Christ-centered, 12-step recovery program for anyone struggling with hurt, pain, or addiction of any kind. Celebrate Recovery is a safe place to find community and freedom from the issues that are controlling one's life.

Caduceus Group for Health Professionals https://caduceusm eeting.blogspot.com

The Caduceus, the staff of the Greek god of healing, has been adopted as a symbol by the medical profession. Caduceus groups are 12-step like mutual support groups for health care professionals. Attendance at a Caduceus meeting is often required by monitoring programs for health professionals. Since it is a specialty group, a Caduceus meeting is not advertised in the AA or NA meeting list. However, meetings often follow a 12-step format. Members share their stories, often inappropriate at an open AA or NA meeting, support each other's recovery, and share strategies for navigating a monitoring program successfully. Confirm a meeting with a recovering health professional.

American Bar Association (ABA) Lawyer Assistance Program (LAP) https://americanbar.org/groups/lawyer_assistance

The American Bar Association provides confidential services and support for judges, lawyers, and law students facing mental health and substance use issues. This site offers many virtual services and provides a Directory of state or local Lawyer Assistance Programs. The Commission on Lawyer Assistance Programs (CoLAP) has jurisdiction over matters relating to lawyer assistance programs as they provide professional assistance to lawyers, judges, and law students who have alcohol and other substance use disorders and mental health issues. The Commission (1) supports and seeks to improve existing services, including diversity outreach, and, as appropriate, assists in the development of new lawyer assistance programs, (2) provides educational and training opportunities for lawyer assistance program staff and volunteers, the legal profession, the judiciary, law students, legal educators, and the public, (3) disseminates information to and creates and fosters platforms for communication among lawyer assistance program staff and volunteers, and (4) develops and advances policies that better enable lawyers and judges to obtain assistance and return to good health, protect the integrity of the legal profession and the judiciary and protect the public.

Human Intervention Motivation for Pilots (HIMS) https://himsp rogram.com/monitoring

The HIMS program is a worldwide, aviation industry-supported, confidential peer mentoring program designed to assist and support airline pilots through recovery and rehabilitation from an addiction or substance dependence diagnosis, facilitating a safe return to work. HIMS is an occupational substance abuse treatment program, specific to pilots, that coordinates the identification, treatment, and return to work process for affected aviators. It is an industry-wide effort in which managers, pilots, healthcare professionals, and the FAA work together to preserve careers and enhance air safety. The HIMS name comes from the Human Intervention Motivation Study in the early 1970s, a joint venture of Air Line Pilots Association (ALPA), the Federal Aviation Administration (FAA), and the National Institute for Alcohol Abuse and Alcoholism. (NIAAA). Although the study is over, the HIMS term persists.

Professional Organizations

National Council on Alcoholism and Drug Dependence, Inc. (NCADD) https://ncadd.org

The National Council on Alcoholism and Drug Dependence, Inc. (NCADD) is an organization, with a nationwide network of affiliates, dedicated to helping people overcome an alcohol use disorder or other substance abuse problem. NCADD focuses on educating the public on the joys and benefits of recovery, working to remove the stigma and discrimination associated with alcohol use and addiction, and encouraging people who are living with the disorder to connect with the help they need. It advocates prevention, intervention, and treatment; and is committed to ridding the disease of its stigma and its sufferers from their denial and shame.

American Society of Addiction Medicine (ASAM) https://asam.org

ASAM, founded in 1954, is a professional medical society representing physicians, clinicians, and associated professionals in the field of addiction medicine. ASAM is dedicated to increasing access and improving the quality of addiction treatment, educating physicians and the public, supporting research and prevention, and promoting the appropriate role of physicians in the care of patients with addiction.

Faces and Voices of Recovery https://facesandvoicesofrecovery.org

Faces and Voices of Recovery is dedicated to organizing and mobilizing the over 23 million Americans in recovery from addiction to alcohol and other drugs, our families, friends, and allies into recovery community organizations and networks, to promote the right and resources to recover through advocacy, education and demonstrating the power and proof of long-term recovery.

The Recovery Research Institute https://www.recoveryanswers.org

A leading nonprofit research institute of Massachusetts General Hospital, an affiliate of Harvard Medical School, is dedicated to the advancement of addiction treatment and recovery. Founded in 2012 by Dr. John F. Kelly, the

Recovery Research Institute is a team of innovative scientists working through research, education, and outreach to *enhance recovery through science*, conducting and disseminating the most up-to-date research findings for individuals, families, healthcare professionals, and policymakers alike.

National Association of Addiction Treatment Providers (NAATP) https://naatp.org

The NAATP Addiction Industry Directory (AID) serves members and the public as a comprehensive source of addiction service providers and supporters. All NAATP members in good standing appear in the AID. All provider members are licensed to provide the addiction services indicated. All listed members agree to abide by the NAATP Code of Ethics regarding marketing and service delivery.

American Academy of Health Care Providers in the Addiction Disorders https://americanacademy.org

Created in 1988, the American Academy of Health Care Providers in the Addictive Disorders is an international credentialing body devoted to establishing and upholding the highest standards for the provision of treatment in the addictive disorders. Membership is comprised of psychologists, medical doctors, nurses, social workers, and counselors from seven countries who provide the highest quality of care. The Certified Addiction Specialist (CAS) is a comprehensive credential that includes specialty areas of competencies for alcoholism, drug addiction, eating disorders, gambling addiction, and sexual addiction.

National Council on Problem Gambling (NCPG) https://ncpgambling.org

Founded in 1972, NCPG leads state and national stakeholders in the development of comprehensive policy and programs for all those affected by problem gambling. The National Council is neither for nor against legalized gambling. Key programs include a 24 Hour Confidential National Helpline as well as training and certification of gambling counselors.

Let's Gamble USA https://letsgambleusa.com

This website offers an extensive contact list of federal, tribal, state, and international gambling associations, commissions, agencies, and regulators for on-site and online gambling/gaming. The site reviews federal and state laws that regulate gambling. Gaming news is current and comprehensive. While the site is a useful resource, Let's Gamble promotes gambling, especially online wagering. "Are you interested in learning how to gamble for real money online in the US, but don't know where to start? Maybe you're wondering if you can legally gamble online from your state, or how online gambling in the United States works exactly. You might even have concerns over the safety and security of U.S. gambling sites. We know it can be confusing. That's why we created this comprehensive guide to U.S. online gambling."

Government Agencies

Office of National Drug Control Policy (ONDCP) https://www.whitehouse.gov/ondcp

The Office of National Drug Control Policy (ONDCP) is a component of the Executive Office of the President. The Director of the ONDCP, colloquially known as the Drug Czar heads the office. The mission of ONDCP is to reduce substance use disorder and its consequences to improve the health and lives of the American people. The principal purpose of ONDCP is to establish policies, priorities, and objectives for the Nation's drug control program. The goals of the program are to reduce illicit drug use, manufacturing, and trafficking, drug-related crime and violence, and drug-related health consequences. ONDCP coordinates the nation's drug control policy through the development and oversight of the National Drug Control Strategy and Budget. ONDCP also administers High-Intensity Drug Trafficking Areas (HIDTA) and Drug-Free Communities (DFC) grant programs.

Substance Abuse Mental Health Services Administration (SAMHSA) https://www.samhsa.gov

The Substance Abuse and Mental Health Services Administration (SAMHSA) is the agency within the U.S. Department of Health and Human Services that leads public health efforts to advance the behavioral health of the nation. SAMHSA's mission is to reduce the impact of substance abuse and mental illness on America's communities. SAMHSA's free treatment referral service connects people with substance abuse services in their community. See especially the work of its CSAP and CSAT. *Developing Competencies for Recovery* builds directly on many SAMHSA resources.

Center for Substance Abuse Prevention (CSAP)

SAMHSA's Center for Substance Abuse Prevention (CSAP) works with federal, state, public, and private organizations to develop comprehensive prevention systems by (1) providing national leadership in the development of policies, programs, and services to prevent the onset of illegal drug use, prescription drug misuse and abuse, alcohol misuse and abuse, and underage alcohol and tobacco use, and (2) promoting effective substance abuse prevention practices that enable states, communities, and other organizations to apply prevention knowledge effectively. CSAP programs foster supportive workplaces, schools, and communities; drug-free and crime-free neighborhoods; and positive connections with family and friends.

Center for Substance Abuse Treatment (CSAT)

The mission of SAMHSA's Center for Substance Abuse Treatment is to promote community-based substance use disorder treatment, and recovery support services for individuals and families in every community. CSAT provides national leadership to improve access, reduce barriers, and promote high-quality, lifesaving, effective treatment, and recovery support services. CSAT works to close the gap between available treatment capacity and demand; supports the adaptation and adoption of evidence-based and best practices by community-based treatment programs and services; and improves and strengthens substance abuse treatment organizations and systems.

National Institute on Alcohol Abuse and Alcoholism (NIAAA) http s://www.niaaa.nih.gov

NIAAA generates and disseminates fundamental knowledge about the effects of alcohol on health and well-being, and applies that knowledge to improve diagnosis, prevention, and treatment of alcohol-related problems, including alcohol use disorder, across the lifespan. NIAAA provides leadership in the national effort to reduce alcohol-related problems by conducting and supporting research, coordinating, and collaborating with other research organizations, and disseminating research findings to health care providers, researchers, policymakers, and the public. Supported research covers a wide range of scientific areas including genetics, neuroscience, epidemiology, health risks and benefits of alcohol consumption, prevention, and treatment.

National Institute on Drug Abuse (NIDA) https://www.drugabuse.gov

NIDA is the lead federal agency supporting scientific research on drug use and its consequences, the mission of the National Institute on Drug Abuse (NIDA) is to advance science on the causes and consequences of drug use (including nicotine) and addiction and to apply that knowledge to improve individual and public health. NIDA supports over 85 percent of the world's research on the health aspects of drug abuse and addiction. NIDA-supported science addresses the most fundamental and essential questions about drug abuse, ranging from the molecule to managed care, and from DNA to community outreach research. NIDA-supported research has revolutionized our understanding of drug use and addiction, driving a new understanding of the neurobiological, genetic, epigenetic, social, and environmental factors that contribute to substance use disorders.

The Bureau of Alcohol, Tobacco, Firearms, and Explosives (ATF) https://www.atf.gov

The Bureau of Alcohol, Tobacco, Firearms and Explosives ATF is a law enforcement agency in the United States Department of Justice that protects our communities from violent criminals, criminal organizations, the illegal use and trafficking of firearms, the illegal use and storage of explosives, acts of arson and bombings, acts of terrorism, and the illegal diversion of alcohol and tobacco products.

National Survey on Drug Use and Health (NSDUH) https://nsduhweb.rti.org

The National Survey on Drug Use and Health, often abbreviated NSDUH, is an annual nationwide survey on the use of legal and illegal drugs, as well as mental disorders, that has been conducted by the United States federal government since 1971. It is funded by the Substance Abuse and Mental Health Services Administration and is supervised by the SAMHSA's Center for Behavioral Health Statistics and Quality. The survey interviews about 70,000 Americans aged 12 and older, through face-to-face interviews conducted where the respondent lives. Information from NSDUH is used to support prevention and treatment programs, monitor substance use trends, estimate the need for treatment, and inform public health policy. The NSDUH, along with the Monitoring the Future, is one of the two main ways the National Institute on Drug Abuse measures drug use in the United States.

Monitoring the Future https://www.monitoringthefuture.org

Monitoring the Future is a long-term epidemiological study ongoing study of the behaviors, attitudes, and values of Americans from adolescence through adulthood. Each year, a total of approximately 50,000 8th, 10th, and 12th-grade students are surveyed. Annual follow-up questionnaires are mailed to a sample of each graduating class for several years after their initial participation. Monitoring the Future is conducted by researchers at the University of Michigan's Institute for Social Research and funded by the National Institute on Drug Abuse (NIDA).

Drug Enforcement Administration (DEA) https://www.dea.gov

The Drug Enforcement Administration is a United States federal law enforcement agency under the U.S. Department of Justice tasked with combating drug trafficking and distribution within the U.S. It is the lead agency for domestic enforcement of the Controlled Substances Act, sharing concurrent jurisdiction with the Federal Bureau of Investigation, the U.S. Immigration and Customs Enforcement, and U.S. Customs and Border Protection. The

DEA has sole responsibility for coordinating and pursuing U.S. drug investigations both domestically and abroad. Check out its useful Drug Fact Sheets from amphetamines to U-47700 ("U4," "pink," or "pinky," a highly potent synthetic opioid).

Food and Drug Administration (FDA) https://www.fda.gov

The Food and Drug Administration is a government agency established in 1906 with the passage of the Federal Food and Drugs Act. The FDA is responsible for protecting and promoting public health through the control and supervision of food safety, tobacco products, dietary supplements, prescription, and over-the-counter pharmaceutical drugs, vaccines, biopharmaceuticals, blood transfusions, medical devices, electromagnetic radiation emitting devices, cosmetics, animal foods and feed and veterinary products. Its Center for Drug Evaluation and Research (CDER) ensures that safe and effective drugs are available to improve the health of the people in the United States.

United Nations

Office of Alcohol, Drugs, and Addictive Behaviours (Search UN Office of Alcohol, Drugs, and Addictive Behaviours)

The Alcohol, Drugs, and Addictive Behaviours Unit is located within the Department of Mental Health and Substance Use. The Unit works globally to improve the health and well-being of populations by articulating, promoting, and supporting evidence-informed policies, strategies, and interventions to reduce the burden associated with alcohol, drugs, and addictive behaviors, and by monitoring their implementation and impact. The Unit develops and disseminates technical guidance on prevention and management of health conditions due to substance use and addictive behaviors to attain Universal Health Coverage (UHC) and strengthen health system responses to emergencies.

Office of Drugs and Crime (UNODC) https://www.unodc.org

The United Nations Office on Drugs and Crime (UNODC) strives to make the world safer from drugs, organized crime, corruption, and terrorism. The Office is committed to achieving health, security, and justice for all by tackling these threats and promoting peace and sustainable well-being as deterrents to them. Because the scale of these problems is often too great for states to confront alone, UNODC offers practical assistance and encourages transnational approaches to action. See also the UNODC publication, *International Standards for the Treatment of Drug Use Disorders* (2020). The guide supports Member States in developing and expanding effective, evidence-based, and ethical treatment for drug use disorders, especially in less-resourced settings. It provides key principles for organizing treatment services for drug use disorders and describes the main components of treatment systems, including treatment settings, modalities, and interventions. The publication includes considerations for populations with special treatment and care needs. Download a free copy.

International Narcotics Control Board (INCB)
https://www.incb.org

Established in 1968, the International Narcotics Control Board is the independent and quasi-judicial monitoring body for the implementation of the United Nations international drug control conventions. The INCB monitors and supports Governments' compliance with international drug control treaties. It had predecessors under the former drug control treaties as far back as the time of the League of Nations.

References

Ahmadi, M., Rakhshanderou, S., Khodakarim, S. & Ghaffari, M. (2021). Internet addiction theory-based intervention among university students: A case of health belief model. *Journal of Education and Health Promotion*, 10, 238. https://www.ncbi.nlm.nih.gov/pmc/articles/PMC8318158.

American Society of Addiction Medicine (2019). *Definition of addiction*. ASAM.

American Society of Addiction Medicine, Mee-Lee, D. (Ed.) (2013). *The ASAM criteria: Treatment criteria for addictive, substance-related, and co-occurring conditions* (3rd ed.). The Change Companies.

Anonymous (1994). *A day at a time Gamblers Anonymous*. Hazelden.

Beattie, M. (1986). *Codependent no more*. Hazelden.

Berger, P. L. & Luckmann, T. (1966). *The social construction of reality*. Anchor Books.

Casey, K. (1982). *Each day a new beginning: Daily meditations for women*. Hazelden.

Conyers, B. (2003). *Addict in the family: Stories of loss, hope, and recovery*. Hazelden.

Covey, S. R. (2020) *The 7 habits of highly effective people* (30th-anniversary edition paperback). Simon & Schuster.

Doran, G. T. (1981). There's a S.M.A.R.T. way to write management's goals and objectives. *Management Review*, 70, 35–36.

Elizabeth, L. (1980). *Food for thought: Daily meditations for overeaters*. Hazelden.

Fisher, C. E. (2022). *The urge: Our history of addiction*. Penguin.

Frisch, M. B. (1993). The Quality of Life Inventory: A cognitive-behavioral tool for complete problem assessment, treatment planning, and outcome evaluation. *Behavior Therapist*, 16, 42–44.

Gorski, T. T. (1992). *The staying sober workbook: A serious solution for the problem of relapse*. Herald House/Independence Press.

Greiner, A. C. & Knebel, E. (Eds.) (2003). *Health professional education: A bridge to quality*. National Academies Press.

Hazelden Meditations (1991). *Touchstones: A book of daily meditations for men*. Hazelden.

Hazelden Meditations (1998). *Day by day meditations for recovering addicts*. 2nd ed. Hazelden.

Helliwell, J. F. *et al.* (2022). *World happiness report*. Sustainable Development Solutions Network.

Hettler, B. (1976). *Six dimensions of wellness*. National Wellness Institute, Inc.

Johnson, V. ([1973]1990). *I'll quit tomorrow: A practical guide to alcoholism treatment*. HarperSanFrancisco.

Levine, R. L. (2021). Healthy people 2030: A beacon for addressing health disparities and health equity. *J Public Health Manag Pract*. 27(6), S220–S221.

Marlatt, G. A. & Donovan, D. M. (Eds.) (2005). *Relapse prevention: Maintenance strategies in the treatment of addictive behaviors.* The Guilford Press.

May, G. G. (2008). *Addiction and grace: Love and spirituality in the healing of addictions (Plus).* Harper One.

McClelland, D. C. (1961). *The achieving society.* Van Nostrand.

Miller, W. R. & Rollnick, S. (2013). *Motivational interviewing. Helping people change.* (3rd ed.). Guilford.

Narcotics Anonymous (1991). *Just for today; Daily meditations for recovering addicts.* Hazelden.

Ortved, J. (2002, January 13). The clouds of smoke return: Cigarettes, once shunned, have made a comeback among young people. *The New York Times,* D1,D7.

Psychology Today (n.d.) Motivational Interviewing. https://www.psychologytoday.com/us/therapy-types/motivational-interviewing

Prochaska, J. O., Norcross, J. C., & DiClemente, C. C. (1994). *Changing for good: A revolutionary six-sage program for overcoming bad habits and moving your life positively forward.* HarperCollins.

Rasmussen, S. (2015). *Ready, set, go! Addiction management for people in recovery.* Balboa Press.

Research Recovery Institute (n.d.) https://www.recoveryanswers.org

Rogers, G. T. (1975). *I'll quit tomorrow* [Film]. The Johnson Institute.

SAMHSA (n.d.) *Eight dimensions of wellness.* SAMHSA.

SAMHSA (2021a) SAMHSA to Launch New "Office of Recovery" to Expand Its Commitment to Recovery for All Americans. https://www.samhsa.gov/newsroom/press-announcements/202109300228

SAMHSA (2021b). SAMHSA Announces Unprecedented $30 Million Harm Reduction Grant Funding Opportunity to Help Address the Nation's Substance Use and Overdose Epidemic (Press Release). SAMHSA. https://www.hhs.gov/about/news/2021/12/08/samhsa

Schalock, R. L. (2001). *Outcome-based evaluation* (2nd ed.). Kluwer Academic/Plenum Publishers.

Shulman, B. H. & Mosak, H. H. (1988). *Manual for lifestyle assessment.* Routledge.

Schwarzer, R., & Jerusalem, M. (1995). General Self-Efficacy Scale. In J. Weinman, S. Wright, & M. Johnston, *Measures in health psychology: A user's portfolio. Causal and control beliefs* (pp. 35–37). NFER-NELSON.

Sifton, E. (2003). *The serenity prayer: Faith and politics in times of peace and war.* W. W. Norton & Company.

The President's New Freedom Commission on Mental Health (2003). *Achieving the Promise: Transforming Mental Health Care in America.* The Commission.

Touré-Tillery, M. & Fishbach, A. (2014). How to measure motivation: A guide for the social psychologists. *Social and Personality Psychology Compass,* 10, 328–341.

U.S. Department of Health and Human Services (HHS), Office of the Surgeon General, *Facing Addiction in America: The Surgeon General's Report on Alcohol, Drugs, and Health.* Washington, DC: HHS, November2016.

Witkiewitz, K. A. & Marlatt, G. A. (Eds.) (2007). *Therapist's guide to evidence-based relapse prevention.* Elsevier.

Wittenberg-Cox, A. (2020). Top countries in the world on wellbeing? Spot the women, yet again. *Forbes.*

World Health Organization and United Nations Office on Drugs and Crime (2020). *International standards for the treatment of drug use disorders.* WHO & UNODC.

Index